THE EARLY ADMISSIONS GAME

W9-CNI-588

THE
Early Admissions Game

Joining the Elite

With a New Chapter

Christopher Avery

Andrew Fairbanks

Richard Zeckhauser

HARVARD UNIVERSITY PRESS
Cambridge, Massachusetts
London, England

Copyright © 2003, 2004 by the President and Fellows of Harvard College
All rights reserved
Printed in the United States of America

Library of Congress Cataloging-in-Publication Data

is on file at the Library of Congress.
ISBN 0-674-01055-8 (alk. paper)
ISBN 0-674-01620-3 (pbk.)

Contents

THE EARLY ADMISSIONS GAME

Introduction:
Joining the Game

The big secret in college admissions is that there is no big secret.

Fred Hargadon, Admissions Director, Princeton University

Each year, hordes of American high school seniors apply to selective colleges. They each spend hundreds of hours improving their grades and undertaking extracurricular activities to strengthen their applications. What they don't know is the true "big secret" of the college admissions process: *Applying early dramatically improves an applicant's chances of admission.*

This book summarizes five years of research on the effects of early admissions programs. Our work combines historical research, interviews, and statistical analysis of two valuable new sets of data. Almost all the selective private colleges now offer an early admissions program, allowing students to apply and receive notification of a decision before the ordinary deadline for submitting applications. Such programs, historically for the special few, have become the portal of entry for more than one-quarter of the class at many of America's most prestigious colleges, and half of each entering class at Harvard.

Of the 281 private institutions ranked as the "Best National Universities" and "Best Liberal Arts Colleges" by the *U.S. News College Guide,* nearly 70 percent offer an early admissions program. Altogether, these colleges receive about one million applications each year, including 100,000 early applications. (They enroll about 170,000 incoming students annually.)[1] Early applications have become so prevalent that, according to the Pulitzer Prize–winning writer Larry McMurtry, they are now a hallmark of class distinction among the upper echelons in Washington, D.C.:

> Nowhere is the Darwinian struggle more bloodily evident than among the princes and princesses of the press, whose hapless children are forced at age two or three to start ascending a formidable ladder of schools: Beauvoir, then St. Albans or Sidwell Friends, then Harvard, Yale, or Princeton, where to uphold the family colors, they must not only get in but secure *early acceptance,* the sine qua non of survivability in that peculiar social gene pool.[2]

[handwritten margin note: faculty tradition / class issue / performance]

There are two major early admissions programs, and most selective colleges offer just one of them. Both require application in (or near) November of the senior year, with a decision—acceptance, rejection, or deferral to the pool of regular applicants—usually by late December. Early Decision (ED) allows an application to just one college, with the requirement that admitted students must attend that college. Early Action (EA) allows multiple applications, and acceptance is not binding.

In this book we speak of "the Early Admissions Game" because early applications programs have transformed college admissions from a relatively straightforward process into a complicated strategic arena. We use the term "game" because the results for each applicant depend on the choices made by others, principally by other applicants and the colleges themselves.

As we emphasize throughout this book, simple play is not always rewarded. For instance, colleges may benefit by reducing the admissions standard for early applicants, meaning that they admit some early applicants whom they would not admit as regular applicants. Colleges favor early applicants for many reasons, not the least of which is to improve their national rankings by making themselves appear more selective. And they adjust their early admissions programs to gain a competitive edge on their closest rivals. Between 1995 and 2001, Brown, Princeton, Stanford, and Yale all adopted Early Decision, while Georgetown and Harvard relaxed the rules they employ for Early Action. Stanford and Yale changed their systems again for 2003–04. Each will drop ED and adopt EA.

In response to the perception that colleges favor early applicants, sophisticated high school students frequently apply Early Decision to improve their chances of admission, making a binding commitment even in cases where they have not identified a clear first-choice college. In our interviews with college students at Harvard, MIT, Princeton, and Yale, we found that more than one-third of Early Decision applicants were not certain of their college preference when they applied. Such strategizing about early applications is to be expected, but it is also disturbing to many observers and participants in the admissions process. According to William Fitzsimmons, the dean of admissions for Harvard University, "This element of gamesmanship and hedging bets is quite destructive. Sometimes smart people can talk themselves out of the things that they really want by trying to play too many games. That's one of the dilemmas of closing things off so early."[3] Larry Momo, the former admissions director at Columbia University and now the college counselor at Trinity School in New York, paraphrased Mark Twain to explain how the trend toward applying early has distorted the academic lives of high school students: "This getting-to-college-early disease of the 90's is producing a high school culture that is destroying the simplicity and repose of adolescence with its carefree spirit, idyllic visions, its ease and frivolity; replacing them with mindless overwork, cynical maneuvering, constant anxiety, and the sleep that does not refresh."[4]

The Benefits of Attending an Elite College

There are two reasons the phenomenon of early applications is important even though early admissions programs are concentrated at top-ranked colleges. First, these colleges provide (or at least are perceived to provide) a clear path to success in many careers and fields. Second, because students and their parents invest so much to gain admission to selective colleges, rejection can leave lasting emotional scars.

One general finding has been quite persistent over time: graduates of highly selective colleges are the most likely to rise to the highest positions in society.[5] In 1969 the historian George W. Pierson produced a massive study of the colleges attended by preeminent Americans of that time. He found that "1 alumnus for every 25 (approximately) of the undergraduates at H-Y-P [Harvard, Yale, Princeton] in the years 1920–49 had achieved recognition in *Who's Who*. This compares with 1 in 36 for Williams, 1 in 48 for Dartmouth, 1 in 82 for Michigan, 1 in 87 for North Carolina, 1 in 89 for Wisconsin, and 1 in 145 for the state universities as a group."[6]

The connection between college and career has long been clear to students, and recent studies are generally supportive of Pierson's findings.[7] But few graduates of any college will rise to become leaders in their fields. To isolate the effect of college choice on future success for a broader set of students, William Bowen and Derek Bok, past presidents of Princeton and Harvard, respectively, gathered information on the lives of graduates from twenty-eight prominent schools some twenty years after college.[8] They studied the results for forty-year-olds (those who had graduated in 1980) in some depth. They found that graduates from the more selective institutions (those with the highest average SAT scores for entering freshmen) had significantly higher average incomes than graduates from the less selective institutions.

There is considerable debate in the current academic literature over the interpretation of these findings. Are the more selective colleges enhancing the positions of their students, or are they merely admitting the "Best and Brightest" and then taking false credit for their subsequent successes? Bowen and Bok concluded from their statistical analysis that if two identical students went to different colleges, the one who attended the more selective college would be predicted to have a more successful career. Many contemporary studies reached similar conclusions. The one prominent dissenting study, by the economists Stacy Dale and Alan Krueger, used a different methodology and found that students who attend more selective colleges have higher earnings because of superior innate qualifications, not because of any feature of selective colleges themselves.[9]

These studies agree on one thing: the students who attend the most selective colleges will have the most successful classmates. Going to a college with successful peers might increase one's career prospects for two important reasons: connections and signaling. Connections and networking are a passion of young elites, who believe that they are the path to social and economic success. In the language of social science, these individuals are building their "social capital," which can be roughly represented as one's number of trusted friends and acquaintances weighted by the importance of those people.[10] For example, knowing a U.S. senator might be the equivalent of knowing ten shopkeepers.

Many if not most jobs come through connections, so the benefits of having a prestigious network of friends are significant. Interestingly, "weak" ties of acquaintance have been found to be just as important as "strong" ties of close friendship.[11] Those who attend a highly selective college can anticipate future network benefits from the connections they will make—not only with close college friends, but also with nodding acquaintances and even some strangers, many of whom will go on to positions of power. Networking has long been argued to be of great importance for (say) Ivy League graduates on Wall Street and in corporate America. In recent times, it has been observed that these networks now extend to Hollywood and jobs in the entertainment industry.[12]

Bowen and Bok quote one student who attributes his success to a combination of signaling and access to a valuable network of alumni:

> Based on my association with some people at Yale, I got a job as paralegal at a law firm in New York. Well, I got there, and the guys at the law firm said, "No, no, no, you don't want to be here. We're going to call over to 'X' corporation and get you a job over there." So I worked in the corporate auditor's office through some Yale connection and got to see the workings of a corporation from an inside—and interesting—position as opposed to doing some sort of scut work. . . . It wasn't that any of these people knew me. They knew the association I belonged to at Yale—one of the secret societies. They took my resume and then they met me. I earned my way and got the job. But it was these connections that got me the introduction.[13]

A signaling advantage arises when people who do not know you well, but who can read your resume or talk to you at a cocktail party, take your association with an elite college to be an indication of high quality. In effect, a job interviewer may use the decisions of college admissions offices as a screening device, favoring graduates from more selective colleges because they gained a stamp of approval in the rigorous evaluation process to gain admission to college.

The Growing Interest in Selective Colleges

Whatever the balance of reasons, there is tremendous competition among students to gain a spot at a prestigious college. For hundreds of thousands of families each year, entry to an elite institution is seen as the route to success. One recent estimate suggests that high school students and their families spend approximately $400 million per year on college-prep products, with companies charg-

who can afford?

ing up to $30,000 to devise individualized strategies for college ad-
mission.[14] Despite rapid rises in tuition, the most selective colleges
have been deluged with consistent increases in applications over the
past two decades. In 1999–2000, each of the eight Ivy League colleges received at least 10,000 applications; all tolled, the Ivy League
colleges received 121,948 applications that year and admitted only
23,532, fewer than one in five.[15]

Today's ambitious students spend hours on music lessons, extracurricular activities, athletics, and academic training, all with an eye
toward producing a winning college application. A 1996 *New York
Times Magazine* article described the applications of four outstanding students from Van Nuys High School in California, all of whom
applied to Harvard. One of them, Maya Turre, took the SATs for the
first time in seventh grade, and subsequently enrolled in two special-
ized summer college-preparatory programs, one at the University of
Southern California and the other at Johns Hopkins. Turre's father
explained, "It's a lot more of a marathon for these kids than it used to
be. It's just become more competitive. And parents feel compelled
to enroll their kids in these programs in order to get them noticed."
Another student, Mira Lew, was very much influenced in her choice
of activities by the experience of her older sister, who was rejected
by Harvard despite high SAT scores and graduating as the valedictorian of Van Nuys. Her father explained, "We prepared our second
daughter differently . . . We pushed Mira not just academically but
into activities and sports. The Ivy League definitely needs Asian athletes."[16]

preparing or from start younger

A number of college students told us that they went to considerable lengths to enhance their chance of admission to the most selective colleges:

> I was interested in whatever it took to get in, including SAT
> preparation courses and hiring this snazzy guy [a private coun-
> selor]. (Amanda, Princeton, '99)[17]

I thought I needed a hook to be admitted so I began rowing just before my senior year in high school. Crew is a fairly obscure sport with limited competition for a varsity team, and I thought I could excel at it. I contacted the Princeton coaches for workout advice and kept them informed of my progress . . . I was put on the recruiting list for regular admission and admitted. (Andy, Princeton, '98)

Just as there is much at stake for students in the admissions game, so there is much at stake for colleges as well. Today's elite schools, though maintaining their status as nonprofit institutions, are founts of great wealth. Private institutions now routinely charge more than $30,000 per year for tuition and room and board, and they raise vast sums from dedicated and grateful alumni. As of July 2001, forty-eight private institutions boasted endowments with market values of $1 billion or more.[18] In part, the financial success of private colleges is a direct result of the success of their graduates. But they will only be able to continue such profitable existences if they preserve their position in the pecking order. Few alumni wish to give a library to a college that has fallen seriously in rank, and which is therefore unlikely to burnish the donor's reputation or to be the college of choice for her progeny. Thus, just as admission to these colleges is fiercely sought, the schools themselves must always be on the prowl for superior students, luring talent however they can.

Components of Our Research

We have been studying the early admissions game for more than five years. Our research involved three different approaches: statistical analysis of college admissions decisions, interviews, and historical research.

Statistical Analysis

The centerpiece of our research is statistical analysis of data about many different applicants. For this study, fourteen highly selective colleges gave us their computer records for every single applicant for at least five years 1991–92 to 1996–97.[19] These files included information on the academic qualifications, demographic backgrounds, and in most cases admissions office ratings for each applicant. Each of those colleges ranks in the top twenty in one of the *U.S. News* lists ("Best National Universities" and "Best Liberal Arts Colleges"). In all, we had records for more than 500,000 applications to these fourteen colleges.

We verified and extended our analysis by using data collected from applicants in "The College Admissions Project," a survey of more than 3,000 applicants from more than 400 prestigious high schools, both private and public, across the United States. This survey, which was conducted during the 1999–2000 academic year, compiled much relevant information about these students and their application outcomes.[20]

We use our two sources to settle the question, "Is it advantageous to apply early?" The detailed information about each applicant enables us to compare the academic qualifications and demographic backgrounds of early and regular applicants. We then isolate the effect of applying early. Our analysis produces a clear and consistent finding: applying early provides an advantage in admissions decisions that is approximately equal to the effect of an increase of 100 points in SAT score.

Interviews

We interviewed and surveyed college admissions deans, current and prospective college students, and high school counselors to get dif-

ferent perspectives on the admissions process. What do the participants believe about early applications, and how do they approach
their decisions about applying early?

We surveyed different colleges about their early application practices and interviewed college admissions deans at Harvard, Yale, and
Swarthmore. One of us, Andrew Fairbanks, is a former associate
dean of admissions at Wesleyan University; he provided additional
insights into the perspective of the college admissions office based
on his own experience. From these sources, we learned that each
college is keenly aware of the nuances of the early admissions programs of its rivals, and that colleges may change their early application practices to gain an advantage over their competitors.

We conducted 30-minute interviews with nearly 350 students
from the graduating classes of 1998 to 2001 at Harvard, MIT,
Princeton, and Yale.[21] We were eager to learn how these students decided whether or not to apply early, and how they would advise
other applicants. Did they believe that applying early would improve their chances of admission? Would they advise high school
seniors to apply early for that reason? We found that most students
believe that colleges favor early applicants; we also found that a significant proportion of students were ill informed and confused
about early admissions programs—even after they arrived on campus at one of these four highly selective institutions.

We also tracked fifty-eight high school students from Choate
Rosemary Hall, a private boarding school in Connecticut, and from
Needham High School, a public school in a suburb of Boston, Massachusetts, during their senior year in high school as they applied to
college. Interviews with these students provide information about
the beliefs and choices of applicants at the time they applied to college, rather than as they remembered the process once they were
college students. About two-thirds of these fifty-eight high school
students applied early, though there was not a consensus among
them about whether it was advantageous to do so.

We conducted formal 30- to 45-minute interviews with fifteen experienced high school counselors around the country and with ten counselors from randomly selected public schools in Massachusetts. We compiled further information from informal interviews with other counselors nationwide throughout the course of the study. From these interviews, we learned that counselors play a vital role both as advisors to students and as third parties in the interaction between colleges and students. Counselors are frequently placed in a difficult position: students ask them questions about early applications that are important but impossible to answer, and they find themselves increasingly confronted with students who appear to be rushing into hasty decisions in order to "beat the system."

Historical Research

We studied the origins of early applications and researched the strategies employed by colleges over time. Most of our information about admissions practices before 1990 comes from our own archival research at Harvard and Yale. We used the College Board's database, augmented by articles in various college newspapers, to quantify the size and nature of early admissions programs in recent years. Finally, we contacted a number of college admissions offices for additional information about their programs.

How This Book Is Organized

This book chronicles the efforts of colleges, particularly elite institutions, to attract terrific students. And it is about the efforts of talented students to get into their preferred colleges. Groucho Marx once remarked, "I don't care to belong to any club that would accept me as a member." Most capable students, and their parents and advisors, think like Groucho, taking the position that they should aim higher than the colleges to which they are likely to be admitted.[22]

We see the whole college admissions process as a giant game, with roughly 1 million new applicants and more than 1,700 four-year colleges playing each year. In this book, we focus on "the Early Admissions Game."[23] The students are competing with one another, as are the colleges. But there is also a subtle game between the applicants and the colleges. The latter are seeking to lure talented applicants and, even better, get them to attend. Applicants are simply trying to get in.

In most games, such as corporate politics, dating, chess, or Monopoly, players get many trials and slowly refine their skills. The college admissions game is different, at least for the applicants. They get to play the game only once. By the time these applicants learn the admissions equivalent of "don't leave the office before your boss does," "don't wait until Thursday to ask for a date on Saturday," and "don't move your knight to the edge of the board," it is too late. They have applied in the wrong way to the wrong colleges.

Our central finding is that it is tremendously valuable to apply early. In some extreme cases, applying early appears to double or triple the chances of admission. (For example, our data analysis indicates that this is the case for well-qualified applicants to Princeton.) But colleges mostly deny that there is any advantage to applying early, either stating that they treat all applicants equally, or admitting grudgingly that the enthusiasm indicated by an early application may serve as a tiebreaker in a small number of cases each year. Moreover, many high school students, particularly those from less competitive high schools, do not recognize the advantage of applying early.

Some applicants, of course, are much more likely than others to learn about the details of the admissions process from well-informed individuals. Prestigious private schools, such as Exeter (New Hampshire), Groton (Massachusetts), Harvard-Westlake (California), John Burroughs (Missouri), and the Westminster Schools (Georgia), have developed their own expertise and wisdom from their considerable experience. By contrast, public schools, particularly those from which relatively few students go to college, are likely to lack knowledge in this area.

This situation would not be consequential if there were some published volume or website that described how the game really works. But none of the many guides to the admission process available in bookstores and on newsstands provides conclusive information on the effect of applying early. Not surprisingly, most published guides to admissions are tinged with some version of the colleges' party line on early applications. This book is dedicated to removing the mystery from the early admissions process, with the expectation that our readers will then be better equipped to play the game.

Even if we succeed in our primary goal and level the playing field of information for prospective applicants, the Early Decision game will remain troubling in some respects. Our research suggests that the current model provides a disproportionate advantage to those who come from privileged backgrounds. These are families with the "insider knowledge" that applying early enhances the chances of admission. They are also families that need not be concerned about comparing financial aid awards (nor about the ability to finance a large number of prospective college visits to identify a favorite one for an early application). The majority of highly selective private colleges use a binding Early Decision program. Under this program, early applicants make a commitment to enroll, agreeing to withdraw their applications from other institutions if they are admitted early. Thus, Early Decision applicants forfeit the option of negotiating financial aid. This barrier often leads financial aid candidates to apply in regular decision, putting them at a disadvantage relative to wealthier students who may gain a boost in admission chances by applying early. As expected, we find in our data analysis that financial aid candidates are significantly less likely than their wealthier counterparts to apply early.

Many colleges are eager to recruit applicants who fall into priority categories—for example, athletic recruits, alumni children, and underrepresented minorities. Such students are sometimes described by admissions officers as "hooked." Hooked applicants often have a substantial edge in admissions chances at selective private institutions regardless of when they apply—early or regular. For this reason, we exclude applicants in these categories from much of our statistical analysis in the book. On average, hooked applicants probably neither gain nor lose from early admissions programs in terms of their chances of getting in. Each private college can, and more than likely does, adjust its admission standards in evaluating regular applications to ensure that it admits a desired number of students in each category. Professor Ronald Ehrenberg, the former vice president for academic programs, planning, and budget at Cornell University, offers the following insight:

> To the extent that students admitted via early applications tend to be white or Asian American, institutions that are committed to enrolling a student body that is racially and ethnically diverse will have [to] put more emphasis on attracting under represented minorities through their regular admissions process. But as they do this, white and Asian American applicants' chances of being admitted through regular admission pools will decrease. Astute high school students, parents, and guidance counselors will realize this is occurring and there will be more pressure on white and Asian American students to apply for early decision.[24]

Thus, the students who will likely lose the most from early admissions programs are those who do not fall into any priority category and who are constrained from applying early because of financial aid considerations or because they do not understand the system.

Chapter 1 provides a short history of the Early Admissions Game. Colleges have been playing this same game for decades, albeit with different formal terminology. Before World War I, Harvard, Princeton, and Yale jockeyed to see who could best enact rules to attract a small number of talented public school students from the Midwest and the West. In the 1950s and 1960s these three schools introduced and then fought over the use of "A-B-C" programs, which gave students at certain schools an assessment of their admissions chances before the application deadline. (Criticisms of today's early admissions programs echo earlier criticisms of Harvard's A-B-C program.) More recently, in the 1990s, Harvard, Princeton, and Yale began changing the rules for their early programs, with immediate and substantial effects in the number of applications they receive.

Chapter 2 describes the current rules of early admissions programs at colleges around the country, as well as the number of early applications that colleges receive. Although most colleges offer one of two main programs (Early Action or Early Decision), there are no universal rules governing these programs. Almost all selective private colleges offer Early Action or Early Decision, and almost all admit a higher percentage of early applicants than of regular applicants. Despite the prevalence of programs, there are no universal rules governing Early Action and Early Decision.

Chapter 3, entitled "Martian Blackjack," looks at how difficult it is for students to pierce the mystery of the early application process. This title suggests that applying to college can be akin to trying to win money in a casino on Mars, where blackjack is played differently than in Las Vegas, but no one will tell you the rules. Why is the early admissions game so little understood? Because each college plays by different rules, frequently changes those rules, and often makes misleading or unintelligible statements—and finally, because college guides make equivocal statements where strong ones would be merited.

Chapter 4 follows two sets of strong students from two different high schools from the summer before their senior year through the admissions process. The students were quite successful: most were admitted to their first- or second-choice college. Yet only a third of them figured out that applying early would almost always provide an advantage in admissions decisions.

Chapter 5 presents the results of our data analysis, computing the advantage from applying early. Although colleges admit higher percentages of early applicants than regular applicants, they assert that this is the case only because early applicants tend to be more attractive candidates than regular applicants. We use detailed information about applicants to assess how appealing they should be to the colleges where they applied. We find that, on average, applying early increases the chances of admission at selective colleges the same amount as a jump of 100 points or more in SAT score.

Chapter 6 discusses the strategies used by colleges, guidance counselors, and applicants in the Early Admissions Game. It identifies three clear lessons. First, colleges benefit greatly from admitting students early. This helps them to identify enthusiasts for their school; plan enrollment levels; constrain financial aid commitments, since early applicants are wealthier on average; and improve their positions in the national college rankings. The implication is that colleges may reduce the admissions standard for early applicants. Reducing the standard for admission will also help to attract more applicants to apply early—so long as those applicants perceive that there is a lower standard for admission.

Second, guidance counselors have opportunities to help their students in the process, but they may also face heavy responsibilities. Acting in the interest of one student may well harm other students. The incentives of guidance counselors, who must place an entire graduating class and also preserve their reputation for future years' dealings with colleges, will at times diverge from those of particular students.

Third, applicants have strong incentives to approach early admissions strategically, and they tend to do so. For example, they may decide to declare a first-choice college by applying early, even though they are still not certain of a preferred college. They may decide to forgo applying to a preferred college that is a "reach," instead apply-ing early to a second-choice college where admission is more likely and there is a larger perceived benefit from applying early.

Chapter 7 draws on the insights from our research to provide ad-vice to applicants who must decide whether or not to apply early. Our main advice is to plan the process to leave open the possibility of applying early, but then to make an individual decision weighing the advantages and disadvantages. Applying early has many benefits, but it is not appropriate for everyone.

The Conclusion distills the essence of the Early Admissions Game and presents some possible reforms. As this book began circu-lating in draft form, the prospects for reform brightened. Richard Levin, the president of Yale University, announced that he was con-sidering eliminating Yale's Early Decision program, and that he hoped some of his rivals would eliminate their early programs as well.[25] By fall 2002, four prominent colleges (Beloit, North Carolina, Stanford, and Yale) had announced that they would change their systems and use Early Action in place of Early Deci-sion, opening the possibility that other colleges would make similar changes in future years.[26] But other prominent institutions such as Columbia and Penn have made it quite clear that they like Early Decision, and no college has abolished its early application program entirely. It will be difficult to enact a widespread agreement to abol-ish Early Decision in favor of Early Action, and even more difficult to institute a universal reform that would limit the size of early appli-cation programs or eliminate them altogether.

More modest reforms may be possible. Great benefits, for exam-ple, would come from changing the rating system at the heart of the *U.S. News* rankings to more closely reflect reality. This would discourage gaming by the colleges. In quite a different vein, high schools, or for that matter colleges, could help applicants find cheaper ways than an early or committing application to indicate college preference. Metaphorically, applicants could be given a single gold star, to be placed on their application to one college, presumably to indicate preference.

If the results in this book become widely known, many more students will apply early in the future. Will that alone end the Early Admissions Game as we know it? The lessons of the past suggest that it will not. We expect instead that colleges may change the title given to early applications, but not their substance. Students who are willing to make a commitment by declaring a first choice early in the admissions process (whatever form or action is required to do so) will always be favored by colleges. And thus students will always have reason to be strategic in applying early and declaring a first-choice college. With neither colleges nor students having the incentive to behave in a straightforward manner, early admissions—indeed any system that allows applicants to declare college preference or commitment—will remain a highly strategic game.

1

The History of
Early Admissions

The current early admissions system is the product of a multitude of decisions by colleges, applicants, and other participants, such as parents and counselors. College admissions is like an ecosystem, with some short-lived and some long-lived species. The students, who pass through briefly, merely respond to the environment they encounter. The colleges, by contrast, reside in the system for many years and play a major role in shaping the environment.

The colleges set the rules in the admissions game, with individual colleges changing their policies to gain competitive advantage over their rivals. They have several goals—attract applicants, admit the best, and then induce them to enroll—but relatively few instruments, primarily admissions decisions and financial aid packages, to achieve them. Since 1954, early admissions programs have proved to be an enormously successful way for colleges to compete with one another.

The purposeful actions of colleges may also prove harmful in the rapidly changing admissions environment. Sometimes colleges simply make mistakes, and in other instances, a policy selected by a college to accomplish one particular goal proves to serve another once applicants and other colleges respond. For example, early admissions programs were designed, in part, to reduce stress for some applicants by guaranteeing admission in the first part of senior year in high school. What no one anticipated was that these programs would grow to the point where applicants felt pressured to apply early. Although terminology has changed over time, colleges have always used early admissions programs for strategic purposes; the motivations and results have remained similar over time. In a story of déjà vu all over again, today's debates about the benefits and costs of early admissions programs echo similar debates from more than thirty years ago.

Admissions from the Seventeenth Century to the Mid-1960s

For more than three hundred years—from the founding of Harvard in 1636 to the end of World War II—college admission was remarkably stable: virtually all academically qualified applicants were accepted.[1] As the 1952–53 report of the Harvard Admissions Office explained: "Until very recent times Harvard, like most colleges, followed essentially a simple laissez faire admission policy. We admitted those who applied and met the admission requirements. There was no surplus of qualified candidates and no effort was made to persuade students to come to Harvard."[2] But there was a catch: the definition of a "qualified candidate" eliminated the vast majority of high school students. Before World War II, most colleges administered their own entrance exams. A number of elite schools, mostly in the East, used the examination written by the College Entrance Examination Board (now known as the College Board) to screen applicants for admission, though some applicants were exempted from the exam.[3] These tests focused on subjects routinely taught by preparatory schools, such as Latin, but beyond the reach of many public schools. In the 1930s and 1940s, twelve prestigious boarding schools sent an average of two-thirds of their graduates to Harvard,

Princeton, or Yale. These twelve schools supplied nearly 30 percent of the entering students at Harvard, Princeton, and Yale in both 1930 and 1940. Public school students made up between 14 and 26 percent of the student body at Princeton and Yale during this period. At Harvard, where 20 percent of the students commuted, somewhat more students were from public high schools.[4]

Most students, particularly those at boarding schools, applied to only one college, were admitted, and then enrolled. In 1932, for example, Yale admitted 959 of 1,330 applicants (72.1 percent), and 884 of them (92.2 percent of those admitted) entered the college.[5] Among these students enrolling at Yale, 29.6 percent (262 of 884) had fathers who had attended before them. The percentage of alumni children in the entering class reflects the remarkable degree of social segregation of that period. Yet some admissions processes were also designed to ease entry for public school students. For instance, Harvard instituted a policy known as the "top seventh" or "New Plan" in 1911 to guarantee admission to students in the top seventh of the class at approved schools, including a number of highly regarded public schools.[6]

Even in those early days, colleges competed fiercely for at least some applicants. Eastern colleges found themselves under pressure to relax their examination requirements, in particular the Latin requirement, from alumni who had moved to the Midwest and the West. Few high schools beyond the East Coast even offered Latin. (Latin was not approved to meet the foreign language requirement in California, for example.) Arthur Hadley, the president of Yale from 1899 to 1921, summarized the problem for his college: "The point is that we are not getting men from the *high schools* of the West . . . The Western boys who come to Yale are mostly going to preparatory schools in the East. That is a serious thing. It means that we are getting somewhat out of connection with the public school system of the country; not in the West alone, but in the West first, and probably in other places afterwards."[7]

Harvard jumped ahead of Yale with two innovations. First, it waived the Latin requirement for students in the sciences who enrolled for a Bachelor of Science degree rather than the traditional Bachelor of Arts degree. Second, Harvard's New Plan, introduced in 1911, opened the door still further to public school students by waiving the entrance exam requirement entirely for those with sufficiently strong grades at certain high schools, and relaxing the exam requirements for all students.[8]

In response to Harvard's new policies, Yale relaxed its examination requirements slightly. This response was not sufficient, and so in 1916 Yale introduced its own New Plan. Thus began a consistent pattern that continued into the twenty-first century. Elite colleges, such as Harvard, Princeton, and Yale, regularly altered their entrance requirements to gain an advantage in the competition for applicants. Once one college moved, others responded. In the early twentieth century the jockeying was over foreign language requirements; since World War II, competition has been primarily in the realm of early admissions programs.

The second half of the century saw significant growth in the number of college applicants. When the GIs returned from World War II, they flooded the colleges. Many soldiers had interrupted their studies. More important, the GI Bill entitled veterans to attend college at government expense. The number of veterans who wanted to go to college, and also could afford to, exploded.

By the Eisenhower years, 1952–1956, when the GI bulge had long since passed through the system, Harvard received 3,500 or so applications per year, roughly three times its prewar levels.[9] And the Baby Boom generation waited in the wings. In 1956 Benjamin Fletcher, the president of Smith College, spoke of the "'tidal wave' of students now in elementary schools who will soon be pressing for admission to the colleges."[10] Fletcher's statement foreshadowed sentiments heard often today. Even in the late 1950s, admissions officers responded with "mixed feelings," or perhaps crocodile tears, to each new increment in applications: "The staff was stretched to the limit to take care of the burden of interviewing, correspondence, and folder-reading; and the number of good candidates who had eventually to be disappointed in their hopes of entering Harvard was painfully large."[11]

As applications increased, colleges moved to more selective admissions practices in order to limit the size of entering classes: "For the first time we can, within limits—and in fact we have to—consciously shape the make-up of our student body instead of allowing natural selection or laissez faire to determine it."[12] Eugene Wilson, the dean of admissions at Amherst, echoed this sentiment in 1959: "For generations prior to the last war, the central problem of admissions at Amherst and similar institutions had been one of *recruitment*—finding enough qualified candidates to fill each entering class. Since 1946, however, the central problem of admissions has increasingly been one of *selection*—picking the 'best' candidates from a great excess of qualified applicants."[13] At that point, it was common for liberal arts and Ivy League colleges alike to receive four applications for each spot in the entering class.[14] Applicants could no longer be confident of admission to a particular college, so they spread their applications to a bevy of colleges. As a result, many applicants were admitted to more than one school, presenting colleges with two new problems: luring the best students to accept, and managing the size of the freshman class in a world with uncertain matriculation rates.

Within a decade of World War II, the Admissions Game had become vastly more complicated. Dean Wilson lamented, "No longer does an admissions committee select an entering class. To-day [sic] the admission committee selects candidates who by their 'yeas' and 'nays' determine the composition of the entering class."[15] Yield rates, which represent the percentages of admitted students who matriculate to a given college, fell to between 50 and 60 percent for top colleges.[16] As a result, competition to attract the top applicants stiffened.[17]

Until 1952, the College Board required students to list a top-choice college as part of the exam registration process. Once this practice was abolished, almost concurrent with the rise of multiple applications, colleges faced the significant danger of over- or undershooting the desired size for the next entering class. In 1955 Amherst enrolled 306 students, 56 more than its desired entering class of 250.[18] Predictably, college administrators found a way to blame their problems on the applicants. Admissions officers decried "ghost applications," "admissions letter collectors," and even "shoppers" (who applied to multiple colleges to increase chances of receiving a scholarship to one of them).[19] They labeled students as selfish if they did not withdraw applications to other colleges immediately after learning of admission to a likely top-choice school.

In 1958 Reverend Miles Fay, the dean of admissions at Holy Cross, wrote that predicting the size of an entering class was an "educator's blind man's bluff," forcing colleges to adopt "an egregiously oversimplified rule of thumb . . . 'capacity plus one-third.'"[20] Safety margins of this scale were unacceptable.

In the mid to late 1950s, colleges realized that they could manipulate the timing of the application process to their own advantage. At first, colleges tried to gain an edge on their rivals by sending admissions letters to applicants before their competitors did so. Williams, for example, tried to preempt Ivy League colleges in this manner.[21] An applicant faced a very hard choice when one college required an answer to its offer of admission *before* other colleges even sent acceptance and rejection letters: "This candidate could find himself with three equally cruel options: (1) accept his 'second choice' and prematurely withdraw his application to his 'first choice' as required; (2) accept the second choice, put down a deposit (up to $300) without withdrawing from his first choice, and then forfeit the money if accepted at the favorite; (3) turn down the second choice and stake everything on getting into his favorite, which may mean ending up with no college at all."[22] Today, more than forty years later, students confront a variant of this problem when they decide whether to apply ED, which requires them to commit to one college before receiving an admission decision from any other college.

The process continued to move forward in time until 1961, when a consortium of leading colleges agreed to adopt uniform dates for application deadlines (January 1) and notification (decisions sent to applicants in mid-April with a deadline of May 1 for selecting a college). The *Boston Sunday Herald* underscored the need for standardized "mail-out" and "candidate's reply" dates: "Up to this year some colleges, including Amherst and Williams, required definite commitments from admitted candidates in early May—often before the large schools like Harvard, Yale, and Princeton had even mailed out their notices."[23]

Seeking competitive advantage, some colleges, including Wesleyan, preempted the common mail-out date. As the *Herald* noted, "such schools are often willing to assure qualified candidates of acceptance several months before formal notices are mailed, if the students withdraw other applications."[24] These programs, in effect a delayed version of Early Decision for regular applicants, were the precursor of today's Early Decision-2 programs (to be explained in detail in Chapter 2). Currently offered at such colleges as Haverford and Wesleyan, Early Decision-2 allows applicants to apply at the regular deadline, while making a commitment to matriculate if admitted.

The A-B-C Programs and the Introduction of Early Decision and Early Action

In 1954–55 Harvard, Princeton, and Yale—then unquestionably the Big Three—introduced the "A-B-C" system. Applicants from feeder schools that commonly sent a sizable number of freshmen to these colleges were given a preliminary indication of the likely outcomes of their applications.[25] A rating of A indicated that an applicant was a "clear admit provided past levels of performance and behavior were maintained during the year." A rating of B indicated that the outcome was "uncertain, with the final decision depending on final Board scores, academic record and the competition." A rating of C meant "certain reject."[26]

The A-B-C program foreshadowed the development of the modern early application system. It channeled eligible students back toward a "one-student, one-application" system, as applicants receiving a rating of A were nearly certain of admission. In the first year of the A-B-C system, 414 applicants received a preliminary rating of A from Harvard, and almost all of them went there. By the second year of the program, Harvard's yield rate had jumped by nearly ten percentage points to 69.2 percent.[27] Harvard's 1954–55 admissions report stressed other advantages to the A-B-C system in words that could be applied to today's Early Action and Early Decision programs: "It gave schools a better basis for realistic advising of their students about their college plans and it gave many students a chance to concentrate on education in their last year in school instead of worrying about their chances of college admission."[28] The A-B-C system also helped to spread the workload for admissions officers: "It lessened considerably the pressure on the Admission Committee in the hectic spring days when the entering class is selected and enabled it to spend more time on the uncertain cases which need the most careful consideration."[29]

In 1959 the Seven Sisters colleges (Barnard, Bryn Mawr, Mount Holyoke, Radcliffe, Smith, Vassar, and Wellesley) introduced Early Decision programs. Amherst, Oberlin, Williams, and other small liberal arts colleges adopted ED between 1961 and 1965, and almost all of them still have these programs.[30] Just as today, Early Decision applicants were notified of a decision in December, either

"Accept," "Defer," or "Reject." In a sense, ED simply gave formalized versions of the A-B-C rankings. The central difference was that Early Decision applicants promised not to apply to other colleges if admitted. By contrast, applicants given ratings of A by Harvard, Princeton, or Yale were free to apply to other colleges, though few of them did so. Still the programs were sufficiently similar that they were sometimes hard to distinguish. For instance, Father Joseph Moffitt, the dean of admissions at Georgetown, seemed to describe a hybrid of EA and ED in his 1963 description of the A-B-C program: "In the strictest form of this A-B-C system, no decisions are given to any students until a certain day on which all are told at the same time, and then all have two weeks to reply. When the first wave of replies has been returned, the college then knows how much room is still left for the freshman class."[31]

From the perspective of colleges, the biggest problem with Early Decision and the A-B-C systems in their early years was that they were almost too successful. Colleges already had a natural incentive to overutilize such programs. After only one year of the A-B-C system, Harvard indicated its intention to "extend the system gradually so that half or more of the entering class will be, in effect, admitted in the fall of their last school year."[32] By 1965, Amherst accepted close to 60 percent of its class from Early Decision.[33] Yet these colleges were also aware of the pitfalls of admitting large percentages of students through such systems. As the Harvard admissions report from 1954–55, the first year of the A-B-C system, continues, "It is important, of course, in so doing to leave enough places to be filled in May so that we do not discriminate against those candidates to whom we are unable to give preliminary ratings. There are obvious practical difficulties in a plan of this sort, and it is clearly not a complete solution to the problem of increasing numbers of applicants."[34]

In 1955 Fred Copeland, the director of admissions at Williams, anticipated today's debates in his wary description of his larger competitors' programs: "This year, Yale, and to some extent Harvard, gave early verbal and written guarantees to many top candidates in an attempt to reduce unnecessary 'safety measure' applications. It seems to me that the practice is going to become more prevalent and that 'early acceptances' will become the rule rather than the exception; the problem will be not to let it go too far."[35]

Beyond overuse, the A-B-C program had other pitfalls. Since no rating was a guarantee of an admission decision, students often felt that the ratings, particularly a B, were hard to interpret: "[The] Yale Staff has decided to concentrate on giving 'A' ratings only in most situations, in view of the growing alarm and uncertainty about the meaning of a 'B' rating."[36] In much the same way, applicants and counselors today complain that deferrals of early applications to the regular pool (today's equivalent of a B rating) are confusing and discouraging. (See Chapter 6 for more details on deferral practices.)

The A-B-C ratings also left the colleges open to criticism when a student with a rating of A was not ultimately admitted. For example, the Yale Alumni Association of Bergen County, New Jersey, wrote an angry letter to the Yale Admissions Office in April 1965 to protest a perceived mismatch between initial ratings and final decisions: "Of the 12 accepted, 6 were rated B while many of our top ratings were turned down."[37]

Interestingly, though the A-B-C system spread the workload for the admissions office through the year, it also imposed significant burdens in the fall. As Fred Glimp, Harvard's dean of admissions from 1960 to 1967, explained, the admissions offices were not prepared to evaluate large numbers of applications before the deadline for regular applications. Ironically, the popularity of the program forced Harvard to trim its size.[38] Harvard cut back its A-B-C program in 1964–65, while Princeton and Yale eliminated theirs altogether the following year. These actions foreshadowed developments more than thirty years later: in the spring of 2001, Brown cited the workload that resulted from the growing popularity of its EA program as the primary reason that it switched to ED.

Under its reduced program, Harvard offered preliminary ratings to students from only 45 secondary schools (down from 131 schools), including only those high schools that sent an average of eight or more students to Harvard each year, along with a small number of additional schools in New England.[39] Despite the reduction in Harvard's A-B-C program, the university still gave 275 students an A rating in 1964–65 for admission to the class of 1969.[40] Its rivals, principally Yale, argued that Harvard achieved a competitive advantage in recruiting by maintaining the A-B-C program; students tended to withdraw their applications from Princeton and Yale upon receiving an A rating from Harvard. In the fall of 1966, Kingman Brewster, Jr., the president of Yale, attacked Harvard in the *Yale Alumni Magazine:* "We felt that the preferential rating of students from some schools, when we could not do it for students from all schools, was most unfair as well as — from Yale's point of view — inefficient policy. We wish our friends at Harvard had done likewise; we are quite willing to admit that the fact that they kept the rating system when we and Princeton abandoned it has worked, temporarily at least, to our disadvantage."[41]

In response to Kingman Brewster's attack, Fred Glimp countered in terms that Harvard's admissions office still uses today to defend its Early Action program.[42] He contended: "If you're really careful about giving A's to fellows you're absolutely sure will be admitted in the Spring, there's nothing at all unfair about it."[43]

Princeton and Yale faced a quandary. They could not reinstitute the A-B-C system after attacking it as unfair, and they did not wish to leave Harvard's newfound advantage unchecked. Kingman Brewster summarized Yale's dilemma: "We must equip [the dean of admissions] with a power to give more affirmative advance assurance [of admission] even though we do not intend to return to the rating system as long as it is thought of as a privilege to be extended to some schools and not to others."[44] Without the A-B-C program, it was difficult to predict the matriculation decisions of students. Within a

year, in May 1966, Yale's dean of admissions, R. Inslee Clark, returned to the language of the 1950s, bemoaning in an internal report the growing phenomenon of "ghost applications" to Yale, particularly among top students.[45]

In 1966–67, both Princeton and Yale responded to their mo-
mentary position of disadvantage by instituting National Scholars
programs, promising to give truly outstanding applicants from all
schools advance assurance of admission. As the *Harvard Crimson* explained, "This incentive has been called by some 'the wild-card A' —
an A rating at any school instead of a restricted number of schools."[46]
In terms of timing, the National Scholars program was equivalent to
a small version of today's Early Action programs. At Yale, for example, guidance counselors could nominate students, who would then
turn in all of their materials by October 31 and be notified of Yale's
decision by the end of November. R. Inslee Clark, Yale's dean of admissions from 1966 to 1972, recommended in the original proposal
that the National Scholars program be limited to less than 10 percent of the entering class, noting that "many candidates will be deferred until the April meetings."[47]

Most liberal arts colleges maintained Early Decision through the
late 1960s but reduced the percentages of their entering classes admitted from the ED pool. Many liberal arts colleges simply did not
have as many early applicants as they once had; as Philip Smith, the
admissions dean of Williams College, observed, there was "a growing trend to delay a final decision on the college choice until mid-
April after all options are in hand."[48] Amherst cut back its program
"in the spirit of 'equal access,'" mirroring the decisions of Princeton
and Yale to eliminate the A-B-C system. Even though Early Decision remained open to all, it tended to attract privileged applicants.
In 1978 Amherst limited Early Decision admissions to one-third of
the class, since "by taking nearly half the class under Early Decision,
we simply ran out of room."[49] As Michael Behnke, now the vice
president and associate dean for enrollment at the University of Chi-

cago, recalls, "When I started in admissions at Amherst in the early 1970s, we admitted more than half of our class early. There was a reaction on the part of the faculty . . . and the admissions office was told to pull back."[50]

In 1973 Harvard, Princeton, and Yale adopted a system known as "Early Evaluation." Students who sent in their applications by a uniform deadline received an official assessment between January 1 and January 15 that admission was "Likely," "Possible," or "Unlikely." In effect, Early Evaluation was simply the A-B-C system extended to all applicants. At least one other top college, Wellesley, adopted Early Evaluation along with its existing Early Decision system. As with the A-B-C program, college administrators cited the benefits to outstanding students, who would no longer have to worry needlessly about their chances of admission. It was rare, but not unheard of, for a "Likely" student to be rejected or for an "Unlikely" student to be admitted in April.[51]

Since a "Likely" rating did not literally guarantee admission, some guidance counselors reported that even the highest rating did not relieve students from worry.[52] Partly in response, the Ivy League schools and MIT agreed to adopt formal early admissions programs in 1976–77.[53] Students who applied by a deadline early in November received a formal admissions decision before the end of December, the usual deadline for applications to other schools. At that time Brown, Harvard, MIT, Princeton, and Yale adopted "Early Action," a program that guaranteed admission to accepted students but allowed them to apply to other schools in the regular admissions period. The remaining Ivy League schools adopted "Early Decision." At first, students were allowed to apply early to more than one Early Action school, but in 1979–80, the five colleges in this group that offered Early Action amended the rules to limit students to a single early application.[54] In 1998–99, Brown's website explained the policy as follows: "Since the goal of both plans [Early Action and Early Decision] is to provide students with an admission decision from their first-choice school in December, the filing of multiple early applications would be inconsistent with the purpose of these plans."

Institutional Changes and the Growth of Early Applications

In the 1980s many colleges redoubled their recruiting efforts, anticipating a decline in applications because birth rates had been low through the mid-1960s—there simply would not be as many eighteen-year-olds to populate the college campuses. As a result, many colleges began to emphasize the use of Early Decision. According to *U.S. News and World Report,* "Many colleges, experiencing a drop in freshman applications as the population of 18-year-olds declines, are heavily promoting early-acceptance plans in recruiting visits to high schools and in campus tours in hopes of corralling top students sooner."[55]

In 1983 a major new player came on the scene. *U.S. News and World Report* began to publish an annual college guide that ranked all colleges throughout the country. Many schools tried to manipulate their rankings, attempting to figure out the *U.S. News* formula and changing policies to increase their score. The stakes were high. Many administrators believed that an increase in ranking attracted applications and provided a significant financial boost, and a recent study of thirty top colleges between 1987 and 1997 found this to be the case.[56] Professor Ronald Ehrenberg of Cornell explains: "Even though colleges and universities constantly criticize the rankings and urge potential students and their parents to ignore them, every institution pays very close attention to the rankings and tries to take actions to improve its own rating."[57]

One of the elements that determines the *U.S. News* rankings is "student selectivity": a college that has a lower "acceptance rate" (the percentage of applicants who are admitted) and a higher "yield" (the percentage of admitted students who enroll) garners a higher ranking. For colleges, the rankings made it much more attractive to admit students early. If admitted, Early Action applicants were very likely to matriculate and Early Decision candidates were required to do so.[58] Favoring early applicants boosted the yield and reduced the acceptance rate because, given that those admitted early were likely (or virtually certain) to attend, the college did not need to admit so many students to fill the class. In other words, both "yield" and "acceptance rate" improve when a college admits more early applicants at the expense of regular applicants. (See Chapter 6 for further details about the *U.S. News* ranking system and the efforts of colleges to manipulate it.)

In the early 1990s, legal developments complicated the admissions game. Through the 1980s, many selective colleges met to ensure that they offered similar or identical financial aid packages to admitted students.[59] These meetings, known as "Overlap," were designed to ensure equity for students and to avoid bidding wars. Members of the Overlap Group were also highly unlikely to negotiate with admitted students on financial aid, since they had agreed to definitions of "demonstrated need" with their peer institutions.

During the Bush (Sr.) Administration, the Justice Department charged that the Overlap process violated antitrust regulations. In 1991 the eight Ivy League colleges settled the case (*U.S. Government vs. Brown University*), agreeing to change their practices; MIT subsequently reached a separate settlement. Just as the Overlap Group was being dissolved, many elite institutions were changing their policies regarding "need-blind" admission and financial aid. Some colleges and universities began to use an applicant's financial aid status as one factor in the admission process, in an attempt to control rapidly escalating financial aid costs.[60] At Brown, for example, the university stated publicly that the last 5 to 10 percent of the class would be admitted with sensitivity to need, meaning that students who were not applying for financial aid would be given preference in the admission process.[61]

The elimination of the Overlap Group added a subtle disadvantage to Early Decision for financial aid applicants. Prospective students can no longer be confident that they will receive comparable financial aid packages if admitted to more than one college. As a result, financial aid applicants face a catch-22: if they apply Early Decision, they cannot compare financial aid awards; if they choose instead not to apply Early Decision, their chances of admission may fall. For this reason, hearkening back to the 1960s, when college administrators argued that A-B-C programs favored the wealthy, Early Decision is frequently criticized on equity grounds today. Indeed, the journalist James Fallows spoke for many admissions officials when he stated: "The system as a whole . . . is grossly unfair in economic terms."[62]

Until about 1987, most observers perceived that admission in an early program was reserved for the very best applicants: "Twenty-three of the thirty COFHE [Consortium on Financing Higher Education] schools use the Early Decision plan, whereby they grant admission to *particularly promising applicants* on December 15th."[63]

The first articles suggesting that applying early could enhance an applicant's chances of admission appeared in the late 1980s, yet early programs were still seen as targeted for only the top students: "For those top-bracket students seeking admission to the top-bracket colleges, the best strategy is to request an 'early decision' by the admission offices, which like to 'lock in' the cream of the high school crop as early as possible . . . Even if a student is denied early admission, [meaning that the student is deferred] the applicant often has improved his or her odds of being accepted in the regular process."[64]

In the 1990s, many applicants and guidance counselors began to believe that colleges favored all early applicants, not necessarily just the best. This in turn stimulated more early applications, which provided more anecdotal evidence of favoritism. The move toward early admissions became self-perpetuating: "Counselors tell of strong candidates who followed the regular timetable . . . and who were rejected because the college had taken weaker applicants from the same school who applied early. As word gets around, it feeds the frenzy."[65]

A few institutions acknowledged that they were favoring Early Decision applicants. At Wesleyan, for example, admission officers stated in information sessions and interviews that there was, in fact, a slight advantage to applying early. They admitted that Early Decision was the one opportunity to recognize students who had completed the college search process and decided that Wesleyan was the "best fit" for them. Their argument was that students who are excited about the environment they are entering will be more likely to succeed at the university. Wesleyan enjoyed an increase in the number of Early Decision applicants as it began to be more open about the advantages of applying early.

Like Wesleyan, Harvard also saw its early applications increase each year, from 1,779 in 1989–90 to 3,000 in 1994–95. Each succeeding year thereafter set a new record for early applications to Harvard (see Figure 1.1). Unlike Wesleyan, Harvard stated that an applicant's chances of admission would not be affected by applying Early Action. But the dramatic increase in Early Action applications during this period is consistent with the view that prospective students (and their parents) were beginning to see early admissions programs as a potential lever for improving their chances of being accepted to a top college or university.

As early applications grew in popularity, colleges without an early program risked competitive disadvantage, much as Princeton and Yale had seen themselves at a disadvantage back when Harvard was the only college retaining the A-B-C system. A 1996 *New York Times* article estimated that one hundred colleges added early admissions programs between 1990 and 1996.[66] Similarly, a 1997 study by the

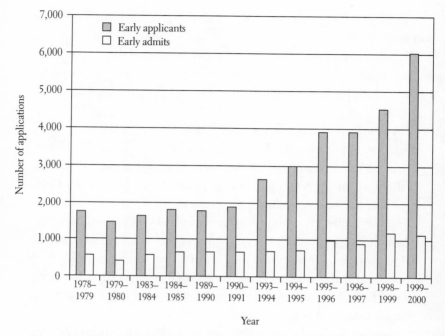

Figure 1.1 Early applications to Harvard, 1978–2000. *(Harvard Crimson)*

National Association for College Admission Counseling (NACAC) found that 35 percent of Early Action colleges and 27 percent of Early Decision colleges had instituted those programs within the past five years.[67] The NACAC study found significant evidence of a trickledown effect: the most selective colleges had long used early admissions, while many of the less selective colleges with such programs had implemented them since 1990.[68]

In 1995–96 Princeton and Yale switched from Early Action to Early Decision, and Stanford adopted Early Decision after years without offering an early application option, in each case allegedly to secure more of the top-ranked students they were losing to Harvard. James Montoya, the dean of admissions at Stanford, explained the motivation for instituting an early program: "We were losing extraordinary students who had Stanford as their first choice, but felt compelled to apply to an early program. By the time they heard from Stanford, Stanford had slipped through their hands."[69]

Widespread publicity surrounding the adoption of Early Decision by Princeton, Stanford, and Yale led to an unprecedented jump in early applications, particularly favoring the relatively few elite colleges that maintained the nonbinding Early Action program. Some colleges registered gains of 30 percent or more in early applications. Admissions officers such as William Fitzsimmons, the dean of admissions at Harvard, likened the decisions of students to a stock-market frenzy: "It almost amounts to panic, with students saying, 'Geez, I better apply early somewhere.'"[70] When its three rivals adopted Early Decision, early applications to Harvard jumped immediately from 3,000 in 1994–95 to 3,909 in 1995–96, and the number of applicants admitted early to the university rose from 725 to 985 (see Figure 1.1).[71]

Ironically, the switch from Early Action to Early Decision had relatively little effect on the enrollment of early applicants to Princeton and Yale. When these colleges offered Early Action, some early admits chose to attend other schools. When these colleges switched to Early Decision, it appeared that those same applicants simply did not apply early. At Yale, for example, between 70 and 80 percent of early admits matriculated in the years when the university offered Early Action.[72] When Yale switched to Early Decision in 1994–95, however, its early applications fell by more than 30 percent.[73] That is, the decline in early applications to Yale more than offset its prior loss of students who were admitted in Early Action and then chose to enroll at other schools.

The enrollment numbers for early admits were still close in the end for the two different systems at Yale. For example, in 1993–94, the next-to-last year of Yale's Early Action program, the university admitted 556 of 1,678 early applicants, and 432 enrolled in the class of 1998.[74] In 1995–96, the first year Yale offered Early Decision, it admitted 415 of 1,096 early applicants in December, and 401 of them enrolled in the class of 2000.[75] Over the next several years, Yale's Early Decision program grew gradually, and the university began to admit more than 500 ED applicants each year.[76]

The Recent Evolution of the System

In 1999 Brown, Georgetown, and Harvard changed their rules to allow students to apply early to more than one Early Action college. Brown amended its website by eliminating a sentence (quoted earlier in this chapter) explaining that Early Action was designed to elicit information about an applicant's first-choice college. As a result, early applications to Brown soared by more than 60 percent in 1999–2000, while early applications to Harvard increased from 4,524 to 6,026. (This change reversed the result from twenty years before. In 1979–80, when these colleges originally adopted the rule that applicants were only allowed to submit one Early Action application, their early applications fell dramatically.)[77]

Other Early Action colleges also benefited from these policy changes. MIT had always allowed its EA applicants to apply early to other Early Action colleges. But once Brown, Georgetown, and Harvard adopted a similar policy, early applications to MIT jumped by 44 percent.[78] It appears that many applicants who previously would only have applied early to one of those other three schools also applied early to MIT in 1999–2000. Perhaps other factors contributed to this increase in early applications as well, for Ivy League colleges offering Early Decision also saw a rise in the number of early applications in 1999–2000 (see Figure 1.2).

Many of Brown's early applicants in 1999–2000 probably submitted multiple early applications. Nevertheless, Michael Goldberger, Brown's admissions dean, indicated that he believed that "many students, who may have only applied to Harvard in the past, will apply to Brown, and then possibly decide to come after being ac-

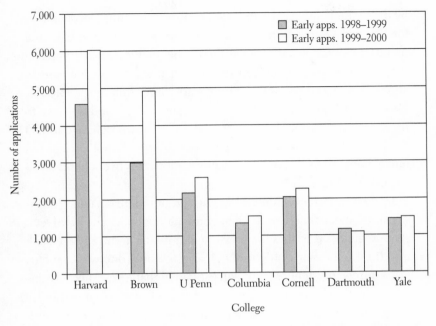

Figure 1.2 Early applications at Ivy League colleges, 1998–2000. (College newspapers)

cepted."[79] This view reflects the uncertainty created when Brown, Georgetown, and Harvard changed their rules; similarly, an internal MIT report noted that the school's increase in early applications makes it "impossible to predict EA yield."

Two years later, Brown made an even bigger change in policy by switching to Early Decision. As Goldberger explained, "After that policy change [allowing multiple Early Action applications], Early Action became a standard admission strategy, an early testing of the waters. Clearly, we are now evaluating application materials from thousands of students who have not yet narrowed their sights on Brown and two years ago would not have applied early. We have, in effect, simply moved the regular admission process several months forward."[80] Goldberger also cited the increase in workload created by the rush of early applications, echoing Fred Glimp's explanation for Harvard's cutback in the A-B-C system in 1965: "We have not had an increase of staff to read them [the additional early applications], no increase in staff to record and file data, no increase in alumni interviews. So we don't have any more time or people . . . Now we have too many applications to get through and we have to move at a faster pace. I think it's hurt us."[81] Brown's change to ED left Harvard as the only Ivy League college not offering ED, and as one of comparatively few of the nation's most selective schools offering EA (see Fig. 2.2).

In December 2001 Richard Levin, the president of Yale University, announced that he wanted to eliminate his college's Early Decision program: "It pushes the pressure of thinking about college back into the junior year of high school, and the only one who benefits is the admissions officers."[82] Levin explained that he is especially disturbed by the discriminatory nature of Early Decision, in particular by the fact that financial aid applicants cannot make an early commitment if they want to compare aid packages across colleges.[83] His statement made clear, however, that Yale could not act alone, for then it "would be seriously disadvantaged relative to other schools."[84] If enough colleges can agree to change their programs, significant change may result, but even Levin conceded that the current system cannot be dismantled overnight: "I don't expect any immediate action. There are some questions about whether these decisions will need to be taken unilaterally, or whether they can be taken in concert. We certainly don't want to run afoul of any antitrust considerations here. It may not be possible to reach a collective decision — we're actually reviewing that right now."[85]

Only two prominent colleges, Beloit College and the University of North Carolina at Chapel Hill, responded to Levin's announcement by the end of the 2001–02 academic year. Beloit and North Carolina stated that they would eliminate their ED program but retain EA (which North Carolina describes as "Early Notification") in

2002–03 (both offered EA and ED in 2001–02). North Carolina explained its decision in a press release:

> We've dropped early decision because we want our applicants to approach their college searches thoughtfully. We believe the best searches are the ones in which students focus on which institution best matches their interests and talents, not on which application plan most improves their chances of being admitted. We hope that our dropping early decision will allow this kind of search to flourish . . .
>
> We simply have come to the conclusion that students choosing Carolina would be best served by making thoughtful, well considered choices. And Carolina will benefit from having students who are certain that the choice they made was for the right educational reasons.[86]

President Levin's comments legitimized open questioning. In the summer of 2002, Harvard officials even hinted that Harvard might ignore Early Decision commitments made by applicants to other colleges, allowing ED admits to apply and enroll at Harvard. Steven Wofsy, a professor who serves on Harvard's Standing Committee on Admissions and Financial Aid, noted, "Why would we honor a system that stinks?"[87] Upon reflection, Harvard decided not to challenge the ED programs of its rivals, meaning that it will continue to remove applicants from consideration once notified that they have been accepted in ED to another college.

In fall 2002, Levin made a blockbuster announcement: Yale would replace Early Decision with Early Action in 2003–04. Later the same day, Stanford announced that it would also change its system from ED to EA in 2003–04. According to John Hennessy, president of Stanford, "This new policy offers those who have set their hearts on attending Stanford the opportunity to apply early in their senior year, without the additional pressure of having to commit before they are ready."[88] Robin Mamlet, Stanford's dean of undergraduate admission and financial aid, said that Stanford finalized its plan to adopt EA independently from Yale, and just decided to move up the timing of its announcement when it learned of Yale's decision. This clarification was important because Yale had not received an antitrust exemption from the Justice Department to enable collective decisions with other institutions to abolish ED.[89] For the moment, there is no possibility that a large group of colleges will jointly abolish Early Decision; any college that gives up ED will have to do so on its own.

In an additional wrinkle, Stanford and Yale announced that they would prohibit EA applicants from applying early to other colleges. This prohibition clashed with the Early Action guidelines established by the NACAC, as well as with the rules of existing EA programs at Georgetown, Harvard, and MIT. These discrepancies suggest the need for further discussion to promote uniformity in the Early Action programs of the nation's leading colleges.

Despite these changes, the system of EA and ED remains in place, though somewhat precariously so. The current combination of greater policy attention and ever-shifting strategic needs of colleges ensures the continued evolution of the early admissions system. We should expect that some other colleges will follow the lead of Stanford and Yale and switch from ED to EA. But it is not certain that very many colleges will do so, and no college has abandoned early admissions. Whatever the specific developments in the future, history indicates that two things will remain constant: colleges will create programs and adopt new strategies to lock in applicants early in the process, and applicants will respond strategically to these measures. Inevitably, some applicants will gain and others will lose from this confluence of strategies.

2

The State of the Game

Early admissions is a complex and constantly changing game. In recent years the cast of characters has grown significantly, with more and more colleges entering the competition for the best students. But still the true rules of applying early are rarely known to students and their parents. In the interest of leveling the playing field, we devote this chapter to uncovering the mystery of early admissions.

We reveal the rules of the game in this chapter and in our data analysis in Chapter 5. Five major points emerge here and are further elaborated in the chapters that follow:

1. Elite private colleges overwhelmingly employ early admissions programs.
2. The system is confusing because the rules and deadlines differ from college to college.
3. Students from advantaged backgrounds are the most likely to apply early.
4. Most early programs are of modest size, but many are substantial, and some have even grown to the point that they leave relatively few spots in the class for regular applicants.

5. Almost every college with an early program admits a higher
   proportion of early applicants than of regular applicants. At
   many colleges this creates a concern about the availability of
   regular admissions slots.

Which Colleges Offer Early Programs?

Currently, only one-third of all four-year colleges in the United
States offer early admissions programs.[1] Yet almost all of the most selective private colleges have such programs, as shown in Figure 2.1.
(This figure measures selectivity using the average SAT scores of
current students. Other measures of selectivity, such as the *U.S.
News* rankings, produce a similar pattern—the higher the ranking,
the more likely that the college is to offer an early program.)

Almost all colleges offer one of two early admissions programs:

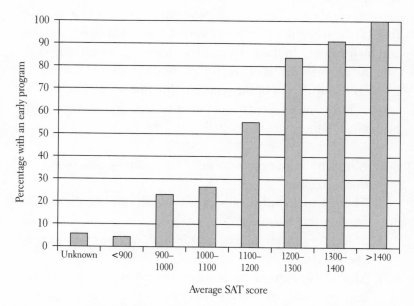

Figure 2.1 Percentage of four-year private colleges offering early admissions programs. (College Board database for 1999–2000)

Early Action (EA) or Early Decision (ED). Early Decision, which requires early applicants to commit to enrolling if admitted, predominates at the most selective colleges. Early Action, which allows early applicants to apply and enroll at other colleges in the regular process, is most common at the least selective colleges. A small number of colleges offer both programs (see Figure 2.2).

Public colleges, which primarily cater to in-state students, usually at dramatically reduced tuition, operate in a less competitive environment than do private schools, with strong built-in demand. Their natural response is to adopt admissions practices that are different from those of their private counterparts. For instance, a survey conducted by the National Association for College Admissions Counselors in 2001–02 found that private institutions were about three times as likely as public institutions to offer early admissions programs.[2] Many public institutions offer rolling admissions pro-

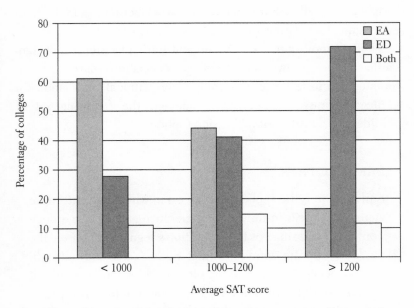

Figure 2.2 Type of early program by average SAT score of college. (College Board database for 1999–2000)

grams and publish standard admissions criteria based on thresholds for grade-point average and SAT scores. For students who meet these criteria, the admission thresholds serve as a form of Early Action — they guarantee admission before the regular application deadlines.

The public institutions that offer early admissions tend to offer Early Action, and some of these programs are quite extensive.[3] The few public institutions that offer Early Decision tend to be the so-called public Ivies that compete for top students nationally, such as the University of North Carolina at Chapel Hill, the University of Virginia, and William and Mary.[4]

The policies of most colleges are relatively stable, though some add or change an early admissions program each year. For example, among the "Top 50 Universities" and "Top 50 Liberal Arts Colleges" named by U.S. News, only four changed the status of their early programs from 1997–98 to 1998–99, and each of these four colleges simply added either Early Action or Early Decision in 1998–99 to complement an existing program.[5]

The terminology of Early Action and Early Decision is not standardized, though two major college associations have each attempted to create some uniformity. The National Association for College Admissions Counseling adopted the following set of "Guidelines for Admission Decision Options":[6]

EARLY ACTION

Early Action is the application process in which students make application to an institution of preference and receive a decision well in advance of the institution's regular response date. Students who are admitted under Early Action are not obligated to accept the institution's offer of admission or to submit a deposit until the regular reply date (not prior to May 1);

A student may apply to other colleges without restriction;

The institution must notify the applicant of the decision within a reasonable and clearly stated period of time after the Early Action deadline;

The student admitted under an Early Action plan may not be required to make a commitment prior to May 1 but may be encouraged to do so as soon as a final college choice is made . . .[7]

EARLY DECISION

Early Decision is the application process in which students make a commitment to a first-choice institution where, if admitted, they will definitely enroll. Should a student who applies for financial aid not be offered an award that makes attendance possible, the student may decline the offer of admission and be released from the Early Decision commitment.

While pursuing admission under an Early Decision plan, students may apply to other institutions, but may have only one Early Decision application pending at any time;

The institution must notify the applicant of the decision within a reasonable and clearly stated period of time after the Early Decision deadline. Usually, a nonrefundable deposit must be made well in advance of May 1;

The institution will respond to an application for financial aid at or near the time an offer of admission is extended;

The Early Decision application supersedes all other applications. Immediately upon acceptance of an offer of admission, a student must withdraw all other applications and make no other applications.

The application form will include a request for a parent and a counselor signature in addition to the student's signature indicating an understanding of the Early Decision commitment and agreement to abide by its terms.[8]

The College Board adopted somewhat different guidelines, referred to as the "Early Decision Plan Agreement" (EDPA):

COLLEGES AGREE TO

1. Act on applications, including applications for financial aid, and notify candidates of action no later than December 15.
2. Consider candidates whose applications are deferred to the college regular admission plan and guarantee that such candidates will receive an unbiased review at that time.

APPLICANT AGREES TO

3. Certify that the college is his or her first choice and that an offer of admission will be accepted if it is extended, provided it includes adequate financial aid if needed.
4. Withdraw applications from all other colleges if admitted by the first-choice college.[9]

These guidelines have done little to clarify the early admissions game. The College Board's EDPA applies only to Early Decision, but fewer than half of the colleges with Early Decision programs subscribe to the agreement.[10] Similarly, some colleges that are members of NACAC employ provisions that put them outside the guidelines for either Early Action or Early Decision, while others do not use the term "Early Action" even though they offer programs that meet NACAC's definition for Early Action. Finally, the details of early admissions programs can vary across institutions. For example, international students can apply early at many colleges, but they cannot do so at MIT.

One reason the rules for early applications have never been standardized is that these two sets of guidelines do not coincide. A particular point of contention is the requirement by the College Board's EDPA that colleges notify Early Decision candidates of a decision (which could be a deferral to the regular pool of applicants) no later than December 15. In contrast, the NACAC guidelines do not identify a deadline for notifying ED applicants of the college's decision.

December 15 is an important milestone because an early applicant who learns of a deferral or rejection by that date still has time to complete applications to other colleges by January 1, which is a common deadline for submitting regular applications. Early Decision applicants who learn after December 15 that they are admitted often submit regular applications to other colleges to meet a January 1 deadline and then have to withdraw those applications. They have lost time and forfeited application fees: "I applied to Harvard and Yale on Friday, and then learned that I'd been admitted to Princeton (as an Early Decision applicant) on Saturday" (Jason, Princeton '01). In fact, more than 25 percent of highly ranked ED colleges notify early applicants of a decision after December 15.[11] A number of them even set their application deadline for early applicants on or after that date.

Interestingly, the College Board is realistic about the fact that many colleges do not follow the December 15 deadline required by its EDPA for notifying Early Decision applicants of an initial decision. A separate discussion of Early Decision in the College Board's *2001 College Handbook* makes no mention of December 15 as an important date: "Some time between mid-December and the beginning of January, the college notifies you whether you have been admitted, deferred to the pool of regular applicants for a spring decision, or denied admission to the college."[12] NACAC and the College Board tried to resolve the differences in the languages of their individual statements in 1999, but they eventually decided to maintain their separate guidelines.[13]

Early programs and deadlines can vary even among colleges

within a single university system. For example, of the seventeen branches of the State University of New York, two offered Early Action in 2000–01, ten offered Early Decision, one offered both programs, three had rolling admissions but no early program, and one had no early program at all. The early application deadlines among these branches ranged from November 1 to December 1.

The Rules of Early Action

Is it permissible to apply Early Decision to one college and Early Action to another (presuming that the Early Decision commitment would take precedence over any Early Action outcome)? Is it permissible to submit Early Action applications to two or more Early Action colleges? The College Board is silent on the issue. Before September 2001, the relevant section of the NACAC guidelines said simply that an EA applicant "may apply to other colleges," and that an EA application is "to an institution of preference." It was not clear from these statements whether those applications to other colleges may include other early applications.

Differing practices among colleges reinforced these ambiguities over time. Throughout much of the 1990s some colleges, such as Cal. Tech and MIT, allowed Early Action applicants to apply early to other colleges, while other schools, such as Brown, Georgetown, and Harvard, prohibited additional early applications. In many cases, the only way to find out about a college's interpretation of Early Action was to call the admissions office, as that information was seldom provided in application materials.[14] Many of the undergraduates we interviewed at MIT and several of our MIT research assistants said that they had not known whether it was allowable to apply early to other colleges while applying early to MIT.

The change in policy in 1999–2000 by Brown, Georgetown, and Harvard to allow multiple early applications eased this confusion to some degree.[15] NACAC has acted to clarify its policy as well. In September 2001 NACAC's members adopted an amendment to their guidelines that states that an Early Action applicant "may apply to other colleges *without restriction*" (emphasis added), as reflected in the guidelines listed above. The amendment is explicit that it is permissible to submit multiple Early Action applications and also to submit Early Action applications in addition to a single Early Decision application.

But ambiguity still remains: Brown and Princeton do not allow their Early Decision applicants to submit an Early Action application to any other college, and similarly, Georgetown discourages its Early Action applicants from applying Early Decision to another college. Further clouding the picture, when Stanford and Yale announced that they would change from Early Decision to Early Action in 2003–04, they each declared that they would not allow Early Action applicants to apply early to any other school.[16] These policies all directly violate the language of the NACAC amendment.

Enforcement of the rules governing multiple Early Action applications has always been haphazard, for EA colleges do not share their lists of applicants.[17] In the past, when admissions offices discovered, usually by coincidence or serendipity, that an applicant had broken the rules and applied Early Action to multiple colleges, they declared that student to be a regular rather than an early applicant.[18] Several college students and two of the high school students we interviewed applied early to multiple colleges when this was not allowed, but none of them was discovered and so none suffered negative consequences.

Some colleges offer more than one early admissions program, which further complicates the process. In 2001–02, forty-eight colleges offered multiple Early Decision programs, usually described as Early Decision 1 (ED1) and Early Decision 2 (ED2).[19] In most cases, the deadline for an Early Decision 2 application is the same as the regular application deadline, or close to it. Early Decision 2 programs are concentrated at the most competitive liberal arts colleges: twenty-four of the Top 50 Liberal Arts Colleges in the 2001 *U.S. News College Guide* offered Early Decision 2 programs in 2001–02.

In its Annual Report for 1997–98, Stanford's Committee on Undergraduate Admission and Financial Aid explained that "Stanford's original justification for offering a two-round early decision program was to provide an opportunity for students from schools with limited counselor resources to apply early."[20] Stanford abolished Early Decision 2 because it did not seem to be fulfilling its objectives. The report continued: "However, ED2 has not attracted as strong an applicant pool as ED1, and targeted minorities have been admitted in greater numbers through ED1 and through the regular admission process. In addition, most of Stanford's competitor schools offer only one early application round."[21]

Wesleyan offers a similar explanation in the description of Early Decision 2 in its application materials: "Option II recognizes that some students arrive at a final college choice later than others. It also accommodates students who wish to have their senior year first semester grades included in their application."[22] Having a later Early Decision program has also helped Wesleyan to attract students who may have considered the institution their second choice. Surveys of admitted students suggest that some applicants apply ED2 to Wesleyan after being deferred or denied admission as early applicants to Brown, Harvard, or Yale. The later deadline attracts top students who might choose another institution in Regular Decision, but who sought the potential advantage of committing Early Decision.

Wesleyan is unusual in that it defers Early Decision 1 candidates to the Early Decision 2 pool (most schools defer to the regular pool). By deferring a decision from December to February, admission officers are able to evaluate midterm grades and thus see a more complete academic picture of the candidate, as complete as for Regular

Decision candidates. In addition, the strength of the Regular Decision applicant pool is known by the time ED2 decisions are finalized. Wesleyan decided that it benefits from deferring applicants to ED2 rather than to the regular pool, for that preserves the commitment made by the student to the institution. If a student opts to be deferred to Regular Decision rather than to Early Decision 2, Wesleyan will release the applicant from the binding commitment, but this choice may reduce the student's chances of being admitted.

Wellesley College offers Early Decision with a deadline of November 1, "Early Evaluation" with a deadline of January 1, and a regular admissions deadline of January 15. Early Evaluation at Wellesley retains the attributes of the A-B-C programs of the 1960s: students apply before the regular deadline and are notified by the end of February that admission is "Likely," "Possible," or "Unlikely." They then receive a final admissions decision at the same time as other regular applicants.

The Early Evaluation program is an important source of students for Wellesley. In 1999–2000 Wellesley received more than five times as many Early Evaluation as Early Decision applications. It enrolled more than twice as many students from Early Evaluation as from Early Decision; the college admitted 70 percent of its Early Decision applicants and more than half of its Early Evaluation applicants, but only 34 percent of its regular applicants. As a result, more than half of Wellesley's entering class in the fall of 2000 consisted of Early Decision and Early Evaluation applicants (see Figure 2.3).

Other colleges also inform some students of decisions before the official notification date in early April, but those early notifications are not part of any official program. In the mid 1990s, for example, Wesleyan began informing a subset of students identified as "institutional priorities" of their admission in early March.[23] Faculty members could then contact those applicants and encourage them to visit campus in April, when Wesleyan hosts various activities for

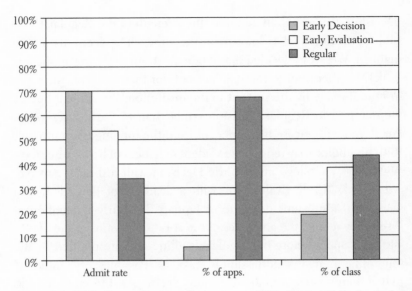

Figure 2.3 Wellesley applications by program, 1999–2000. (Wellesley College Admissions Office webpage)

newly admitted students. The policy was developed to allow less wealthy applicants to purchase the lowest-fare airline tickets, which may require twenty-one days' advance purchase.

The Rules of Early Decision

Both the NACAC guidelines and the College Board's EDPA make it clear that an Early Decision applicant's commitment to enroll is contingent upon an adequate financial aid offer. But what constitutes inadequate financial aid? The NACAC guidelines offer little clarification. In its essay on Early Decision and Early Action plans in the *2001 College Handbook* (separate from the EDPA), the College Board states that "you are only released from an ED decision if the college is unable to meet your need for financial aid as demonstrated by the completion of a financial aid form. It is vitally important for you and your family to understand that 'need,' as used in the college admission process, does not refer to a subjective determination of a family's willingness to pay, but rather to the federal and institutional financial aid methodologies used to determine a family's ability to pay."[24] In other words, an Early Decision commitment is binding so long as the college does not require a student's family to pay more than its Expected Family Contribution, as determined from the filing of the FAFSA ("Free Application for Federal Student Aid").

In theory, a college that meets this minimal stipulation on financial aid awards can expect all of its Early Decision admits to enroll the following fall. In practice, according to a 1997 NACAC study, an average of 91.7 percent of Early Decision admits enrolled at the ED college. Of those who did not enroll, slightly more than half (54.1 percent) stated that financial aid was not sufficient, while almost one-third (32 percent) simply wanted to consider other options.[25] As Martin Wilder, the vice president for admission, counseling, and enrollment practices at NACAC, commented in 2002, a student's Early Decision commitment to a college is an "honor-bound agreement" that "doesn't have any legal standing."[26]

Early Decision commitments are primarily enforced by way of implicit agreements by the most selective colleges. Many private colleges exchange lists of the students they have admitted in Early Decision.[27] As Michele Hernandez, the former assistant director of admissions at Dartmouth, explained, "When Dartmouth finishes its final decisions for the early-decision applicants, it mails a list to the Ivies and several other highly selective colleges."[28] Her subsequent description suggests that Dartmouth sends the list to approximately thirty to fifty colleges. When one college receives a list of ED admits from another institution, it routinely removes those students from its own applicant pool. Early Decision colleges practice this form of reciprocity for self-protection.

Early Action colleges also honor Early Decision commitments

made to other colleges, generally for more complicated reasons. First, EA colleges may wish to maintain a climate of cooperation with their ED counterparts, recognizing that their interactions span many realms beyond admissions. Both NACAC and the College Board support the current Early Decision system and exert influence over their members to uphold it. When Harvard announced that it was considering a policy change to ignore Early Decision commitments made to other colleges, the College Board swiftly registered its disapproval. Renee Gernand of the College Board called Harvard's proposal "appalling," adding, "It's encouraging students to go back on a commitment they have made to other schools. We like to think we're building a nation of people who abide by their commitments, but Harvard is going back on that."[29] Harvard ultimately decided in July 2002 to continue to honor Early Decision commitments to other colleges.

Second, an Early Action college may not wish to admit an applicant who has reneged on an Early Decision commitment to another school. As Marlyn McGrath Lewis, the director of Harvard's admissions office, explained, "If we admitted someone and then found out they murdered someone, we probably would rethink that case as well. It is not proper for us to be enforcing or policing other institutions' rules, but we are very concerned about the ethical behavior of students who might be Harvard students."[30] Harvard is not alone in this concern, as the following story about Fred Hargadon, the dean of admissions at Princeton, indicates:

> One day the mother of a student who had been admitted early action to Princeton called to tell Hargadon that her son had also been accepted by an institution that had a binding early decision program. The mother said she understood that her child had made a mistake, but she begged the dean not to withdraw her child's offer of admission, because Princeton was where her son really wanted to go. Hargadon listened, but he

didn't sympathize with the mother. When these things happen, he later said, and it looks to him as if the family is unsophisticated about the differences between early action and early decision, he will make a call to the admissions head of the other institution to see whether the candidate might be released from his or her obligation. This time, no call was made.[31]

Admission offices also raise the stakes for early admits who seek release from their commitment for financial reasons. Many schools rescind the offer of admission when they release an Early Decision admit from the commitment to enroll. In that case, the student is considered separately for admission in the regular decision pool. Families that question the financial aid offer or suspect that they could secure a better deal from other schools may be hesitant to ask for the commitment to be released when the price is to reopen the admissions decision.

Some colleges consider it an affront when Early Decision admits do not follow through on their commitment to enroll. At the May 2001 New England Association for College Admission Counseling (NEACAC) meetings, Judith Dobai, the acting director of admissions at Fairfield University, explained that she phoned all Early Decision admits who did not submit a deposit by the January 2001 deadline to remind them of their commitment to enroll. Similarly, one student we interviewed told us that she did not withdraw her applications from other colleges promptly after she was admitted Early Decision. She received angry phone calls from the other admissions offices where she had applied.

A number of the admissions office representatives at the NEACAC meeting argued that a parent and a guidance counselor should be required to sign the Early Decision commitment along with the student. The guidance counselors at the meeting were dismayed. They do not feel that it should be their responsibility to "police Early Decision," particularly since they have very little authority once a student has completed college applications. In fact, NACAC adopted a new guideline for ED in 2001 that included a "request" for the counselor to sign each ED application to certify that the student understands the nature of the Early Decision commitment.

Because the ED commitment is binding, financial aid applicants are often directed to avoid getting locked into an unfavorable financial package. The College Board's website is emphatic on this point: "Do not apply under an early decision plan if you plan to weigh offers and financial aid packages from several colleges later in the spring."[32] As described in Chapter 1, this advice disturbs some observers because it suggests that Early Decision is a program that offers the most benefits to the most privileged students. Financial aid applicants who do not fit into a priority category (such as alumni child, athletic recruit, or targeted minority) stand to lose the most by not applying ED; they have no counterbalancing advantage in the process to offset the relative disadvantage of only applying in the regular pool.

Who Applies Early?

Jean Fetter, the former dean of admissions at Stanford, wrote: "I would be willing to wager that an overwhelming percentage of Early Action and Early Decision candidates are white students who come either from select private high schools or from established public high schools in higher-income neighborhoods with well-informed college guidance counselors. They are mostly the children of college graduates who are also well-informed."[33] Similarly, Charles Guerrero, a counselor for the Prep for Prep program in New York, which enrolls solely students of color who are usually in the first generation in their families to attend college, stated, "[Students eligible for Prep for Prep] lack sophisticated understanding of the college admission process and are ill informed about the differences between individual institutions."[34]

Data that we collected from the admissions offices at fourteen

highly selective colleges reveal the differences in demographics between the pools of early and regular applicants. Jean Fetter was
right: Early Action and Early Decision applicants are disproportion-
ately nonminorities from advantaged backgrounds. At each college
in the admissions office data, African Americans and Hispanics applied early at lower rates than the overall early application rate.
Across the schools, African Americans applied early about half as often as others; Hispanics about two-thirds as often as others. Specifically, 11.9 percent of African Americans and 13.5 percent of Hispanics applied early at Early Action schools, while 20.5 percent of
all applicants to those schools applied early. The pattern is the same
at Early Decision schools: 3.6 percent of African Americans and 4.8
percent of Hispanics applied early at ED schools, while 7.4 percent
of all applicants to those schools applied early. Similarly, financial
aid applicants were less likely than others to apply early.

Our interviews with college students at Harvard, MIT, Princeton,
and Yale augment these findings. Among these college students who
attended high school in the United States, 70.3 percent applied
early to some college.[35] The students who attended prominent private high schools and who were not relying on financial aid were
even more likely to apply early. Among those who went to a prominent private high school, 83.5 percent applied early; among those
students for whom financial aid was not a concern, 78.0 percent applied early to some college. In contrast, of the students who went to
a less competitive public high school (where it is common for graduates not to go on to college), only 42.6 percent applied early. Similarly, among the college students who reported that financial aid was
important to their choice of college, only 48.0 percent applied early
to some college.

A likely reason for these disparities is a difference in the timing of
college visits, which is probably due in part to the geographic loca-
tion and the comparative lack of wealth of financial aid applicants.
Some students can only afford to visit a small number of colleges.
For these budget-constrained students, it may be an extravagance to

visit a college before being admitted to it; if rejected by the college, the expense of the trip is a loss. In our interviews, 83.3 percent of the students from prominent private high schools and 69.1 percent of the students who were not relying on financial aid reported that they had visited the college they ended up attending (or had a close family member attend the school) before the early application deadline. In contrast, only 34.6 percent of the students from less competitive public high schools and 41.1 percent of students for whom financial aid was a major concern had visited the college (or had a close family member attend the college) that they ended up attending before the early application deadline.

By contrast, a greater percentage of alumni children, recruited athletes, and those not seeking financial aid applied early than did students overall in the admissions office data. For example, 34.0 percent of alumni children applied early at Early Action colleges, and 17.1 percent of alumni children applied early at Early Decision colleges—rates that are significantly higher than the 20.5 percent and 7.4 percent of all applicants who applied early at those schools. For five of the fourteen colleges, we have the zip code for each applicant. In general, we found that applicants from zip codes with unusually high per capita incomes or unusually high percentages of college graduates applied early more frequently than did others.[36] Figures 2.4 and 2.5 compare the percentages of early applicants from eleven groups. Identified minorities, public school students, and financial aid applicants constitute a noticeably smaller proportion of the early application pool than of the regular pool at both Early Action and Early Decision colleges.

Recruited athletes quite often apply early at selective colleges. At these colleges most athletic recruiting occurs in the fall, and coaches tend to emphasize early applications. A student at Princeton summarized her experiences as a recruit for the golf team: "Coaches prefer for you to apply early to demonstrate interest; if you apply early, they might move you up the list of their preferred appli-

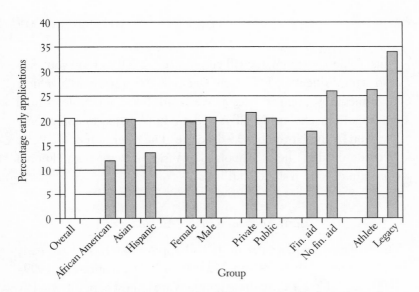

Figure 2.4 Early application rates for different groups: Early Action colleges. (Admissions office data)

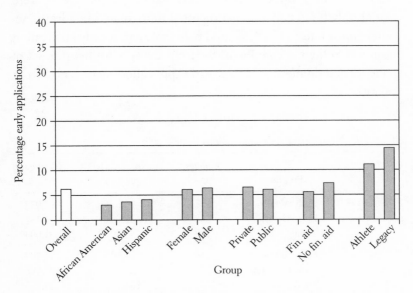

Figure 2.5 Early application rates for different groups: Early Decision colleges. (Admissions office data)

cants. Potential teammates will emphasize this if they want you to attend" (Jill, Princeton, '00). Early Decision 2 also serves as a vehicle for attracting student-athletes at Wesleyan. Some top athletes hold out hopes for scholarship offers and are unprepared to apply Early Decision by the November 15 deadline. The extension of the Early Decision deadline helps schools like Wesleyan to secure additional commitments from student athletes.

Early Applicants across All Colleges

The College Board's database tallied approximately 159,000 early applications in 1998–99 and 162,000 early applications in 1999–2000 (see Table 2.1). But these numbers are almost certainly too low because in each year more than 30 percent of the colleges did not report their early application numbers to the College Board. For instance, Miami University (Ohio) and North Carolina State were two of only three colleges that reported more than 5,000 Early Action applications in 1998–99, and neither reported early application numbers to the College Board for 1999–2000.[37] Further, the set of colleges that do not report their early applications can change from year to year.

Table 2.1   Numbers of early applications, 1998–2000

Year	Program	Colleges reporting	No. of early applications	No. of early admits
1998–1999	Early Action	107	96,871	57,932
	Early Decision	208	62,001	33,152
	Total	292*	158,897	91,094
1999–2000	Early Action	115	95,506	55,799
	Early Decision	210	66,046	33,596
	Total	298*	161,552	89,395

* A total of twenty-three colleges in 1998–1999 and twenty-seven colleges in 1999–2000 reported numbers for both Early Action and Early Decision.

Source: College Board Database.

To assess whether early applications have increased over time, we compared the numbers reported for 1997–98, 1998–99, and 1999–2000 for those colleges that reported early applications in all three years.[38] Among the 64 colleges that reported Early Action applications in each year, early applications rose by 25 percent from 1997–98 to 1999–2000, whereas regular applications declined slightly.[39] Among the 169 colleges that reported Early Decision applications in each year, early applications rose by 9 percent from 1997–98 to 1999–2000, but regular applications increased by even more than that.

The size of early admissions programs varies widely. In 1999–2000, 15 Early Decision colleges and 26 Early Action colleges received more than 1,000 early applications each. By themselves, these 41 colleges accounted for more than 92,000 early applications, or approximately 60 percent of the nationwide total. The University of Maryland received the largest number of Early Action applications, while New York University received the largest number of Early Decision applications for 1999–2000 (see Table 2.2). The set of most popular Early Action and Early Decision colleges varies little from year to year. The colleges that ranked in the top ten in Early Action or Early Decision applications for 1999–2000 all ranked in the top twenty in early applications for 1998–99.[40]

At the other extreme, some colleges receive very few early applications: five colleges reported that they received fewer than ten Early Decision applications, and fifty-two colleges reported that they received fewer than fifty Early Decision applications in 1999–2000. Early Action programs tend to attract more applicants. Only four colleges reported that they received fewer than ten Early Action applications, and nine colleges reported that they received fewer than fifty Early Action applications in 1999–2000.[41]

Not surprisingly, the highest-ranked colleges are among those that tend to receive the most early applications, whether Early Action or Early Decision. EA colleges with the highest average SAT scores among current students received more than one-quarter of all appli-

Table 2.2   Colleges with the largest numbers of early applications, 1999–2000

Early Action colleges	No. of early applications	Early Decision colleges	No. of early applications
University of Maryland	13,171	New York University	2,718
Harvard College	6,026	University of Pennsylvania	2,370
Brown University	4,923	Virginia Tech	2,300
Georgetown University	3,732	Cornell University	2,264
University of Miami (Fla.)	3,057	University of North Carolina	2,157
University of Connecticut	2,935	Stanford University	2,009
MIT	2,921	University of Florida	1,997
Rice University	2,384	University of Virginia	1,847
Villanova University	2,311	Princeton University	1,669
University of New Hampshire	1,914	California Polytechnic: San Luis Obispo	1,531

Source: College Board Database.

cations from early applicants in 1999–2000. But ED colleges in each category received fewer than 10 percent of their applications in ED (see Figure 2.6).

Since almost all Early Decision admits fulfill their commitment to enroll, a more accurate measure of the magnitude of Early Decision is the percentage of spaces in the entering class that are offered in Early Decision. This measure suggests that early admits make up slightly more than 20 percent of the entering class at the top universities and colleges that offer Early Decision. The figure tends to be somewhat higher at institutions offering Early Action. At the most selective colleges offering Early Action, an average of 25 percent of admitted students are admitted early.[42] Given that Early Action applicants are more likely than regular applicants to matriculate, the percentage of early applicants in the entering class at these EA colleges is probably more than 30 percent.

The popularity of early applications creates the appearance that there are few spots left for regular applicants. Table 2.3 summarizes author Bill Paul's tally of admitted students for Princeton's class of

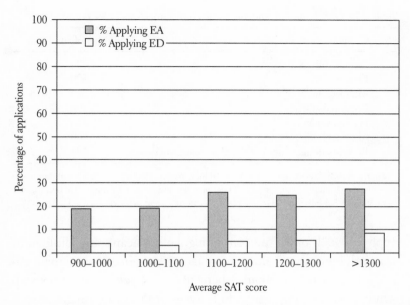

Figure 2.6 Percentage of early applications. (College Board database for 1999–2000)

1999, the last year (1994–95) that the school offered Early Action for its applicants. Princeton admitted 2,000 students overall in that year, and Paul estimated that more than 1,500 fall into at least one of the priority categories listed in the table; some students fall into two or more. According to this estimate, Princeton admitted fewer than 500 applicants in the regular pool (including deferred applicants) who failed to fit into a priority category. In the admissions lexicon, applicants who fall into a priority category are known as "hooked," and applicants who do not are "unhooked." With 12,000 regular applicants, the chances of admission for those who were unhooked were poor.

Bruce Breimer, the college counselor at the Collegiate School in New York, concluded that many of the students admitted in the regular pool must be minorities, given that minorities generally do not

Table 2.3   Distribution of students admitted to Princeton, 1994–95

Category	Number of admits
Total admits	2,000
Early admits	600
Minority students	600
Recruited athletes	300
Foreign students	100
Alumni children	200
Regular admits in none of the above categories	500

Source: Bill Paul, *Getting In* (New York: Addison-Wesley, 1995), pp. 127, 225. All numbers are estimates (from p. 127 and p. 225). These numbers add up to more than 2,000 because some students fall into more than one of the six categories and so are counted at least twice.

apply early: "If only 7 percent of regular applicants are admitted to Harvard, then what is the percentage of 'unhooked' white male applicants? It must be about 3 percent . . . If you're an 'unhooked' white male applying regular to Harvard or Princeton, might as well just stick a fork in you, because you're done."[43]

Breimer made clear that he sees Harvard and Princeton as rarities even among the most selective colleges. Yet if there was a crunch for spots for regular applicants at Princeton in 1994–95, when Bill Paul developed the estimates shown in Table 2.3, then there may well be a similar crunch for spots at the competitive private universities that admit relatively large numbers of students early.

The Percentage of Early Applicants in Our Interviews and Surveys

What percentage of students at selective colleges applied early to some college, not necessarily the one where they enrolled? We calculated this percentage for three groups of students. First, approximately two-thirds (65.5 percent) of the high school seniors we interviewed at Choate Rosemary Hall and Needham High School in 1998–99 applied early. Second, of our interview subjects who were undergraduates at Harvard, MIT, Princeton, Wesleyan, and Yale, almost two-thirds had applied early to some college. But among those from high schools where many of their classmates do not go on to college, less than half applied early. Given the complexity of the system, it is not surprising that even the most talented students at such schools do not understand the early applications game well enough to play it.

Third, more than half of the more than 3,000 high school seniors who participated in the College Admissions Project in 1999–2000 applied early to some college. An even higher percentage of those who applied to highly selective colleges did so. Sixty-five percent of the participants who applied to an Ivy League college, MIT, or Stanford applied early to some college. Most striking, of the students who enrolled in one of those ten highly selective colleges, 81 percent applied early somewhere and more than half applied early to the college where they enrolled. These figures tell a strong story: the evidence indicates that if you want to attend an Ivy League college, MIT, or Stanford, then you should apply early. As one Harvard student explained in an interview, "That's just how you apply to Harvard" (Amy, Harvard '98).

Given that the students who participated in the College Admissions Project were selected because they had strong records at outstanding high schools, they do not represent the ordinary population of high school students—they do represent the population of applicants who are the most competitive for admission to elite colleges. Our results show that the majority of the most talented high school students in America are now applying early, and an even higher percentage of those who are applying to selective private colleges are doing so.

Admissions Rates for Early and Regular Applicants

To our knowledge, every selective school admits a higher percentage of early applicants than of regular applicants. When NACAC conducted a survey of colleges in 1996, Early Action schools reported an average admissions rate of 65 percent for early applicants and 59 percent for regular applicants. In that same survey, Early Decision schools reported an average admissions rate of 66 percent for early applicants and 60 percent for regular applicants, a difference of 6 percent for both programs.

But the difference between the rates of admission for early and regular applicants is almost certainly considerably larger than 6 percent. The College Board asks each school to report how many students are admitted early—it does not ask about early applicants who are initially deferred and then later admitted.[44] This understates the true chance of admission for early applicants. For example, almost 10 percent of early applicants to MIT in 1999–2000 were deferred and then subsequently admitted. According to the College Board's database, MIT admitted 18.6 percent of its early applicants in 1999–2000. Including those who were admitted after a deferral, however, MIT admitted 28.5 percent of its early applicants that year. (See Chapter 6 for a more detailed discussion of the deferral practices by colleges.)

We contacted seven admissions offices in the summer of 2000 to compile statistics on the number of deferrals and the number of students admitted after deferral. We recalculated the overall rates of admission for these colleges, to compute the percentages of early applicants who were eventually admitted, and we found very large differences in the admission rates for early and regular applicants. MIT was the only college where the admission rate for regular applicants was within 10 percentage points of the admission rate for early applicants. Three colleges, Harvard, Princeton, and Stanford, had admissions rates for early applicants that were at least double their admissions rates for regular applicants. (See Figure 2.7, which reports percentages for 1999–2000; the results were very similar for 1998–99.)

We do not have information about the outcomes for deferred ap-

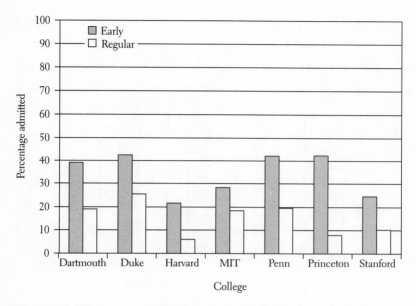

Figure 2.7 Admission rates after accounting for deferrals, 1999–2000. (Phone interviews with admissions offices)

plicants at other colleges. The statistics for these schools, based on the College Board's database, count applicants who are deferred and then admitted in the regular pool as *regular admits* but as *early applicants*. Thus these statistics, which still indicate that early applicants are admitted at higher rates than regular applicants, *understate* the admission rates for early applicants and *overstate* the admission rates for regular applicants.

Figure 2.8 shows a comparison of admission rates for Early Decision colleges of different rankings; the results are similar for Early Action colleges. Among the most selective schools, that is, those with the highest average SAT scores among their current students, early applicants are admitted at noticeably higher rates than are regular applicants.

Previous studies and these graphs suggest that applying early will

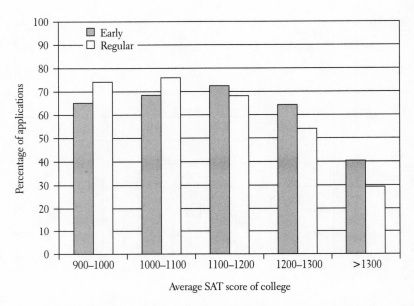

Figure 2.8 Admission rates at Early Decision colleges, not including deferred admits. (College Board database for 1999–2000)

improve an applicant's chances of admission at the most selective colleges. But they do not prove it, because we have not yet looked at whether the differences between early and regular applicants account for the full differences in admission rates. After all, many college admissions offices assert that early applicants are stronger candidates than regular applicants in terms of academic and extracurricular qualifications. Fortunately, we have statistics on such qualifications, enabling us to assess the true effect of applying early, after adjusting for variations between early and regular applicants. Chapter 5 provides a more detailed analysis.

Absent a complicated statistical analysis, high school students have for years been reaching their own conclusions about the effect of applying early. Chapters 3 and 4 analyze their assessments and responses.

3

❧❦❧

Martian Blackjack: What Do Applicants Understand about Early Admissions?

You wander into a casino on Mars and stride up to a blackjack table. An old man is watching. The first player secures an 18, the dealer a 16. The player gets paid off and departs. A new player sits in and gets a 20, but the dealer hits 21. That player gets paid as well. She doesn't understand but doesn't question the dealer, opting instead to wander away. A third player, who has been monitoring the proceedings, takes a seat and scores 19 to the dealer's 18, but the player's chips are swept away, and he leaves dejected. The old man offers a surmise: "Here an even score beats an odd score." The theory survives until the next deal, when a new player gets a 19 to the dealer's 20 yet still gets paid.[1]

Martian Blackjack is a metaphor for the Early Admissions Game. The players (applicants) do not know the rules (that is, the standards for admission), and the casinos (college admissions offices) do not describe them, at least not fully or accurately. The players' perceptions depend on their own experiences, and perhaps the experiences of others at their high school. And each player participates just once.

The old man is the everyman of guidance counselors. He sees many plays but analyzes them mostly anecdotally, often reaching premature or incorrect conclusions. His task is made harder in that a college, like a Martian casino, may change its rules periodically to capitalize on its patrons' changing behavior. Moreover, the rules differ from casino to casino. But there is a big difference between the Early Admissions Game and Martian blackjack: the first significantly determines who gets admitted to which elite college, with all that implies. The second is just about money.

In both settings, market forces limit how much the rulemaker can exploit his clients. On average, the casino can only secure a moderate take lest competitors steal its business, and colleges cannot employ extreme differences in standards for early and regular admissions, or very few would apply to the tough regular process. But there are ill-informed suckers at the casino, and naïve players among college applicants, and there may be a wide gap between the expected fortunes of those who are well informed about the rules and those who can only guess. Some people—card counters and highly informed college applicants alike—gain a considerable advantage.

This chapter has three purposes: to see how college students, who have completed the admissions process successfully, understand the game; to examine the sources (such as guidebooks, counselors, and the colleges themselves) from which applicants can learn about early admissions; and to discover what students conclude about the effects of applying early.

We were curious to see how well students understood the early admissions process, so we interviewed nearly 350 students at Harvard, MIT, Princeton, and Yale. Clearly, these students must have navigated the admissions process successfully. Yet even they were confused about the early applications system. Nearly a quarter (22.9 percent) of these college students had only a "fair" or "poor" understanding of early applications when they applied to college.[2] They either described themselves as poorly informed (6.1 percent), did not understand the difference between Early Action and Early Decision (10.7 percent), did not understand the rules of early applications, or made contradictory statements about early applications during the course of the interview (11.6 percent), generally about the effect of applying early.[3] A few did not even know that it was possible to apply early until after they had been admitted to college.

We wondered if college students from more prominent high schools were better informed than those from less competitive schools. Such students likely had the most experienced college counselors and the most savvy classmates. We began by dividing the high schools into two groups, those prominent schools included in the College Admissions Project (CAP) survey (see Appendix B), and those from all other schools.[4] In general, schools classified as "in the CAP survey" are known for sending a substantial percentage of their graduates to the most selective colleges. We then further classified them into private and public and divided the remaining public schools into two categories, depending on how many of their graduates go to college.

Table 3.1 tells the story. First, the college students' levels of understanding fall as we move down the table, from more elite to less elite schools. Second, the disparities are great. Among those students in the CAP study of prominent high schools, 90 percent of those from private schools and 84 percent of those from public schools had a full understanding of early applications when they applied to college. By contrast, nearly half the students from public schools where many graduates do not attend college—and remember these students were attending Harvard, MIT, Princeton, and Yale—had a full understanding of early applications when they applied to college.

Sources of Information on Early Applications

The official sources for information on early admissions are college guidebooks, the colleges themselves, and guidance counselors. Un-

Table 3.1   Knowledge of early applications when applying to college: students at Harvard, MIT, Princeton, and Yale (classes of 1998 to 2001)[a]

	"Good" understanding of early applications	"Fair" or "Poor" understanding of early applications	Applied early
Private school, included in CAP survey	71 of 79 (90%)	8 of 79 (10%)	66 of 79 (84%)
Public school, included in CAP survey	76 of 91 (86%)	15 of 91 (14%)	71 of 91 (78%)
Private school, not included in CAP survey	30 of 35 (84%)	5 of 35 (16%)	25 of 35 (71%)
Public school, not included in CAP survey, where most attend college	44 of 57 (77%)	13 of 57 (23%)	39 of 57 (68%)
Public school, not included in CAP survey, where many don't attend college	32 of 61 (52%)	29 of 61 (48%)	26 of 61 (43%)
Overall	253 of 323 (79%)	69 of 323 (21%)	227 of 323 (70%)

a. We exclude from the tabulations throughout most of this chapter college students who attended high school outside of the United States.
Source: Interviews with college students.

officially, students learn by anecdote, from conversations with their high school classmates and predecessors, from relatives, from the media, and from the rumor network. As this chapter will show, the official sources are inconsistent, often misleading, and insufficient to make an informed estimate of the effect of applying early.

U.S. News College Guide and Its Competitors

The *U.S. News College Guide* has become a bible for many students; indeed, it is so influential that it has significantly affected the behavior of colleges, which strive mightily to improve their ranking in the report.[5] How does this authoritative source assess the situation, and what does it advise? For the past several years, the *U.S. News College Guide* has reported widespread belief among students and some counselors that colleges favor early applicants in admission decisions. But it has taken slightly different positions regarding the actual practices of the most selective colleges.

The 1997 *U.S. News College Guide* (for applicants in the school year 1996–97) asserted that the differences in admissions rates for early and regular applicants demonstrate that early applicants gain an advantage in admissions decisions at even the most competitive colleges: "Admissions officials at some prestigious universities like Harvard and Stanford insist that they give early applicants no special edge. But as at Williams, the numbers tell a different story." But from 1998–99 to 2000–02, the *U.S. News College Guide* took the dramatically different position that early applications only gain an advantage in admissions decisions at "lower-profile colleges engaged in aggressive recruiting" (1999 *Guide*). The 2000 *Guide* elaborates:

> But at the most competitive schools, the dynamic is very different. They use early decision to garner prospects with impeccable qualifications; if they have any doubts about candidates, they defer them into the regular admissions pool. Some of these schools let in a higher fraction of applicants through early decision than through regular admissions, but going early decision does not typically give the less qualified a better shot. Although acceptance rates may be higher, early decision candidates are competing against a more qualified set of peers.

Both the 2000 and the 2001 guides repeated that same claim, namely, that the most selective colleges use deferrals to ensure that early applicants do not gain an advantage over regular applicants. The 2001 issue quoted William Fitzsimmons, Harvard's dean of admissions, making a similar point: "[Before accepting anyone early], we have to be 100 percent sure that [he or she] will get in later."[6]

The 2001 *Newsweek College Guide* took a similar position, suggesting that differences in the percentages of early and regular applicants admitted at a given school need not indicate a difference in standards: "Penn recently took more than half of its early applicants, who fill more than a third of freshman classes. But what the numbers don't tell you is that the early competition is often stiffer."

In contrast, the 2001 *Time/Princeton Review College Guide* asserted, much like the 1997 *U.S. News Guide,* that aggregate statistics indicated that all colleges, even the most selective, were favoring early applicants. This assertion represents a dramatic change in stance from that of the 2000 *Time/Princeton Review College Guide,* which had said almost nothing about the possibility that applying early can affect an applicant's chances of admission.

The 2001 *Time/Princeton Guide* emphasized the small number of spaces that are left in the freshman class at certain colleges by the time regular admissions rolls around: "Harvard and Brown accepted enough students under nonbinding EA to make up 69% and 73% of their classes, respectively. It doesn't take a math wizard to figure out that this leaves a lot fewer places for regular admissions. 'You must apply early, or you have almost no chance,' said a Harvard alumnus who has interviewed prospective students for a decade. 'Just look at the numbers.'"

At the same time, all three guides emphasized the "hidden pitfalls" of early applications. All were concerned with the possibility that students would apply Early Decision to one college and then decide that another college was their first choice:

The downside: early decision is rushing many students into hasty decisions. (2001 *Newsweek Guide*)

When kids cut their research into colleges short, they often limit their choices much more than they ought to. (2001 *U.S. News Guide*)

Many educators believe students are being drafted far too early into the admissions game—being encouraged to turn in college applications that aren't ready or to make hasty college decisions at a time when real maturation is taking place. (2001 *Time/Princeton Review Guide*)

These publications also emphasized the fact that students who apply early may lose out in their financial aid packages. The 2001 *U.S. News Guide* concluded by describing the case of a student who benefited in financial aid by deciding not to apply early: "Even though Sara Strasser had her heart set on Grinnell College in Iowa, the Crete, IL senior didn't apply early so she wouldn't be 'stuck going there' if she got a lot of money from another school. Strasser was smart: Grinnell offered her the lowest amount of the four schools she applied to, so she chose Lawrence University in Appleton, Wis., instead." The 2001 *Time/Princeton Review Guide* concurred that financial aid considerations complicate the decision to apply early: "Devising a strategy to get the best shot at acceptance and aid is nearly impossible, since students don't have access to either set of odds."

Thus each of the three most popular college guides has vacillated about the effect of applying early, and their discussions of early applications have varied substantially in quality, accuracy, and detail. Even when they did conclude that an early application significantly improves the chance of admission at the most selective colleges, they still tended to discourage students from applying early. For instance, the 2001 *U.S. News Guide* highlighted a single sentence: "There are compelling reasons to resist early-bird urges."

Similarly, we examined the other leading college guides in the fall of 1999 and found them to be highly inconsistent and for the most part uninformative, as Table 3.2 shows.[7] Most of these guides told whether schools offered early admissions and, if so, when the application deadlines were. Beyond that, they reported some pub-

Table 3.2   Information in college guides, fall 1999

Source	Effect of applying early	Recommended strategy
U.S. *News College Guide*	"Statistically better chance" at less competitive schools	Aim for Early Action if possible
Newsweek College Guide	Advantageous at some (less competitive) schools	"Don't even think about applying [ED] if . . . you aren't sure about your first choice"
Barron's	Does not mention	None
Fiske	More advantageous for colleges than for students	None
Kaplan	Advantageous in some cases (not clear which ones)	Apply early to signal preference, if you have one
Peterson's ("4-Year Colleges")	Does not mention	None
Peterson's Insider's Guide	Equivocal	Unclear
Princeton Review	Lists admissions rates, but does not interpret them	None
A Is for Admission	Applying Early Decision will generally help your chances of admission	"You have to be sure that the college is truly your first choice [to apply ED]"
College Planning for Dummies	Focuses on disadvantages of applying early	"Because you're reading this book, you won't succumb to the pressure [to apply early]"
Secrets of Harvard Students	Equivocal	Apply early (EA or ED) "only if you are sure that the school is your first choice and you definitely want to go there"
Yale Daily News, Insider's Guide	Does not mention	None

licly available facts incorrectly, sometimes in embarrassing fashion. (The *Yale Daily News Insider's 1999 Guide,* for example, stated that Yale uses Early Action, even though it switched to Early Decision in 1995–96.) Most of the guides were silent on the advantages and disadvantages of applying early, and those that spoke missed most important factors. Only a few gave statistics on numbers from early admissions, and only one gave percentages of those admitted among early and regular applicants. Only one, *A Is for Admission*, clearly stated that applying Early Decision will improve the chances of getting into highly selective colleges.

Most of these guidebooks directed students away from applying early. Almost all emphasized that students who are not absolutely certain of a first-choice college should not apply in Early Decision. The College Board website epitomizes this view: "You should only apply under an early decision plan if you are very, very sure of the college you want to attend. These plans make a lot of sense if one college is your clear preference and if your profile closely matches that of the students at that college."[8]

Two guides, *College Planning for Dummies* and the *U.S. News College Guide*, seemed to argue at times that even those students who have identified a first-choice college should not apply early. The former even suggested that applying early is tantamount to succumbing to a psychological weakness: "Peer pressure builds on students to apply early . . . Because you're reading this book, you won't succumb to the pressure [to apply early for prestige]."

Whereas the *Newsweek, Time,* and *U.S. News* guides cite disadvantages of early applications that apply almost exclusively to Early Decision, the *Peterson's Insider's Guide* discouraged students from applying Early Action, which it described in wholly negative terms.[9]

A Is for Admission was the most informative of these guides. Its author, Michele Hernandez, the former assistant director of admission at Dartmouth, revealed that admissions rates were higher for early applicants to Dartmouth than for regular applicants (the same was true at the other Ivy League colleges). Hernandez also offered the valuable insight that deferred applicants may be able to improve their chances of success through contact with admissions officers. Yet even this guide fell short of providing a complete picture of early admissions. It did not offer a sense of the magnitude of the advantage for early applicants, and it made some mistakes. For example, it identified Cornell as one school that does not give preference to early applicants, even though Cornell contradicts that statement on its website: "Because enthusiasm for Cornell is considered a plus, early-decision applicants stand a better chance of gaining admission—a fact reflected in the statistics."[10] Further, *A Is for Admission* stated that all the Ivy League schools are "100% need-blind." This was not true when the book was published; at that time Brown, for instance, openly admitted that it takes financial status into account in admission decisions for the last 5 to 10 percent of its entering class.[11]

College Websites

In spring 2002 we examined the websites of the eight Ivy League colleges, along with MIT and Stanford.[12] Two of those colleges provide little or no useful information about the effect of applying early. MIT and Stanford describe the procedures for applying early but make no mention of whether or not doing so will enhance an applicant's chance of admission. In contrast, three colleges take a clear position that applies to all applicants. As quoted above, Cornell states that it gives an advantage to early applicants, whereas Brown and Harvard say that they give no advantage whatsoever to early applicants. The remaining five colleges (Columbia, Dartmouth, Penn, Princeton, and Yale) provide partial but unsatisfying information.

Penn explains that "children of alumni receive some preference" if they apply early, but it says nothing about other applicants.[13] This omission is surprising given that Penn's admissions director, Lee Stetson, stated in the 1997 *U.S. News Guide* that early applicants receive special consideration at Penn.

Columbia notes that its admission rate for applicants for the fall of 2000 was 36 percent for early applicants as opposed to 13 percent overall; it also states that early applicants made up 47 percent of the entering class.[14] The college makes no comment about the overall effect of applying early, not even to note that the early and regular pools might contain different proportions of competitive applicants. It is possible that Columbia is indicating in coy fashion that Early Decision offers an advantage, presumably because it is trying to use these statistics as a lure to induce applicants to apply early. (Hilary Ballon, a professor at Columbia and chair of the Columbia Committee on Admissions and Financial Aid, has been one of the most vigorous defenders of the Early Decision system.)[15]

Dartmouth says that "Early Decision candidates are judged according to the same criteria as those in regular decision."[16] Yale makes a similar statement, but with a twist: "Early Decision candidates are evaluated in the same way as are those who apply as Regular Decision candidates, but with the understanding that Yale is the student's first choice."[17]

These statements are as notable for what they don't say as for what they do say. For example, does the "understanding that Yale is the student's first choice" work in favor of Yale's Early Decision applicants? Perhaps, or perhaps not.

Princeton's website provided a particularly confusing statement:[18]

Are my chances for admission better if I apply under the Early Decision program?

Well, in one sense the answer to that question is "no." A candidate to whom we otherwise would not offer admission is not going to be offered admission simply because he or she applied Early Decision. However, it *is* the case that the rate of admission of early applicants is invariably higher than our overall admission rate. In part, that's simply a matter of there being a rather large number of compelling candidates in the early applicant pool (which also explains why we invariably end up, after reviewing the *entire* applicant pool, making yet more offers of admission in April to candidates whose early applications

were deferred back in December). And in part, it's undoubtedly the most efficient way in which to effect a match between
the kinds of students Princeton seeks to enroll and those among
them who seek to enroll at Princeton.[19]

But if it is true that early admits would also be regular admits at
Princeton, then no part of the difference in admission rates should
be attributed to the efficient matching promoted by Early Deci-
sion. We interpret the last sentence of the statement to mean that
Princeton wants to favor applicants who have a particular interest in
Princeton, but that's certainly not clear.[20]

Many of the counselors we interviewed decried such lack of clar-
ity on the part of the colleges. For example, Scotte Gordon, the
college counselor at the Moses Brown School (R.I.), complained
that "colleges are not fully candid about ED. They do not provide
full information unless pressed. They tend to hide glaring discrepancies in admit rates and try to gloss over these gaps with flowery language."[21]

Why don't colleges make straightforward statements about their
early and regular admissions standards? The explanation, we believe, is that colleges face conflicting pressures, including major
pressure to maintain that they treat all applicants equally. Any ac-
knowledgment of favoritism for early applicants—a wealthy and
well-connected group—would play poorly with many constituen-
cies. In fact, the 2001 *Time Guide* suggested a potential class-action
suit against colleges that favor early applicants.

Similarly, colleges are often loath to admit that they give preference to athletes, alumni children, and minority applicants, despite
clear evidence that they do so.[22] Colleges are no more forthcoming
on the subject of affirmative action than on standards for early applications, with few providing relevant statistics when not compelled to
do so by law. When questioned about their policies on affirmative
action, colleges, which are seeking simultaneously to satisfy con-

flicting goals, generally obfuscate with complex language and conflicting statements of principle. But it can also be advantageous in
some instances, depending on the audience, for colleges to state that
they have enacted energetic affirmative action policies. Similarly in
the case of Early Action and Early Decision, both stances ("all applicants are treated equally," "early applicants are favored in admissions
decisions") have their advantages, depending on time and place.
Thus, it is not surprising that colleges such as Princeton try to take
both positions at once.[23]

Perhaps colleges believe that the most desirable group of applicants—better-connected students who tend to be full-payers from
leading feeder schools—will be able to ferret out the information
that early applicants are favored, and that others will not. Then a
garbled message, but one decipherable with hints or considerable
experience, may be the preferred message to disseminate.

College Admissions Officers

College admissions officers provide information to prospective applicants at information sessions and in personal conversations on
campus and at high schools. A relatively small number (18.8 percent) of the college students we interviewed reported specific
statements by admissions officers about the effect of applying early.
Some 7.3 percent of the college students were told (or felt that it was
implied) by admissions officers that early applicants would receive
special consideration. Another 7.3 percent were told that early applicants were treated the same (or approximately the same) as regular
applicants, while 4.2 percent felt that the admissions officer evaded
the question or gave an answer that was difficult to evaluate.

One intrepid candidate reported that he asked the admissions
directors at Harvard, Princeton, and Yale during his campus visits whether they gave preference to early applicants. William Fitzsimmons said that Harvard did not, whereas the others said that they

do give a slight preference to early applicants. Harvard students were more likely to have been told by an admissions officer that early applications do not affect admissions decisions, but not all of them got that message. Of nineteen Harvard students who described conversations with admissions officers, twelve said they were told that early applications have no effect on admissions chances (including three who said they were told that applying early might help a very small amount). Three others said that they concluded from their conversations that applying early would help their chances. It seems clear that different admissions officers left different impressions with the students:[24]

> Harvard said that the Early Action process is beneficial if you are a strong candidate, and I figured that it did not hurt. If it was not explicitly stated, it was implied. (Carolyn, Harvard '00)

> The Harvard admissions officer said, "Apply early only if you think you can walk on water." He referred to rejected students as "roadkill." (Roger, Harvard '98)

Several of the counselors and a smaller proportion of the college students we interviewed felt that admissions officers were not always forthright in their statements. Rory Bled, a counselor at Berkeley High School, believed that she had observed a significant advantage in admission decisions for students applying Early Decision to Columbia, even though Columbia stated that its standards were no different for early and regular applicants. Among the thirty college students in our interviews who reported that they were told directly by an admissions officer that an early application has literally no effect on outcomes, seventeen doubted the claim. The following comment from a student from Palo Alto High School typifies the views of these students:

Admissions officials gave their supposedly generic answer that admissions treats all applicants, whether early or regular, the same. I was skeptical. (Anne, Yale '00)

Two students from the Thomas Jefferson High School for Science and Technology in Fairfax County, Va., felt that admissions officers made misleading statements:

Admissions office talks are deceptive. In particular, Ivy League schools seemed to be very political in their approach. I didn't always believe what they said, and I hope they believed what they said. (Robin, Princeton '00)

Princeton claimed that there would not be a big effect from applying early, but I thought that the statistics that I'd seen indicated that there would be. (Akash, Princeton '00)

A student from nearby Montgomery County, Md., summarized this cynical view of college information sessions:

Admissions officers will say what they need to say to get you to apply. (Sean, Harvard '01)

Guidance Counselors and Others

All the counselors we interviewed at nationally prominent high schools stated that applying early—at least applying Early Decision—would help a student gain admission. Some drew logical inferences from the advantage that an early admit provides to the college, or from their discussions with college admissions offices. Others drew on experience and anecdote. In some cases, stark experiences made it obvious to counselors that early applicants gain an advantage in the admissions process. Bill Matthews, who headed the college counseling office at St. Paul's School in New Hampshire for many years, described his observations in some detail in an article for the *Boston Globe*: "If you want to get admitted to a competitive college, your chances are dramatically better if you apply early. Let me cite just three examples from this past year. Princeton accepted 8 of our 17 early applicants, but not 1 of 31 in the regular pool. At Yale, 14 were accepted early and 4 of 26 later on. Williams took two of three early ones, then one of nine in April."[25]

Most of the counselors we interviewed concurred that smaller colleges tended to favor early applicants more than larger schools did, but they disagreed about the practices of particular colleges. Rory Bled of Berkeley High School and Alice Purington of Andover both cited Duke and Penn as colleges that favor early applicants. Beyond this, however, there was little overlap in the counselors' observations. In fact, whereas one identified Northwestern as a school that favors early applicants, another cited Northwestern as a school that does not.

The college students we interviewed described widely varying advice from their counselors concerning early applications. About the same number had a counselor who specifically indicated that applying early would help the student's chances of admission (18.8 percent), as had a counselor who encouraged students in general to apply early (18.0 percent).[26] Only 2.6 percent had a counselor indicate that applying early would have no effect. Most of the remaining students did not remember the counselor's taking any particular stance about early applications.

At the other extreme, 16.5 percent of the students felt that the counselor had hindered the application process, if anything. They did not receive information about early applications from the counselor and frequently had to sidestep unhelpful guidance in other areas:

I said that I wanted to go to a small liberal arts college in the East. He suggested two state schools in the Midwest. (Leah, Harvard '01)

The counselor told me to consider [the local] community college. In fact, the counselor told everyone to consider community college. (Yael, Princeton '00)

Some students, generally those in wealthy suburban areas, hired private counselors. A student from Winnetka, Ill., shared her experience: "My high school counselors showed some statistics on acceptance rates. But my private counselor really knew the strategies of applying more than the high school counselors. He showed me some graphs that showed the effect applying early had on certain types of students" (Jessica, Yale '00).

The college students also received information from other sources—in particular, from SAT tutors, teachers, and athletic coaches at colleges. Most of these people suggested that applying early would help.

Our interviews also provided evidence that information travels within families. Several students said that older siblings who went to Ivy League schools directed them to apply early. Similarly, several students who did not know about early admissions when they applied said that they are telling their younger siblings to apply early.

Information about recent graduates can spread within a high school. Since experiences vary across schools, students at different schools can reach markedly different conclusions, as did the following two students, one from Virginia's Thomas Jefferson High School and the other from a public school in nearby Bethesda, Md.:

The rap in the school was that early admits were less qualified than regular applicants who were not admitted. That seemed to be the case the year that I applied. After the experience of my class, everyone knew that they had to apply early. (Robin, Princeton '00)

Only one out of eight or ten students who applied under Early Action was admitted. Many more were accepted under regular admissions to those Early Action schools. I would have had a better chance of getting into Brown if I had applied under regular decision. (Elena, Yale '01)

As these stories indicate, information dissemination is unpredictable. The results for only a few graduates of a high school in one year may well serve as the entire base of knowledge for students in the next class. Phyllis MacKay, the counselor at Oyster River High School in New Hampshire, told us of a single case that had a long-lasting effect on decisions for subsequent students. After the explosion of early applications to Harvard in 1995–96, most Oyster River students and their families were convinced that there was very little chance of being admitted as a regular applicant to Harvard. Yet one Oyster River applicant was admitted as a regular applicant to Harvard that year. As MacKay explained, "the admission of this one student to Harvard considerably reduced the emphasis on early applications in the minds of later applicants."[27]

Assessments of the Effect of Early Applications

At the end of each interview we asked students and counselors to assess the effect of applying Early Action and Early Decision on separate scales of 1 to 5, where a response of 3 corresponded to "no effect" in admissions and responses of 4 and 5 indicated that an early application provided an advantage.[28] Most of the students and almost all the counselors agreed that applying early would help the chances of admission (see Table 3.3).

Table 3.3 Percentage who believe that applying early provides an advantage in admissions decisions

	College students	High school seniors	Counselors in competitive high schools	Counselors in Mass. public schools
Early Action	73.8%	34.5%	73.3%	50%
Early Decision	83.9%	70.7%	100%	60%
Number of respondents	317	58	15	10

Source: Interviews with college students.

Twice as many college as high school students felt that Early Action provides an admissions advantage. We suspect this is at least partially the result of information-sharing among college students. Several students at Princeton referred to articles in the college newspaper to bolster their views that early applications provide an admissions edge: *"The Daily Princetonian* had an article this morning stating that one out of three early applicants was admitted as opposed to one out of fourteen regular applicants" (Mary, Princeton '00).

Many students employed common sense and logic to determine the effect of applying early, but since so many factors might and do play a role, their conclusions varied wildly. Table 3.4 lists the factors in the early admissions game that college students mentioned in our interviews and the different conclusions they drew.

Table 3.4 illustrates the challenge of assessing the effect of an early application without solid empirical information. The students' overall conclusions depended on the individual factors upon which they focused. Students often disagreed about the likely consequence of a factor, to the point where some students argued that some factor made it an advantage to apply early, while others argued that the same factor could lead to a disadvantage—not always with the greatest logic. In the three sections that follow, we outline patterns of student reasoning.

Table 3.4   Logical conclusions drawn by interview subjects

Factor	Consequence	Implication for early applicants
Large number of early admits	Few spaces in the class for regular applicants	Advantage
Possibility of deferral	Two chances at admission	Advantage
	Can improve one's application	Advantage
	Deferral is tantamount to rejection; also, could be rejected immediately	Disadvantage
The early and regular pools of applicants differ	Easier to stand out in a smaller pool	Advantage
	Better to be compared against regular than early applicants	Disadvantage
Absolute standard for admissions decisions	Would be admitted as regular applicant if admitted early	No effect
	Adm. officers subconsciously set a higher standard for regular applicants	Advantage
Signaling	Applying early demonstrates enthusiasm and organization	Advantage
College rankings	Colleges improve their ranking by admitting early applicants	Advantage
Diversity	May have to apply early to have a chance of admission if "unhooked"	Advantage

Source: Interviews with college students.

Aggregate Statistics

Some students simply extrapolated from the difference in published statistics for the percentage of early and regular applicants admitted at various colleges. Other students found that the proportion of early admits in the entering class was telling:

> Let's face it, by the numbers, a higher percentage [of early applicants] get in. (Karen, Princeton '01)

> The spots are half filled by the time regular applicants are considered. (Miriam, Princeton '98)

Although the simple comparison of admission rates is naïve—it neglects the fact that early and regular applicants have different attributes—it may give a more accurate conclusion than many more sophisticated approaches.

The Possibility of Deferral or Rejection as an Early Applicant

Many applicants focused on the possibility of being deferred from the early to the regular pool of applicants. However, drawing inferences here is challenging since colleges differ substantially in their practices. Some, such as Cornell, defer virtually all early applicants who are not accepts. Others, such as Stanford, defer only a relatively small percentage. (See Chapter 5 for further details of the deferral practices of various colleges.) On the positive side, some students felt that deferral provided an advantage:

> It gives you two chances instead of one. The second review may take a different view of you. (Barbara, Harvard '01)

Beyond this advantage, deferral might give a student the opportunity to improve his or her application.[29] For example, some MIT students we interviewed said that they solicited and received guidance from the admissions office on how to improve their applications after they were deferred. On the negative side, students cited two reasons the possibility of deferral is a disadvantage for early applicants: deferred applicants are less likely to be admitted than regular applicants; and if not deferred, some early applicants are rejected immediately, leaving them out of the running thereafter:

> If you get deferred, the fact that you applied early can hurt your application under regular admissions, so you should only apply early if you're an exceptional candidate. (Michelle, Princeton '98)

> Deferrals go into the throwaway pile. (Kenneth, Harvard '00)

The specter of immediate rejection is a powerful influence in the minds of many participants, with most adhering to the view that this sudden-death possibility makes it a disadvantage to apply early:

> My friend was told that Early Action couldn't hurt [his chances of admission], but then he was rejected. (Bruce, MIT '01)

One counselor who stated in our interview that Northwestern does not seem to give an advantage to ED applicants cited as evidence the fact that Northwestern is willing to deny students outright in Early Decision. The 2000 *U.S. News Guide* makes a similar argument: "But going EA can also be risky. At Notre Dame and some other schools, if you apply early and you are rejected, you're automatically denied consideration in the regular admissions cycle, which may be less competitive than the EA cycle."

These comments exaggerate the importance of an immediate rejection. As we discuss in Chapter 6, colleges generally defer the vast majority of early applicants who are not admitted early. An outright rejection of an early applicant indicates that the applicant had no real chance of admission, regardless of when he or she applied.

The possibility of deferral need not give an advantage to early applicants, because a deferred application is generally assigned to the same admissions officer(s) who evaluated it during the early application process.

Motives of Admissions Offices

A number of students tried to assess what motivates the admissions officers as they sift through their piles of early applications. These students cited four major goals of admissions offices that might influence their evaluations: rewarding enthusiasm, maintaining standards, improving college rankings, and facilitating enrollment planning. Some students also mentioned the lessened demand for financial aid as a motive for colleges to favor early applicants.

Nearly half of the interview subjects (44.3 percent) felt that an early application sends an important signal of interest to colleges.[30] Nearly one-third (29.9 percent) felt that applying Early Action is also an important indication of enthusiasm, while 34.5 percent (there was some overlap) stated that Early Decision sends an even more powerful signal:

> Admissions is based on four things: where you're from, your scores, your grades, and how interested you are. I don't know why everyone doesn't do it [apply early]. (Nelson, Harvard '00)

Nevertheless, at the end of the interview when we asked for a numerical rating of the effect of applying early, 9.2 percent of those who said that applying Early Action is an important signal went on to rate EA as offering no advantage in admissions. Similarly, 17.9 percent of those who said that applying Early Decision is a more powerful signal than applying Early Action later indicated that the two programs had equivalent effects on admissions.[31]

Many of the strategically oriented students we interviewed talked about the connection between early applications and college rankings, noting that a college can make itself appear more selective by admitting more applicants from the early pool:

> [Colleges are] competing for good statistics in all those viewbooks [promotional guides] and *U.S. News* . . . [Why not] make your own student body better by admitting people psyched to be there [and] make competitors look bad for next year. (Amy, Harvard '98)

> It also helps universities to stay ahead of the curve and to improve the statistics that they demonstrate to governing boards. (Richard, Princeton '99)

A few students who thought about the perspective of the college mentioned that favoring early applicants helps schools gauge the number of students to admit, both overall and in certain desirable categories (such as athletes, musicians, and so on). Beyond that, the demographic differences between Early Decision applicants and regular applicants allow the admissions office to manage better several other goals. As one cynical student explained,

> The best way is to lock them in ED, so college admissions officials can make sure about taking care of legacies, about people they are trying to get donations from, and getting students from each state and culture. More white students get in early . . . [then there is] more affirmative action in the spring to affirm that admission is blind. (Steve, Yale '01)

These students are correct in determining that admissions offices face a variety of incentives for favoring early applicants. The outstanding question is how strongly these incentives tip the scales. We will answer this question in Chapter 5.

An Absolute Standard of Admissions Decisions

Many of the students we interviewed liked to believe that "if you are admitted early, then you would have been admitted from the regular pool as well." Indeed, it was common for students to say this almost reflexively, without realizing that what they were in fact saying was that the early and regular admissions standards are identical, meaning that applying early provides no advantage in admissions chances. Other students started with the supposition that it might be the goal of admissions offices to equate the early and regular standards, and then went on to consider whether that goal is achievable. One respondent noted that admissions officers face this problem every year:

[The problem of maintaining standards] is a solvable system for admissions officers. (Will, Princeton '99)

Interestingly, this argument almost mirrors that given by Harvard's admissions deans:

[Early applicants] are admitted because the Admissions Committee, with many years of collective experience to draw upon, is convinced that each is 100 percent certain to be admitted when compared to the full slate of candidates who will be considered in the spring. Yearly variations in the rigor of the admissions competition here are relatively small and the Committee will defer a candidate if there is any doubt.[32]

At the same time, many students were aware that the pool of early applicants is generally much smaller and more competitive (at least at extremely selective colleges) than the pool of regular applicants. To some, the small early pool suggested an immediate link to an effect in terms of admissions chances, though they disagreed on the likely effect:

Your application has a better chance of standing out in a smaller pool of applications from exceptional people. (Claudia, Princeton '00)

They [the early applicants] are a bunch of legacies, the super-eager beavers, and the people with Emmys—I gotta go against that? No thanks. (Kenneth, Harvard '00)

Maybe they [admissions officers] just get tired of reading applications by the time they get to [the] regular people. (Diane, Harvard '98)

Rachel Toor, a former admissions officer at Duke, supported the claim that the process is not so scientifically precise in a discussion on National Public Radio:

> One of the things that surprised me is how intensely personal the process is. Not only for kids and the parents, but also for the admissions officer. So even though at Duke, for example, we didn't require interviews, when a kid came to campus and you interviewed them and you thought they were great in person, even if they didn't shine on their application, you'd push a little bit harder for them because you had that personal connection.[33]

Toor admits that, faced with a pile of more than a thousand applications to read, an admissions officer might well tend to lose energy:

> Even when you're an admissions officer and you're reading applications, if you've already read 50 applications that evening and you have to read the 51st, and you're not reading it as carefully and as closely, you may miss something in the application and you may not argue as hard for the kid.[34]

If this is the case, then timing would tend to favor early applicants, for admissions officers necessarily read them at the start of the process, when they have the most energy and enthusiasm.

Why is there so much confusion about the effect of applying early? First, understanding the basic mechanics of early applications requires some effort. To begin with, there is a plethora of programs. Beyond the distinction between Early Action and Early Decision, some colleges offer other programs, such as Early Decision 2, Early Evaluation, and so on; in some cases, the rules for programs with the same name have even varied from college to college.[35] In addition, there have been four dramatic changes in early applications at elite colleges in recent years: (1) a general increase in early applications; (2) adoption of Early Decision by Princeton, Stanford, and Yale in 1996; (3) a change by Brown, Georgetown, and Harvard to allow multiple early applications, and subsequent adoption of Early Decision by Brown in 2001; and (4) a change by Stanford and Yale from Early Decision to Early Action in 2003. Such frequent changes make it hard to determine the effects of the current system, as insights from past experience may or may not be relevant to the present.

Second, though there is much anecdotal evidence—"Joe was admitted early, Mary was denied regular"—there is little solid information from which to draw inferences about whether applying early improves the chances of admission. Colleges are evasive and often inaccurate in their promotional materials, while books and articles tend to be incomplete and equivocal. Moreover, with the exception of this study, we know of no published analyses on the admissions chances of early and regular applicants.

This leaves students and counselors either to try to reason their way through a very complicated system, or to draw inferences based on observation of a limited number of prior applicants. The difficulty is that reasoning alone cannot distinguish among a variety of plausible conclusions. Strikingly, though not surprisingly, we repeatedly found dramatic variations in understanding of early applications among enrolled students at four highly selective colleges. Some students, like Amy and Richard, understood the system better than the authors of best-selling college guidebooks. Others did not even know that it was possible to apply early. Almost one-quarter of the college students we interviewed revealed that they simply did not understand the mechanics or implications of early application programs. Many others believe, incorrectly, according to our data analysis in Chapter 5, that applying early does not enhance an applicant's chances of admission. Although counselors tended to concur that Early Decision applicants are favored in admissions decisions, they disagreed on many more specific assessments.

In the next chapter, we examine the experiences of college applicants from two different high schools, one public and one private, both highly regarded. We follow the applicants through the admissions year, to see how well informed they were about the early admissions game, and how their understanding of the system influenced their application choices. This detailed picture reinforces the general findings of this chapter. For a host of understandable reasons, applicants are confused about the operation of early admissions programs—no less confused than would be the patrons at our Martian casinos, where the house picks its own rules, the rules change regularly, and each player gets a single trial. Those applicants who do not believe that admissions offices favor early applicants, by whatever process and for whatever reasons they reached that conclusion, are at a significant disadvantage in gaining admission to elite colleges.

4

The Innocents Abroad:
The Admissions Voyage

Congratulations, you're off to Paris! You've heard that the city is incredible, but you don't speak a word of French and you don't know the Eiffel Tower from the Arc de Triomphe. Few of your hometown friends from Podunk have been there. From the moment you arrive, your learning curve will be steep. You may choose to stay at the Sheraton, well recommended in your guidebook, only to find that you would have been happier in a small hotel on the Left Bank. You may not know which cafés to frequent on the Champs-Elysées, and it may be difficult to find restaurants that are both affordable and good. After a week in the city, however, you may have met other people who told you about their fabulous, small hotel, and introduced you to excellent, little-known restaurants. Once you're back in Podunk, your friends will ask how it was. "Wonderful," you may say, "but if I had it to do over again, boy would I know what to do this time."

There is another traveler to Paris on the same plane, a man from the Upper East Side of Manhattan. Many of his friends have been to Paris before, even if he has not. Before he departs, he collects their opinions on where to stay and where to eat; he can judge how simi-

lar his tastes are to those of his friends and uses their advice accordingly. This man does not know everything about Paris. He may very
well find a new restaurant, or realize that he would have been even
happier in a different hotel that he ran across in his wanderings.
Nonetheless, the Manhattanite starts with much more information
than you did coming from Podunk.

In many ways, high school juniors at the start of the college applications process are like these travelers — except that the travelers can
get a second chance at Paris if they wish. Students begin with varying degrees of knowledge about the application process, and they
come from very different backgrounds. But even the most informed
students have not actually "been to Paris."

Fortunately, many students can draw on a sophisticated network
of their peers who pass on information about college admissions,
and it may seem as if these students are applying more as a part of
that network than all alone. These are the "Manhattanites." But
what about the applicants from "Podunk"? Their information network is sorely lacking. And even the Manhattanites are seldom truly
well informed. Much of their knowledge comes from their peers,
and much of it is more speculation than fact. All applicants lack important information because they have not been through the process
themselves. Many college students will look back and imagine how
they might have been more successful, and even those who end up
at a top-choice school must wonder whether they could have done
even better.

This chapter looks at how high school students perceive the rules
of the admissions game, especially Early Action and Early Decision. Our primary source of data is interviews with top students at
one private and one public school in New England, Choate Rosemary Hall and Needham High School, respectively. Choate Rosemary Hall is an elite private boarding school in Wallingford, Connecticut. Choate attracts students from all over the country and the
world, although it draws primarily from the Northeast, and consis-

tently sends 100 percent of its graduates to the top four-year colleges in the country. The second school, Needham High School, is a well-regarded suburban high school in Needham, Massachusetts, a suburb of Boston. Needham is a long-established, relatively affluent community.

The analogy between Manhattanites and Podunk residents does not quite fit the students we interviewed for this chapter. While the Choate students represent extremely sophisticated applicants—Manhattanites to be sure—the Needham students represent some of the most informed public school students rather than the average traveler from Podunk. Needham High School ranked 10th of 310 Massachusetts high schools in standardized test scores in a recent *Boston Globe* compilation.[1]

For our purposes, the two schools bear many similarities. Both consistently send students to high-quality colleges and have well-developed college counseling programs. They offer Advanced Placement classes and a high level of instruction to their students. Yet they also differ in major ways. The first and most obvious difference is that Choate is private, whereas Needham is public. In fact, Choate is very expensive—$23,000 a year for boarding students, $17,000 for those who don't live on campus—while Needham, being public, is free. Although many students at Choate receive substantial financial aid at college (and while they're at Choate), a smaller percentage of the students at Choate than at Needham were considering financial aid as part of their decisions. Even when aid is a factor in the college choices of Choate students, they often need less financial aid than their Needham counterparts. Second, there are obvious differences associated with private secondary schooling, such as smaller classes. Third, the Choate students we surveyed were much less involved than Needham students in activities outside school, such as part-time jobs and community service. Even for students who do not live at school, Choate can be an all-consuming experience, with Saturday classes every other week, for example.

Few students at Choate manage outside activities. Presumably, a comparison of Choate students with students from a randomly selected public school would have demonstrated even more dramatic differences.

We examine what students learn as they travel through the applications process. How do high school students perceive the advantages and disadvantages of Early Action and Early Decision programs, and how does that understanding affect their decisions about whether and where to apply early?

There are two important distinctions between our interviews with these high school seniors and our interviews with college students. First, the college students in the study were all unusually successful in the application process, as they all attended extremely selective colleges. In contrast, two-thirds (67.2 percent) of the high school students were rejected from at least one college, though they were all in the top tier of their graduating class in terms of rank. Thus the high school students provide one of our main sources of information about frustrations and regrets related to early applications.

Second, the college students provided a synthesis of their experience in a single conversation. They sometimes expressed regrets or recalled changes of heart during the course of the admissions process, but they probably described their decisions with greater certainty than they actually felt at the time they were applying. The interviews with high school seniors discussed in this chapter represent the equivalent of time-lapse photography. We conducted four brief interviews with each student, from the start of summer before their senior year. This let us observe the timing and evolution of their decisions. In the fourth and final interview, at the time of high school graduation, we learned the students' opinions about the effects of early applications—before they went to college and compared notes with college classmates from other high schools.

We selected students in spring 1998 and then followed them over the course of the next year, from the summer between junior and senior year (junior summer) until the summer before college. The 28 students we interviewed from Choate were randomly selected from the top 100 students in their class of 250 (ranked by junior grade-point average, or GPA). The 30 students from Needham were chosen randomly from a list of the top 50 students in a class of approximately 250, again ranked by GPA.

We interviewed students four times during the year: the summer of 1998, before their senior year; December 1998; late March or early April 1999; and June or July 1999, when they could reflect on the whole admissions process. The response rate was virtually 100 percent—students who agreed to be part of the study followed through.[2]

The Beginning: Summer 1998

Both Choate and Needham students begin the college process in the winter or early spring of their junior year. Students from both schools entered their senior year with significant advantages over typical college applicants. Both schools have experienced counselors who are dedicated to advising students on the application process. Students applying to selective colleges also have the benefit of their peers' and predecessors' wisdom, as it is common for top students at both high schools to apply to a varied group of prestigious colleges. These students also gain an advantage in the process because some of their classes are geared toward helping them complete their applications:

> Teachers give us some room around college deadlines. They provide some leeway about homework due dates and help prep us with SAT-2 study material. (Rebecca, Needham)

> Teachers assigned essays that we could use for our applications. (Mark, Needham)

Choate incorporates the college process in almost every department, so it has been present throughout my senior year. (Simon, Choate)

By the end of their junior year, students at both schools had met
with their counselors several times, were developing a list of colleges, and were ready to start visiting them. Many similarities and a
few sharp differences between the students emerged in our interviews in the summer. At that point, most (73 percent of Needham
students and 85 percent of Choate students) cited their college
counselors as an important source of information. Furthermore, 90
percent of the students at both schools had identified a set of schools
on which to focus, most of them with the help of their counselors.
At Needham, the counselors used a "1, 2, 3" system to describe a
student's chances; at Choate it was a "Reach, Possible, Probable"
system.

Only three students from Choate and two from Needham mentioned their college counselors in later interviews during the school
year. Perhaps the college counselors are most useful as an initial
source of important background information, but as time goes on,
students begin to look elsewhere, principally to their peers, for more
guidance. The importance of college counselors at the outset indicates that the students lacked basic information when the process
began. They are like first-time travelers to Paris who, before the trip
looms on the horizon, need to consult a guidebook.

In the summer interviews, less than half (fourteen of thirty) of the
Needham students even mentioned the possibility of an early application. In contrast, every one of the Choate students responded to
the question, "How do you plan to proceed with applications?", by
discussing the possibility of applying early. Most of them had some
clearly defined thoughts on the early process, with twenty-one of
twenty-eight saying that they might apply early (see Table 4.1).

A number of these students seemed committed to applying early
without having identified a preferred school:

Table 4.1 Comments about early application before senior year

Comment	Choate students	Needham students
Planned to apply early to a particular college	3 (10.7%)	5 (16.7%)
Planned to apply early, not certain of the college	8 (28.6%)	7 (23.3%)
Considering the possibility of applying early	10 (35.7%)	1 (3.3%)
Planned not to apply early	7 (25.0%)	1 (3.3%)
Did not mention early application	0 (0%)	16 (53.3%)

Source: Interviews with high school students.

There are some schools I want to consider, but nothing definite and I have no final list . . . I'll probably go early somewhere — it depends on where I decide to apply. I want to find a place that I really like early enough in the process that I can apply Early Action or Early Decision and have it over with. (Frank, Choate)

This statement strongly indicates sophisticated information, in part because this student has not gotten his information about an early program from a specific school. It is not as if he were looking carefully at Yale and found that it has an Early Decision program; rather, he has heard from others about early applications and their possible benefits. Several other Choate students made it clear that they had already thought in depth about the possibility of applying early:

I dream about doing my applications in August, but it really may not happen. I have no definite first choice right now, so I may go Early Action at Brown. I don't have one "dream" school, so unless one really jumps out at me in the next couple of months, I won't do Early Decision anyplace. (Tim, Choate)

Two of the seven Choate students who said they planned not to apply early provided compelling explanations for that decision:

Whether I go anywhere early or not really depends on whether the school can guarantee financial aid. Columbia only guarantees 50 percent of demonstrated need. I most likely wouldn't try that [Early Decision to Columbia] unless I had a good outside scholarship. (Emily, Choate)

I probably won't go early anywhere. I really am interested in the Naval Academy, and they don't have any kind of early program.[3] (Andrew, Choate)

A few of the Needham students had detailed plans for early applications before the start of senior year:

I have a clear-cut plan. Brown is the number-one choice and I will apply Early Action there. (Joey, Needham)

But many of the Needham students had not considered the possibility of applying early at all:

Next fall and winter, I plan to talk to some other friends who have applied and to my counselor about how to proceed. (Paul, Needham)

A significant minority of the Needham students who discussed early applications in the summer interviews seemed confused about their plans and about the rules of the system:

I will not apply early. Penn and Northwestern might be hard to get into, so I may apply early there. I haven't done any research on Early Action programs yet. (Bill, Needham)

A couple of the Needham students mentioned the possibility of applying to more than one school early, a practice that was generally not allowed at the time:

I hope to apply to a couple schools early in November. (Julie, Needham)

This student, like a number of others at Needham, eventually learned the rules more concretely: she applied Early Decision to the University of Vermont and was admitted.

Summer Plans and Winter Actions

In the end, nineteen of the students we interviewed from each school (68 percent of the students from Choate and 63 percent of those from Needham) applied early. Many Needham students who did not mention the possibility of applying early in the summer interview learned enough to change their views in time to apply early and meet the fall deadlines.

The actions of the Choate students were consistent with their earlier statements. Almost all the Choate students who were even considering the possibility of applying early did so, while only one of the seven Choate students who stated that they would not apply early changed their minds and did apply early. The two Choate students who said that they intended to apply early but did not do so were admitted to all the colleges to which they applied (a total of nineteen schools). One chose to attend Harvard and the other chose Stanford. The outstanding success of these two applicants suggests that they didn't need the boost an early application would provide. In other words, the Choate students who considered applying early and had the most to gain all applied early.

In sharp contrast, there was little or no connection between the earlier statements of the Needham students and their decisions regarding early applications. Twelve of the sixteen students (75 percent) who did *not* mention early applications applied early, while only 58 percent of the Needham students who said they planned to apply early did so. This pattern suggests some initial confusion; for example, Needham students who mentioned early admissions in summer interviews probably did not fully understand their costs and benefits at that time. Indeed, several students in the Needham survey were initially strongly in favor of applying early, but did not do so in the end (see Table 4.2).

Tables 4.2 and 4.3 show that students at the two schools made remarkably similar choices. Slightly more than one-third of the students applied Early Action; slightly less than one-third applied Early Decision; and the remaining one-third of the students did not apply early. Brown was a very popular choice, as almost half of the EA applicants applied early to that school (eleven of twenty-three).[4]

It appears that the Needham students became about as well-informed and sophisticated as the Choate students by the time early applications were due. Yet almost one-third (eight of thirty) of the Needham students stated after the fact that they had started the process too late. Table 4.4 shows students' main reason for not applying early. Eight of the Needham students said either that they could

Table 4.2   Early application decisions and initial plans of students: percentage applying early as a function of plans in the summer

	Choate students	Needham students
Planning to apply early	11	12
Did apply early	9 (82%)	7 (58%)
Considering applying early	10	1
Did apply early	9 (90%)	0 (0%)
Did not mention early application	0	16
Did apply early	—	12 (75%)
Planning not to apply early	7	1
Did apply early	1 (14%)	0 (0%)
Total	28	30
Did apply early	19 (68%)	19 (63%)

Source: Interviews with high school students.

Table 4.3 Early applications by high school and early program

	Choate applicants	Needham applicants
EARLY ACTION		
Boston College		1
Brown	5	6
Chicago	1	
Georgetown	2	
Harvard	2	1
MIT	2	2
New Hampshire		1
North Carolina	1	1
Total	12*	11*
EARLY DECISION		
Bates		1
Columbia	1	1
Dartmouth	1	
Drew		1
Duke	1	
Penn	1	
Princeton		1
Tufts		3
Vermont		1
Williams		1
Yale	3	
Total	7	8*

*The numbers in these columns do not add up to the total at the bottom, because of multiple early applications. One student from Needham applied Early Action to both Boston College and North Carolina, while another applied Early Action to Brown and then Early Decision-2 to Tufts. One student from Choate applied Early Action to both Brown and North Carolina. Each of these students is counted twice in the table.

Source: Interviews with high school students.

not complete a strong application by the early deadline or that they did not have sufficiently strong preference to apply early. Each of these factors indicates that the students might have applied early had they started sooner with campus visits, essays, and standardized tests:

Table 4.4   Why students did not apply early

Reason	Choate students who did not apply early	Needham students who did not apply early
Financial aid	2	1
Problems with due date (too early to complete application/needed to retake standardized tests)	1	2
Did not have strong enough preference to apply early	3	6
Spent one semester abroad during critical time	2	0
Other/unknown	1	2
Total	9	11

Source: Interviews with high school students.

I really was not ready to apply early. I hadn't visited any of the colleges I was considering, and I hadn't decided how far away I wanted to go for college. I didn't have my act together by the Early Decision deadline. (Mark, Needham)

Two of the Choate students who did not apply early had a more compelling explanation than that given by Mark above. They had enrolled in Choate's semester abroad program, one during the spring of junior year and the other during the fall of senior year, so that they did not have enough time or information at the critical moment in the application process to apply early.

Student Strategies for Early Applications

The students from both schools followed a relatively limited set of strategies. Students with very strong preferences applied Early Decision or Early Action to their favorite college. Others applied Early Action or did not apply early at all. EA applicants from Needham, however, tended to apply to their first-choice schools, whereas EA applicants from Choate more often applied to safety schools. In addition, Early Decision applicants from Needham tended to apply to less selective schools.

Each of the seven Choate students and nine Needham students who applied Early Decision expressed at least a slight preference for the college when they applied. EA applicants from Choate, by contrast, were sometimes strategic. While 90 percent (nine of ten) of the Early Action candidates from Needham ranked their early application school as one of their top two choices, only 58 percent (seven of twelve) of the EA candidates from Choate did so. All nine of the students who were admitted Early Action (six from Choate and three from Needham) applied to other colleges at the regular deadline, and in the end four of those early admits chose to attend another college.[5]

Several Choate students emphasized that Early Action simplified the process:

> It's really nice to get one [application] done in the beginning. A lot of people who are not sure how they'll stack up tend to apply early as a judgment call . . . it relieved a lot of pressure if you're [admitted]. [An early rejection] was a chance to re-evaluate where people want to go and how they would stack up in general. (Alexis, Choate)

> I know a lot of people who applied early to a place that wasn't exactly a reach, and they just did it to get a safety. Then, they could apply to other, more desirable places later and go there. Brown was a popular place to do that with this year. (John, Choate)

At Needham, in contrast to Choate, EA applications were more often to schools that were a "reach." Six Needham students applied early to Brown but only one was admitted. In all, only three of Needham's eleven Early Action candidates were admitted early. This implies that they were "reaching for the stars." By contrast, three of five of Choate's early applicants in the study were admitted to Brown; as the above quotation suggests, some of those students viewed Brown as a safety school where they would likely be admitted, rather than as a top choice.

Brown is a surprising choice for a safety school, given that it is among the ten most selective colleges in the country.[6] Yet only one of the four students admitted early to Brown (three from Choate and one from Needham) chose to attend that school. The others all ended up choosing yet more selective colleges and programs, with two choosing Yale and the third choosing the Morehead Scholarship at North Carolina.[7] For some students, this "safety" approach to Early Action schools turned out to be more burden than relief, even if they were admitted early:

I think you have to be careful about the safety thing because some people didn't get in to their safety schools and that is demoralizing if everyone says you should get in and you don't. (Kendal, Choate)

Yes, I definitely would have done things differently. I didn't really know what I wanted to do in the fall because I didn't have a definite first choice so I applied to Brown because it was Early Action . . . In the end I really didn't want to go to Brown, so even when I got in it really wasn't that relieving or exciting. (Chris, Choate)

The most successful applicants were the Early Decision applicants from Needham, as more than three-quarters of them were admitted early (see Table 4.5). One reason for the relative success

Table 4.5   Outcomes for early applicants at Choate and Needham

	Choate		Needham	
Outcome	Early Action	Early Decision	Early Action	Early Decision
Admitted early	50%	57%	33%	78%
	(6 of 12)	(4 of 7)	(4 of 12)	(7 of 9)
Deferred and then admitted	0%	14%	8%	0%
	(0 of 12)	(1 of 7)	(1 of 12)	(2 of 9)
Deferred and then rejected	50%	28%	58%	22%
	(6 of 12)	(2 of 7)	(7 of 12)	(2 of 9)
Matriculated	25%	57%	17%	78%
	(3 of 12)	(4 of 7)	(2 of 12)	(7 of 9)

Source: Interviews with high school students.

of these applicants is that they chose slightly less selective colleges than the Early Action applicants or any of the early applicants from Choate. The Choate students applied early to the Ivy League schools, Chicago, Duke, Georgetown, and MIT. By contrast, the Needham students who were admitted Early Decision applied to Bates, Drew, Tufts, Vermont, and Williams. With the exception of Williams, these are generally considered less selective than any of the colleges to which Choate students applied early.

The choice of ED colleges among the Needham students is an interesting phenomenon that we did not explore thoroughly. All of these students expressed enthusiasm for the Early Decision college both before and after they were admitted. We wondered if they had taken account of their admissibility in selecting a first-choice college—did they rule out yet more selective colleges on the basis of the assessment (right or wrong) that they were unlikely to be admitted? We did not inquire into these subjects, and it is not clear that the students would have been able to provide cogent responses had we done so.

One applicant, a Needham student who was admitted Early Action to Brown, indicated that her initial preferences probably were influenced by her assessment of her admission chances. In December she said that Brown was her top choice, but when she was admitted as a regular applicant to Yale in the spring, she said that she was no longer certain. When we asked about this change of mind, she commented:

> I hadn't thought that I would get into Yale since it was a "reach school" for me. I found out about my acceptance [to Yale] when I got back from spring break. Now I have no idea [of my top choice]. (Chrissy, Needham)

Three students submitted multiple early applications.[8] One student from each school applied simultaneously to two Early Action schools, with one applying to Brown and North Carolina and the other applying to Boston College and North Carolina. (At the time, Brown had a formal rule against applying to multiple EA colleges.)

A third Needham student chose a sequential strategy. First, she applied Early Action to Brown. When Brown deferred her, she then applied Early Decision 2 to Tufts, where she was admitted. To an outsider, this may appear to be a cynical strategy, representing an early application to a second-choice college (Tufts) rather than a change in preferences, but the student felt that her actions were straightforward. She, like many students, responded to the deferral by deciding that she did not want to attend the college that deferred her. She explained her change of preferences in the December interview (after she learned of her deferral at Brown) and in June:

> I made a list of their pros and cons. I'm interested in education, and the secondary education certification program is better at Tufts than at Brown. Also, Brown has Division I sports and student athletes are not encouraged to play more than one sport, but Tufts has Division III sports, which is better for me because I want to play two sports. (Eliza, Needham, December 1998)

The students are more realistic and down to earth [at Tufts] than the ones I met at Brown . . . I would have applied Early Decision to Brown [if Brown offered Early Decision], but that would have been a mistake. (Eliza, Needham, June 1999)

Such mid-course changes in preference, which occur after applicants receive bad news from a top-choice college, may be a means of self-protection in a game that can damage young peoples' egos. Just as a person who is turned down as a job applicant often responds by saying, "Well, I really didn't want to work for that company anyway," so do rejected applicants turn their favor to a college where they have prospects for admission.

There is ample evidence that this dynamic is real. The Higher Education Research Institute at UCLA surveys nearly 4,000 college freshmen across the country each year. According to the institute, nearly 70 percent of college freshmen in 2000–01 reported that they were attending their first-choice college, while more than 90 percent said that they were attending at least a second-choice college.[9] These statistics can only be believed if one accepts the premise that applicants' ranking of schools is shaped profoundly by expectations of success and by the reactions they receive from the schools to which they apply.[10]

Students with Special Attributes

The early application decision had different consequences for students in two categories: those applying for financial aid and those who were recruited athletes.

Financial Aid Candidates

Many of the students who were not locked into an Early Decision school made their college choices with financial aid in the front of their minds:

I ruled out BC and Brandeis because they only offered small scholarships. BU offered almost a half scholarship and I like it a lot and would love to go there, but if Northeastern offers more money then I'll probably go to Northeastern. (Margaret, Needham)

I'm not from a family that can "throw it around." My financial aid package at Vassar will cover approximately the entire tuition. I had to go for that. (Joey, Needham)

Students who expect to rely on financial aid face an especially difficult decision about whether to apply early (Chapter 6 discusses the difficulties in detail). If you apply Early Decision and are admitted, it is possible that you would also have been admitted as a regular applicant and would have had the chance to compare and negotiate financial aid packages. If you do not apply early and are rejected as a regular applicant at some college, it is possible that you would have been admitted there as an early applicant.

Two Choate students expressed these complementary regrets:

Because I applied early, I didn't have any options with aid and I got screwed. I couldn't compare other aid packages with Yale, and they also knew I had to come to their school, so they could give me any package they wanted. (John, Choate)

Presumably, John would have felt differently had he discovered that applying ED was just the boost that got him into Yale. Melanie's situation was similar:

I had my heart set on going there [Northwestern] and I didn't apply early because it is binding and I was worried that I wouldn't get enough financial aid. Then I found out that that is the one way at Northwestern that you can get out of it being binding. Applying early there in the first place would have made everything so much easier. (Melanie, Choate)

A possibility that Melanie didn't mention is the one emphasized by John—that she might have been offered an unsatisfactory package as an early applicant, but not one so unsatisfactory that she would have been released from her commitment. In the end, however, she was not admitted to Northwestern as a regular applicant. As her comment suggests, she is well aware of the tradeoff between competitive financial aid and improved admissions chances, and it surely still stirs in her mind.

Some of the Choate students who needed financial aid, and did not apply early for that reason, mentioned that fact in the summer. While many more of the Needham students than the Choate students mentioned financial aid as a concern during the summer, not one connected the financial aid issue with early applications. The issues surrounding financial aid are incredibly subtle—only a particularly well informed group of students would identify this issue as early as the summer before senior year. Conceivably, some of the Needham students who originally mentioned applying early but switched to regular admissions may have changed their plans once they recognized that regular admission might help with financial aid negotiations.

Recruited Athletes

A number of students in the sample group had a special talent, such as outstanding athletic or artistic or musical ability. For the athletes—by far the largest of these groups—early applications were viewed as a necessity:

I would say certainly [apply early] if you're an athlete because coaches like you to commit. Also, because it has become more popular for athletes recently, it's become more expected. (Lindsey, Choate)

Applying early may be even more important for recruited athletes than for other members of the applicant pool. Decisions about which recruited athletes to admit are often based—in part—on lists submitted by coaches.[11] Anecdotal evidence from admissions officers and college counselors strongly suggests that coaches are inducing applicants to apply through binding early admission programs by threatening to lower their position on the list if they do not do so.

The coach's interest can also secure an athlete some leeway in the timing of his or her application:

I got into Tufts Early Decision, although I missed the early deadline (the lacrosse coach made that okay for me). The lacrosse coach there kind of got me started, since I wasn't that sure about Tufts in the beginning. I really hadn't thought about it, and I had wanted to go to Johns Hopkins. Then I saw that Tufts had a good science program and it started to seem like the right thing to do. Also, the coach said that I'd get in. (Joan, Needham)

Athletes who did not apply in formal early application programs still clearly received favored treatment:

At Stanford, if you are a recruited athlete, you can submit your application by October 11 and the admissions committee does an "early read." I got in. (Alexis, Choate)

In effect, Stanford offered a limited Early Action program solely for athletic recruits.

Student Beliefs about Early Applications

The students in our study drew most of their information about the effect of applying early from experienced sources—primarily their counselors and friends who had already been through the process. By the end of the year, when we asked them directly about their views on early applications, they could also draw on their own experiences and the experiences of their classmates. Fundamentally, there are three possible views about whether applying early helps the chances of admission:

1. applying early never helps;
2. applying Early Decision helps because the applicant must commit, but applying Early Action does not help;
3. applying either Early Decision or Early Action helps.

Some students also believe that the effect of applying early varies by college or depends on whether an applicant falls into a special category, such as athlete or alumni child.

About equal numbers of students held each of the three possible views, and opinions at Choate and Needham were almost identical (see Table 4.6). This result is striking for several reasons. First, whatever the truth about the effect of applying early, less than half the students at each school understood it. Second, by the time the Choate and Needham students had finished the admissions process, they had arrived at virtually identical breakdowns in beliefs, despite their initial disparities in information. Nonetheless, at both schools many students still disagreed or were ill informed.

Even the college counselors at Needham said they didn't know if applying early would help a student's acceptance possibilities.[12] Such uncertainty is not surprising given the reluctance of colleges

Table 4.6 Views about the effects of applying early

	Applying early never helps	Applying ED helps, but applying EA does not	Applying EA and ED both help
Choate	32%	36%	32%
	(9 of 28)	(10 of 28)	(9 of 28)
Needham	27%	37%	37%
	(8 of 30)	(11 of 30)	(11 of 30)
Total	29%	36%	34%
	(17 of 58)	(21 of 58)	(20 of 58)

Source: Interviews with high school students.

to provide clear statistics or precise statements about the consequences of early applications.

Learning from Experience

Why might so many students conclude that applying early does not improve the chance of admission? Perhaps they were most influenced by happiness or unhappiness with the process—if they were not accepted early, they were much more likely to think that early applications do not help. Indeed, across the two schools, 80 percent of those who were admitted in Early Decision thought that applying ED would help their chances of admission, but only 40 percent of those who were deferred in Early Decision thought so. Similarly, 44 percent of those who were admitted in Early Action thought that applying EA would help their chances of admission, but only 21 percent of those who were deferred in Early Action thought so.

Such reasoning is a classic example of what psychologists call the "availability bias."[13] Individuals judge characteristics, such as probability of admission, by the cases that are most easily brought to mind, rather than all the evidence at hand. Therefore, we can expect that students who have just applied to college will vastly overemphasize their personal experiences in assessing the workings of the system as a whole.

Some students who extrapolated from the aggregate results of their classmates reached the right conclusion:

> I was not admitted to Tufts, yet classmates with weaker records were admitted ED to Tufts. I wonder if Tufts puts special emphasis on ED. (Mary, Needham)

> From what I observed at Needham, I think that applying early helps your chances of admission. ED has a stronger pull than EA since it is binding. (James, Needham)

> Most of the people I heard from, and my friends . . . said they got in early, so from that it seems like a great idea. (Jane, Choate)

> I know it [applying early] does [help], but I think people sometimes think it will get them in just because they're applying early even if they're not qualified. (Adella, Choate)

But student networks, with their arbitrary connections, also have failings. Some information never gets put on the network, and some gets distorted. As our study shows, students apparently draw inferences from extremely small samples, with students at different high schools getting different tidbits of information. In particular, many Choate students focused on the importance of athletics in early admissions outcomes because so many athletic recruits applied early and were successful. Among the students in the study, five athletes from Choate applied early and four were admitted early—just less than half of the ten Choate students in the study who were admitted early. The success of these athletic recruits tells us that athletes are highly prized, probably regardless of when they apply, but it tells us little or nothing about whether non-athletes gain an advantage from applying early. Psychologically, however, this implication may be difficult for less athletically oriented students to decipher:

> It seems that if you have a certain hook—like a sport or something—the hook can have more weight if you apply early. (Peter, Choate)

For many of the Needham students, the most obvious experience of their classmates was that very few early applicants were admitted, particularly those who applied Early Action. The immediate response for many Needham students was thus to conclude that applying Early Action does not help, and may even hinder, chances of admission:

> Based on my classmates' results, I don't think that it really makes a difference. (Mary, Needham)

> I think that Needham students had better success in the regular pool. (Paul, Needham)

Yet many of the applicants from Needham applied to "reach schools" early, meaning that their applications were not likely to be successful no matter when they applied. As one student explained, of the twenty Needham students (overall, not just those in our study) who applied early to Brown, only two were admitted.

Not surprisingly, we saw evidence of developing "urban myths" at both high schools; in particular, individual outcomes became salient cases that grew into legends and shaped the overall views of many students. Two students described the seemingly paranoid view that applying Early Action to one college might diminish an individual's chances at other colleges. Our interviews suggested that this view derived entirely from the speculation of a single classmate (not included in the study) who was admitted early to Harvard and denied admission as a regular applicant to Yale:

> For Early Action, I think when people apply Early Action and get in, then when they apply to other schools regular—schools that also had an Early Action program—that could hurt the student because the [second] school thinks that they would really rather go to the first school. I saw this happen with people [who were admitted early to] Brown and Harvard. (Lisa, Choate)

Similarly, Needham students were influenced by the number of students admitted early to Tufts (three out of thirty Needham students in our sample), and by the case of a particular classmate. That classmate, not included in the study, was admitted to Williams but rejected by Boston College, normally considered a much less selective school:

> In retrospect, I might have applied to more schools because the process was more competitive and unpredictable than I'd expected. For example, there was a girl in my class who was admitted to Williams and rejected by BC. (Mark, Needham)

> I might have tried more stretch schools [since some admission decisions seemed slightly odd]. I had friends who, for example, didn't get into BC but got into Williams. (Paul, Needham)

As these quotations indicate, the salient but uncharacteristic case often gets accepted as the norm.

Only one student at each school got admitted to a college after being deferred from the early to the regular pool. To the typical student, this data may be discouraging—and may indicate that it is not, in fact, a good idea to apply early:

It seems like the stereotype is [that] if you apply early and you're a good candidate, you'll get [a] better chance because you've somehow assured them of your commitment. However, it seemed like a lot of people who were deferred weren't accepted in the regular round. I think if you're qualified, you should apply early, and it probably won't make a difference. (Alexis, Choate)

Using Logic

In Chapter 3 we described attempts by the college students to use logical reasoning to understand the Early Applications Game (see Table 3.4). Similarly, a number of the Choate and Needham students referred to individual factors that might influence an admissions office, and many were right on the mark in their analysis:

[There are some schools] that accept so many people early because it makes them look good to have such a good yield. (Ellen, Choate)

I think that ED has to make a big difference: it makes a statement that "I want to go here more than anywhere else on the planet." Admissions officers must be flattered by such a strong statement of interest. (Mary, Needham)

Yet just as we found in Chapter 3, the system is sufficiently complicated that seemingly logical reasoning can lead students to almost certainly unfounded conclusions:

There was a time when it totally helped you to apply early because a school would have accepted half their class early. Since then, everything has gotten reversed and now you have lots of people applying to places where they don't have a shot. I know a girl who applied to Stanford early and I thought she was totally qualified and she didn't even get deferred early—she was rejected. I wondered why and I wondered if she had waited, would she have gotten in? (Whitney, Choate)

The logic underlying this statement is very difficult to establish. There is no rational reason for schools to reject early applicants who would be competitive in the regular pool, since they can simply defer such students into that regular pool. (We discuss the logic of deferrals from the perspective of college admissions offices in Chapter 6.)

Student Recommendations for Early Applications

In June and July we asked the students whether they would advise others to apply early. Table 4.7 categorizes their responses. A majority of the Needham students and one-third of the Choate students recommended a straightforward strategy: apply Early Decision if you have identified a strong first-choice college. Otherwise, apply Early Action to your favorite EA school or to a safety school.

The Needham students used remarkably similar language in expounding the reasoning for a straightforward approach. This unifor-

Table 4.7   Strategies recommended at the end of the year

Strategy	Choate students	Needham students
Always apply early; apply ED if you have a solid first-choice college, otherwise apply early to your favorite EA college	9 (33%)	22 (73%)
Apply ED if you have a solid first-choice college, otherwise, apply EA, but only to a college that is at least an (equal) first choice	17 (63%)	5 (17%)
Other	1 (4%)	3 (10%)
Total	27	30

Source: Interviews with high school students.

mity may reflect the attitudes of the Needham college counselors, who encourage students who are uncertain about their preferences to consider applying Early Action to "second-tier–level schools, as the application and admission will reduce anxiety."[14]

Choate's counselors sometimes make similar recommendations. Terry Giffen, the director of college counseling, explained: "Early Action can be the foundation for further applications. For colleges in the top three or four on a student's list, I might suggest Early Action."[15]

It was more common for Choate students than for Needham students to recommend a conservative strategy, one that required greater interest in an Early Action school to apply early. The majority (63 percent) of the Choate students suggested that students with only a slight preference for an Early Decision school should not apply there early. Once again, the response by the Choate students reflects the advice of at least some of the college counselors at the school:

> Our college counselors told us that you really shouldn't apply early anything just to do it—that early admission was reserved for people who really know where they want to go. (Lindsey, Choate)

It is striking that the strategies recommended by students at the end of the year were not always consistent with the strategies they followed during the year. The Needham students tended to recommend that those without a strong preference should apply Early Action, even to a second- or third-choice college. Yet Needham students who applied to a school Early Action tended to prefer that college. The Choate students tended to recommend that students should only apply Early Action to a school that was at least a weak first choice. Yet a number of Choate students applied Early Action to colleges that were not among their top two choices. (Two Choate students who said they would only recommend Early Action to a weak or a strong first-choice college had actually applied

Early Action to a college that was clearly not their first choice, while several others offered advice that at least mildly clashed with their own actions.)

The recommendations from the Choate students may have been influenced by two developments during the year. First, there was something of a backlash against the students who gained admission to an Early Action college that was not a first choice. Two Choate students expressed the feeling that such applicants were harming their classmates:

> I think a lot of people used Early Action just to have a school they got into. It didn't affect them, but it did affect other people who really wanted to go to those schools, but didn't get in because the smarter people who were using the school as a safety got in instead. (Kendal, Choate)

> I know a lot of people who applied to Brown early and then only apply to Harvard, Yale, and Princeton [as regular applicants]. I don't agree with that because there are lots of people who are applying to Harvard, Yale, and Princeton and really want to go there, [yet] they're competing with these other people who've already gotten into Brown and might go there. (Leslie, Choate)

Second, as noted, some Choate students suggested that applying Early Action to one college could harm their own chances for admission as regular applicants to other colleges. Students who subscribe to either of these views should not be inclined to apply EA to anything other than a first choice, both to avoid hurting classmates applying to the same schools and also to avoid the possibility of hurting their own chances at a more preferred college. Interestingly, though at least one student at Needham expressed each of these views, such opinions did not seem to influence the recommendations of the Needham students as they had the Choate students.

Table 4.8   Choate master chart

Name	Early application	Choice rank of early app.*	Outcome**	Other apps.	Attend	Perception of early advantage
Adella	None	N/A	N/A	10	Harvard	EA and ED
Alexis	Brown EA	1/2	Admit	3	Brown	None
Andrew	None	N/A	N/A	1	Naval Acad.	None
Carlin	Harvard EA	Not 1/2	Def./Rej.	6	Brown	ED only
Chris	Brown EA	Not 1/2	Admit	3	Yale	EA and ED
Derek	Penn ED	1	Admit	0	Penn	EA and ED
Elizabeth	Columbia ED	1	Def./Rej.	5	NYU-Tisch	ED only
Ellen	Georgetown EA	1/2	Admit	2	Georgetown	None
Emily	None	N/A	N/A	9	Columbia	ED only
Frank	MIT EA	Not 1/2	Admit	2	Yale	ED only
Jane	None	N/A	N/A	7	Rochester	EA and ED
John	Yale ED	1	Admit	0	Yale	ED only
Kathy	None	N/A	N/A	10	Richmond	None
Katie	Chicago EA	1	Def./Rej.	2	NYU-Tisch	None
Kendal	Dartmouth ED	1	Def./Rej.	6	Penn	EA and ED

Name	Early application	Choice rank of early app.*	Outcome**	Other apps.	Attend	Perception of early advantage
Leslie	Duke ED	1	Def./Adm.	9	Yale	None
Lindsey	Yale ED	1	Admit	0	Yale	ED only
Lisa	Brown EA	1/2	Def./Rej.	4	Penn	ED only
	UNC EA		Admit			
Mary	Harvard EA	2	Def./Rej.	5	Yale	ED only
Melanie	None	N/A	N/A	6	Tufts	EA and ED
Peter	Yale ED	1	Admit	0	Yale	None
Raoul	None	N/A	N/A	9	Emory	EA and ED
Scott	MIT EA	1/2	Admit	1	MIT	EA and ED
Shawana	None	N/A	N/A	7	Georgetown	None
Simon	Brown EA	1/2	Def./Rej.	13	Reed	ED only
Ted	Georgetown EA	1	Def./Rej.	7	George Washington	EA and ED
Tim	Brown EA	Not 1/2	Admit	4	UNC–Morehead	ED only
Whitney	None	N/A	N/A	9	Stanford	None

* 1 = first-choice college; 2 = second-choice college; 1/2 = uncertain as to first- or second-choice college; not 1/2 = not first- or second-choice college.

** Admit = admitted early; Def./Adm. = deferred and admitted; Def./Rej. = deferred and rejected.

Note: First names of students have been changed to protect their anonymity.

Source: Interviews with high school students.

Table 4.9 Needham master chart

Name	Early application	Choice rank of early app.*	Outcome**	Other apps.	Attend	Perception of early advantage
Akshay	MIT EA	1	Def./Rej.	13	Carnegie Mellon	ED only
Austen	Brown EA	1	Def./Rej.	4	Brandeis	None
Bill	None	N/A	N/A	6	Wake Forest	ED only
Chrissy	Brown EA	1	Admit	3	Yale	EA and ED
Dara	Drew ED	1/2	Admit	4	Drew	None
Eliza	Brown EA	1/2	Deferred	0	Tufts	None
	Tufts ED2***		Admitted			
Fred	Brown EA	1	Def./Rej.	5	Boston College	ED only
Garfield	None	N/A	N/A	7	McGill	ED only
Gretchen	Columbia ED	1	Def./Rej.	3	Tufts	None
James	Harvard EA	1/2	Admit	5	Harvard	EA and ED
Jane	Brown EA	1	Def./Adm.	7	Brown	ED only
Jason	MIT EA	1/2	Def./Rej.	4	Cornell	EA and ED
Joan	Tufts ED	1/2	Admit	0	Tufts	EA and ED
Joey	Brown EA	1	Def./Rej.	5	Vassar	None
Julie	Vermont ED	1	Admit	0	Vermont	EA and ED
Kristin	BC EA	Not 1/2	Admit	7	Bates	EA and ED
	UNC EA	Not 1/2	Def./Rej.			

Name	Early application	Choice rank of early app.*	Outcome**	Other apps.	Attend	Perception of early advantage
Margret	None	N/A	N/A	4	Boston University	EA and ED
Mark	None	N/A	N/A	6	Wesleyan	EA and ED
Mary	None	N/A	N/A	11	Johns Hopkins	ED only
Matt	Williams ED	1	Admit	0	Williams	ED only
Melissa	None	N/A	N/A	8	George Washington	None
Michael	None	N/A	N/A	2	U.Mass-Amherst	ED only
Monica	None	N/A	N/A	6	James Madison	EA and ED
Namdi	Princeton ED	1	Def./Rej.	11	Wash & Lee	None
Neve	Bates ED	1	Admit	0	Bates	ED only
Paul	None	N/A	N/A	8	Conn. College	ED only
Rebecca	UNH EA	1/2	N/A	1	UNH	None
Sandy	Tufts ED	1	Admit	0	Tufts	EA and ED
Steven	None	N/A	N/A	6	Rochester	ED only
Tricia	None	N/A	N/A	7	Notre Dame	EA and ED

* 1 = first-choice college; 2 = second-choice college; 1/2 = uncertain as to first- or second-choice college; not 1/2 = not first- or second-choice college.

** Admit = admitted early; Def./Adm. = deferred and admitted; Def./Rej. = deferred and rejected.

*** Eliza was accepted to Tufts in second-round Early Decision.

Note: First names of students have been changed to protect their anonymity.

Source: Interviews with high school students.

The Outcomes

In the end, nearly all the students in our survey seemed quite happy with their college choice, even if it was not an initial first choice (see Tables 4.8 and 4.9). On a more objective basis, how did they do? Figure 4.1, a graphical "scorecard" for the overall process, shows the number of students who were accepted to their first- or second-choice school according to their initial preferences. For the computations in this figure, we used the initial college preferences rather than those expressed at the end of the year to avoid distortions due to acceptances and rejections—a student who is rejected by a first-choice college is likely to report thereafter that this school is no longer his first choice, but this report is unreliable.

Most of the students did very well: more than two-thirds of the students at each school were admitted to their first- or second-choice school. These statistics are impressive, particularly given the caliber of schools to which the students were applying.[16] Second, relative to their preferences and decisions of where to apply, students at the two schools have eerily similar results. Although the pool of schools to which the students applied varied somewhat—Choate students on average applied to and attended more highly ranked schools—both pools of students gauged their chances accurately and applied well.

In one sense, Figure 4.1 indicates a great performance by the two high schools. In the end, students at both schools were well informed and well advised about the details of the application process, and they reached desirable outcomes. But their application successes were not without costs. Students at both schools described suffering considerable stresses throughout the process—stresses less likely to be encountered by students at high schools that are not so oriented to college applications.

At Choate, the endless discussions about admissions decisions and strategies, which provide sophisticated information, also make the atmosphere tense and competitive:

I think being in an atmosphere where many students are very competitive about college admission has made the process more difficult. I am not, for example, extremely comfortable announcing the places to which I have applied to certain members of my class because I don't like the competitive atmosphere. (Emily, Choate)

I've had a couple of weird dreams about admissions officers getting a kick out of telling me I'm in, and then rejecting me. (Ellen, Choate)

Students at Needham may have encountered the same issues, though no one mentioned dreams or nightmares. The atmosphere at Needham was less affected by stress over college applications than was the case at Choate, but students at Needham were more focused on getting the grades to get into college. This was true in the fall of senior year, but students also cited the mountain of work assigned during junior year:

I spend an extreme amount of time on schoolwork. Junior year was the most stressful one. I easily stayed up after twelve and got up before five. I was also doing a lot of activities . . . it was extremely, extremely stressful. (Joey, Needham)

The Choate students did not describe much of a difference in workload during their later years at school, but they probably had more work than the Needham students in earlier years owing to the nature of preparatory school. Some students at Needham said they were actually forced to quit activities and part-time jobs, often under pressure from their parents:

I'm not doing winter sports this year, because my parents said I couldn't. (Mary, Needham)

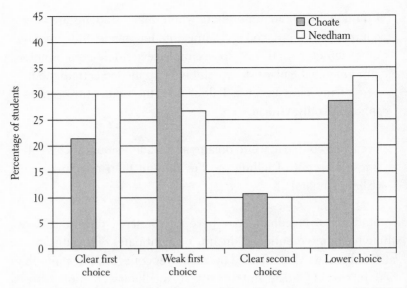

Figure 4.1 Admission results, Choate and Needham. (Interviews with high school students)

The week that colleges send out their letters must be a tense time for most every student. At both Choate and Needham, there were undoubtedly times during the year when it seemed like nothing mattered but an acceptance letter. However, the pressure seemed to build much earlier at Choate than at Needham. Even in the summer interviews, a few students mentioned the competitive aspect of the process, and once students returned to school it was omnipresent. Since 80 percent of Choate students live at school, they have at least eight additional hours each day for oppressive discussion. Unlike their public school peers, they can't go home and leave talk of college behind at the high school. Even late at night in a Choate dorm, someone is always writing an application, a reminder that one's own is soon due, and that the competition is at work.

5

The Truth about Early Applications

The truth about early admissions is hard to discern. Elite colleges accept higher percentages of early applicants than of regular applicants. But college admissions deans frequently claim that this difference in admission rates arises because early applicants are more attractive than regular applicants, not because they are favoring early applicants in their decisions. Despite this claim, the majority of students believe that colleges favor early applicants, as explained in Chapters 3 and 4.

Now we seek a hard answer to the central question, "Will applying early help me to get admitted?" The answer requires access to detailed admission records—records that are not available to guidance counselors or applicants. We are fortunate to have extensive original data from two sources, college admissions offices and the College Admissions Project survey of high school seniors in 1999–2000. In this chapter we examine these data to determine the magnitude of the advantage, if any, held by early applicants.

Fourteen highly selective colleges provided us with complete records for all their applicants for at least five years, from 1990–91 to 1996–97.[1] Each of those colleges ranks in the top 20 in one of the

U.S. News lists in 2002–03 ("Best National Universities" and "Best Liberal Arts Colleges"), with most in the top 10. In all, we had records for 505,054 applications at these 14 colleges, with at least 15,000 applications from each college. (We promised to maintain the anonymity of these 14 colleges when they gave us access to their data, so we cannot name them here.) Our second source of data is from 3,000 high school seniors who completed surveys about their backgrounds, academic qualifications, and college admissions outcomes in 1999–2000. This survey, called the "College Admissions Project," selected students at random from the top of the senior classes at prominent high schools around the country.[2] Most of these students applied to selective colleges, and more than half of them applied early.

The records provided by admissions offices, which we call the *admissions office data*, provide a complete picture of their decisions about which students to admit over several years at 14 particular colleges. The results for students in the survey, which we call the *survey data*, update the results from the admissions office data to 1999–2000 and provide information about a greater number of selective colleges. The survey data allow us to study the results at individual colleges by name, something we cannot do with the admissions office data because of our agreement to maintain anonymity.

In general, the results from the survey data closely mirror the results from the admissions data, with the caveat that the participants in the survey were chosen because they had particularly high grades at prominent high schools. As a result, average academic qualifications and admission rates are higher in the survey data than in the admissions office data.

Using these two sets of data, we can learn how much an early application improves a student's chance of admission, even though the early and regular pools of applicants differ in average qualifications and demographic backgrounds (recruited athletes and alumni children tend to apply early and minority applicants tend not to). We have enough data to exclude so-called hooked applicants (recruited athletes, alumni children, and targeted minorities) for whom admission may be an institutional priority and still be able to compare early and regular applicants with similar qualifications.

Our analysis of both sets of data leads to a consistent and emphatic conclusion: *Applying early provides a significant admissions advantage, approximately equivalent to the effect of a jump of 100 points in SAT-1 score. Applying early to an ED college provides a slightly larger advantage than applying early to an EA college.* Although some colleges, specifically Brown and Harvard, state that they do not favor early applicants, the survey data provide strong evidence that they do. Moreover, we find that the claim made by some colleges that the pool of early applicants is much stronger than the pool of regular applicants is part exaggeration and part myth. Early applicants have *slightly higher* test scores and high school class ranks than regular applicants at the most selective EA colleges, but early applicants tend to be *slightly weaker* in these qualifications than regular applicants at ED colleges.

In this chapter we describe our methods and then apply them to two main questions: Are early applicants stronger than regular applicants? Comparing early applicants with regular applicants with similar qualifications, do the early applicants get an edge in admissions chances? We perform separate analyses for each of these questions with the admissions office data and with the survey data.

Our Methods

Baseball fans love to debate the relative skills of players from various eras. How would Barry Bonds stack up against Babe Ruth, Pedro Martinez against Grover Cleveland Alexander? In answering such questions, they don't just compare the players on the basis of their numbers of homeruns and strikeouts. They also evaluate the liveliness of the ball, the configuration of the home stadium, the quality of the opposing players, and many other factors.

Assessing the effects of early applications presents a similar problem. Since the pools of early and regular applicants differ in many ways, simple comparisons of percentages of early and regular applicants admitted could be highly misleading. For this reason we take early and regular applicants with various common characteristics — for example, on SAT scores, high school grades, and extracurricular activities — and compare their outcomes.

We use two main approaches in our analysis. First, we use *analysis by categories*, which is designed to isolate groups of similar students. In order to compare likes with likes, we exclude minorities, alumni children, and recruited athletes wherever we could identify them in these categories, as studies have shown that they are given distinct advantages in admissions decisions.[3]

All the results in this chapter for the admissions office data are reported for the restricted sample; that is, for the set of applicants who are not minorities, alumni children, or recruited athletes. Within this restricted sample, we then classify applicants by different measures of academic performance, and look at the early and regular admission rates for applicants in the same category — for example, for early and regular applicants with SAT-1 scores ranging from 1300 to 1390.

For expositional purposes, we usually average the results across colleges when we report our findings for analysis by categories for the admissions office data. This averaging procedure enables us to preserve the anonymity of individual colleges in the admissions office data, and also helps us to summarize our findings for all colleges in individual graphs and tables.[4]

Second, we employ *multivariate regression analysis* (MRA). Regression analysis is a standard technique in formal research in areas stretching from finance and business to medicine and social policy. Despite its widespread use, its results are more difficult to interpret than the results of analysis by categories. Regression analysis estimates the separate impact of many different variables in producing an outcome, such as how much one earns or whether one gets admitted to college. In the case of earnings, a regression analysis would look at information about many individuals—their work experience, whether they went to college, where they live—to determine the average effect of each element on individual salaries. All else being equal, how much does a college degree increase salary on average? All else being equal, how much does an additional year of work experience increase salary on average? Regression analysis is designed to estimate the answers to questions like these.

We use regression analysis to assess the effect of each of many factors—in particular, SAT-1 scores, high school grades, status as a recruited athlete or alumni child, and type of high school—on admissions chances.[5] We particularly want to know the effect of applying Early Action or Early Decision, and how it varies with a student's other characteristics and by college. For example, a hypothetical student with a score of 1100 on the SAT-1 and grades that put her in the bottom half of her high school class is hardly likely to get into (say) Brown or Bryn Mawr, no matter when she applies. But a student in the top-tenth of her class with a 1350 score on the SAT-1 might gain a noticeable boost in admission chances by applying early.

In the figures throughout this chapter, we generally compare students and their outcomes on the basis of their SAT-1 scores. In fact, these scores were only one of several ways we measured an applicant's attractiveness—we also used SAT-2 scores, class rank, and a numerical ranking of extracurricular activities. The results based only on SAT-1 scores are relatively close to the results when we use a much more comprehensive approach, so we use the former to ease exposition.

Are Early Applicants Stronger Than Regular Applicants?

Many college admissions officials and offices emphasize that their early applicants are generally stronger than their regular applicants in test scores and class rank. Princeton's dean of admissions, Fred

Hargadon, advanced this view in 1996: "The fact that a higher fraction get admitted early is misleading. There is no big advantage to applying early, except to have it out of the way. The early pools are stronger; they don't have a bottom half to them."[6]

The Brown and Harvard admissions offices have developed official statements that summarize this argument:

You can see that the admit rate for those students who apply early to Brown is slightly higher than the overall admit rate, but you will also note that these rates are relatively close . . . Yes, there is a difference. However, this difference reflects a difference in quality rather than a policy that favors early applications.[7] (*Brown Admissions Office Report to Schools*, Fall 1999)

Higher Early Action acceptance rates reflect the remarkable strength of Early Action applicant pools — not less rigorous admissions standards.[8] (*Harvard Admissions Office Statement on Early Action*)

We found some support for these claims at Early Action colleges; we discovered that early applicants usually have somewhat higher SAT scores and class rank, and slightly more impressive extracurricular records, than regular applicants at Early Action colleges. On average, these early applicants scored about 10 to 20 points higher on each section of the SAT-1 than did regular applicants to the same colleges (see Figure 5.1).[9] These differences are important, but they hardly explain the gaps in the admission rates for early and regular applicants at Early Action colleges.

We found no support for the claims that early applicants are stronger than regular applicants at Early Decision colleges. Early applicants have slightly lower SAT scores and class rank, and slightly less impressive extracurricular records, than do regular applicants at Early Decision colleges. On average, these early applicants scored

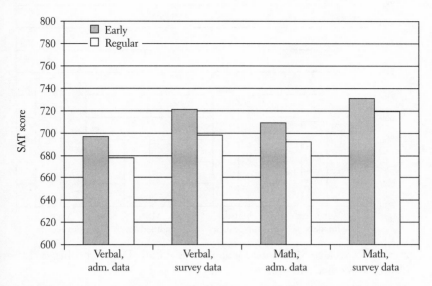

Figure 5.1 Average SAT scores for applicants at Early Action colleges. (Admissions office data and survey data)

between 0 and 5 points lower on each section of the SAT-1 than regular applicants to the same colleges (see Figure 5.2).

We used the survey data to compare early and regular applicants at fourteen individual colleges that received more than thirty early applications from participants in the survey.[10] At the most selective colleges offering Early Action—Brown, Harvard, and MIT—early applicants were noticeably stronger than regular applicants. At the three less selective colleges offering Early Action—Boston College, Chicago, and Georgetown—early applicants were similar to or even weaker than regular applicants in test scores (see Figure 5.3).

At the more selective colleges offering Early Decision—Columbia, Princeton, Stanford, and Yale—early applicants were broadly comparable to regular applicants in average SAT-1 scores. But at the four less selective schools offering Early Decision—Cornell, Dartmouth, Duke, and Penn— early applicants had average SAT-1

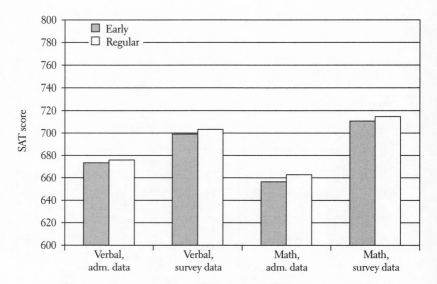

Figure 5.2 Average SAT scores for applicants at Early Decision colleges. (Admissions office data and survey data)

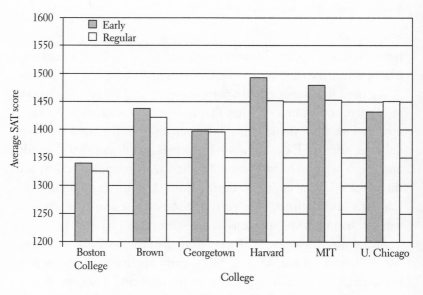

Figure 5.3 Average SAT scores for applicants to Early Action colleges. (Survey data)

scores at least 10 points lower than regular applicants (see Figure 5.4).

Fred Hargadon of Princeton asserted that there is "no bottom half" to the early applicant pool. To see if this is so, we returned to the admissions office data and looked at the distribution of SAT scores.[11] At the four Early Action schools in the admissions data, early applicants are slightly more concentrated at higher SAT-1 scores than regular applicants to the same colleges. At the ten Early Decision schools in the admissions data, early and regular applicants to those same colleges have nearly identical distributions of SAT-1 scores. At least at these ten colleges, the early pool has just as much a bottom half as the regular pool of applicants (see Figures 5.5 and 5.6).

While the finding that Early Decision applicants tend to be

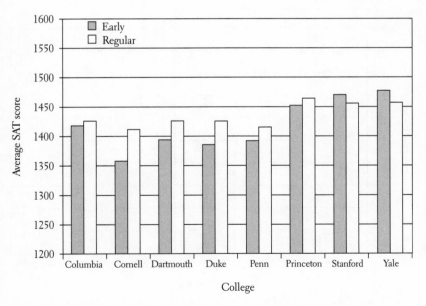

Figure 5.4 Average SAT scores for applicants to Early Decision colleges. (Survey data)

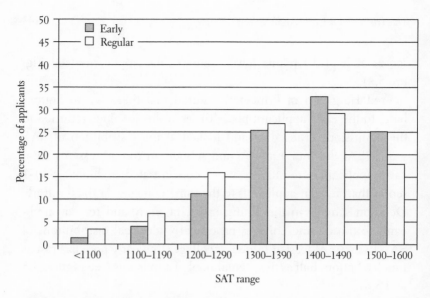

Figure 5.5 Composition of applicant pools by SAT scores, Early Action colleges. (Admissions office data)

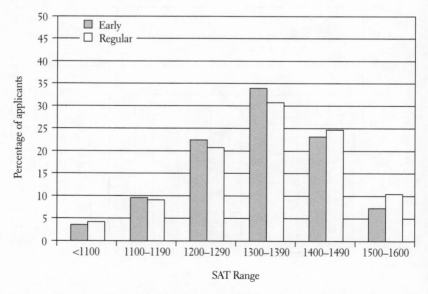

Figure 5.6 Composition of applicant pools by SAT scores, Early Decision colleges. (Admissions office data)

weaker on average than their regular counterparts contradicts much of the conventional wisdom, some sophisticated participants have long been aware of this pattern. Bill Matthews, the former college counselor at St. Paul's School in New Hampshire, wrote, "Many admissions officers say that most of the admitted-early applicants would fall somewhere in the middle of the pack of their regular decision group, and many would not be admitted in April, particularly those who need financial aid."[12] Similarly, Michele Hernandez, the former assistant director of admissions at Dartmouth College, observed that the advantage of applying Early Decision looms largest for applicants who are not at the top of the application pool in qualifications: "In almost every case, the early-decision pool is much more homogenous [than the regular pool of applicants]. Dartmouth, for example, receives many more [early] applications from candidates in the middle of the academic range than it does in the very high end or the very low end . . . I surmise that the most spectacular applicants know that they will get into almost any college they apply to, so those very highly qualified applicants don't feel the need to apply early."[13]

Admissions Rates for Early and Regular Applicants

Our analytic methods are designed to go beyond a simple comparison of admission rates for early and regular applicants. It is a useful preliminary, however, to consider these admission rates by themselves as preparation for more detailed analysis.

On average, the admission rate for early applicants is at least ten percentage points higher than the admission rate for regular applicants at both Early Action and Early Decision colleges.[14] This is true in both the admissions office data and the survey data (see Figure 5.7). These differences are consistent with the numbers we showed for a different set of colleges at the end of Chapter 2.

The differences in admission rates vary considerably from college

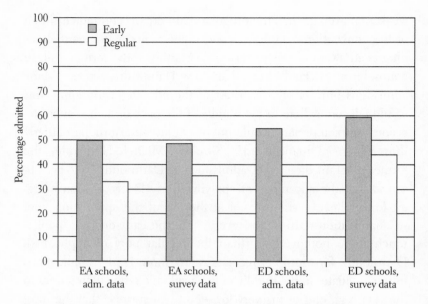

Figure 5.7 Admission rates for early and regular applicants. (Admissions office data and survey data)

to college. Admission rates from the survey data for six Early Action colleges are shown in Figure 5.8. For instance, Harvard accepted early applicants at more than three times the rate for regular applicants in the survey. Similarly, Brown accepted early applicants at almost twice the rate for regular applicants in the survey. The admission rates are higher for early than for regular applicants at the other four Early Action colleges that received more than thirty early applications in the survey data, but the differences are smaller.

At most of the Early Decision colleges that we studied in the survey data, early applicants were admitted at much higher rates than regular applicants. Columbia, Penn, Princeton, and Yale have the largest differences in rates of admission. Their early applicants were admitted at rates that were at least thirty percentage points higher than the admissions rates for regular applicants at those colleges.

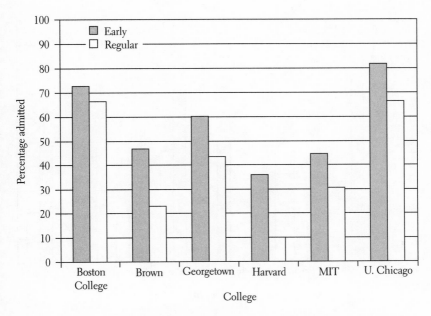

Figure 5.8 Admission rates for individual Early Action colleges. (Survey data)

While the admissions rates are closer at the other four Early Decision schools, the rate of admission for early applicants is at least five, and usually ten, percentage points higher than the rate of admission for regular applicants at each school (see Figure 5.9).

The results for Princeton stand out. Early applicants in the survey were admitted at almost three times the rate of regular applicants. Yet in the survey early applicants to Princeton actually had lower average SAT-1 scores than did regular applicants to Princeton. The survey also found that regular applicants to Princeton were quite similar on average to its early applicants in terms of extracurricular activities and the quality of high school.[15] Yet Princeton admitted 55 percent of early applicants and only 19 percent of regular applicants among students participating in the survey. The implication is clear: if you want to be a Princeton Tiger, apply early.

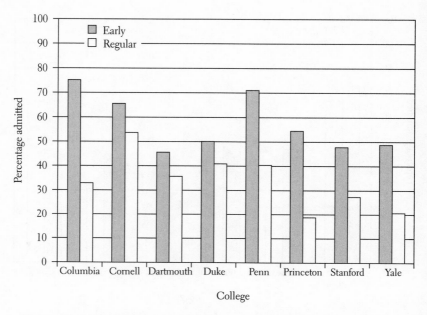

Figure 5.9 Admission rates for Early Decision colleges. (Survey data)

At six of the eight Early Decision colleges (the exceptions are Stanford and Yale), the early applicants had lower average SAT scores than the regular applicants. Academic qualifications simply do not explain why early applicants were admitted at higher rates than regular applicants at these colleges. We now turn to a more detailed analysis to estimate the exact benefit from applying early.

Detailed Analysis of the Admissions Office Data

Figure 5.10 depicts the difference in admissions rates at Early Action colleges for early and regular applicants within each 100-point range for SAT-1 scores. Within each 100-point range, the admissions rate for early applicants exceeds the admissions rate for regular applicants by at least 5 percentage points. In most cases, the admissions rate for regular applicants in one range is very close to the ad-

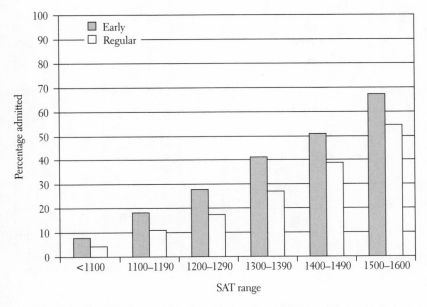

Figure 5.10 Admission rates by SAT scores, Early Action colleges. (Admissions office data)

missions rate for early applicants in the next range up. In other words, applying Early Action improves an applicant's chances of admission by about as much as a 100-point increase in SAT score. (To reiterate, this analysis excludes applicants who are minorities, alumni children, or recruited athletes.)

The difference in admissions rates is somewhat more pronounced at Early Decision schools than at Early Action schools, as shown in Figure 5.11. Within each 100-point range for SAT-1 scores from 1100 to 1490, the admissions rate for early applicants exceeds the admissions rate for regular applicants by at least 15 percentage points. In most cases, the admissions rate for early applicants in one range is slightly higher than the admissions rate for regular applicants in the next range up. For example, these Early Decision colleges admitted a higher percentage of early applicants with scores from 1200 to

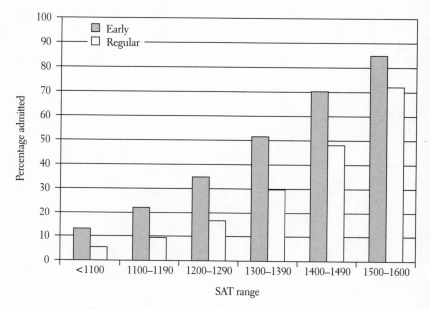

Figure 5.11 Admission rates by SAT score, Early Decision colleges. (Admissions office data)

1290 than of regular applicants with scores from 1300 to 1390. That is, applying ED improves an applicant's chances of admission more than would a 100-point increase in SAT score.

To check our results, we repeated our analysis using three different measures of applicant quality: class rank, SAT-1 score combined with class rank, and admissions office ratings. All tests gave the same result: early applicants were much more likely to be admitted than regular applicants with the same qualifications.

The admissions office ratings provide an especially important way to assess applicant quality. These ratings are assigned by two or three committee members who read a student's application before the committee reaches a consensus on whether to admit or reject. The ratings procedure varies from college to college: some colleges use a single composite rating, while others have different sets of categories, such as "Academic-Extracurricular-Personal." These ratings are important because admissions officers also consider essays and personal interviews when they assign ratings to applicants. Thus if early applicants write better essays and are stronger in their interviews than regular applicants, this difference should be reflected in their admissions office ratings. Eleven colleges provided us with their ratings of applicants as part of the admissions office data.

We compared the admissions outcomes for early and regular applicants with the same admissions office ratings at each of these eleven colleges. Once again, we found that colleges were much more likely to admit an early applicant than a regular applicant with the same qualifications. Figure 5.12 illustrates the results for early and regular applicants with the same admission ratings at one partic-

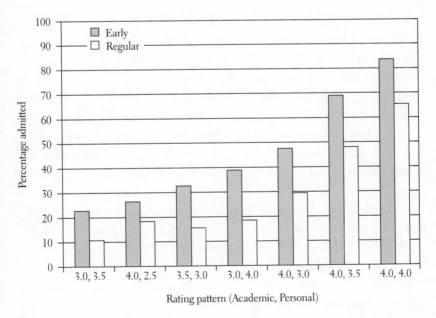

Figure 5.12 Admission rates by reader ratings: common rating categories at one Early Action college. (Admissions office data)

ular Early Action college in the admissions office data. This college gives each applicant an Academic rating and a Personal rating, with higher ratings being better. A rating higher than 4 is quite rare. The figure compares the outcomes for applicants with the seven combinations of Academic and Personal ratings that occurred most frequently.[16] The college admitted a higher percentage of early than regular applicants in each category. The early admit rate was at least ten percentage points higher in six of the seven categories. Some comparisons are stark; for example, applicants with ratings of (4.0, 3.0) should be admitted at higher rates than applicants with ratings of (3.5, 3.0). Yet 33 percent of early applicants with ratings of (3.5, 3.0) were admitted while only 29 percent of regular applicants with ratings of (4.0, 3.0) were admitted.

Results from the Survey Data for Individual Colleges

We now return to the survey, which contains data for more than 3,000 students who applied to college in 1999–2000. The immediate advantage of the survey data is that they allow us to identify individual colleges and study their decisions in 1999–2000. Figures 5.13a through 5.13f depict the results for early and regular applicants at the six most selective colleges in the survey. Once again, we excluded alumni children, recruited athletes, and minorities so that the early and regular pools of applicants contain truly similar students.

These graphs show striking differences in the results of early and regular applicants at three Early Action colleges: Brown, Harvard, and MIT. At Harvard, the early applicants in each range above 1400 were admitted at approximately two to three times the rate of regular applicants in the same categories. Similarly, early applicants to Brown with SAT-1 scores up to 1500 had much higher rates of admission than regular applicants in the same SAT-1 range.

The three Early Decision colleges in these figures (Princeton,

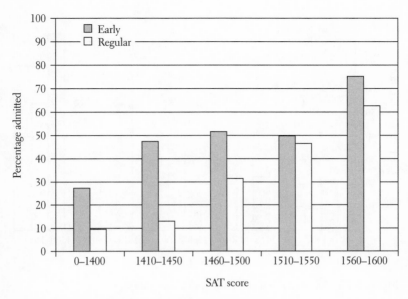

Figure 5.13a Admission rates for Brown. (Survey data)

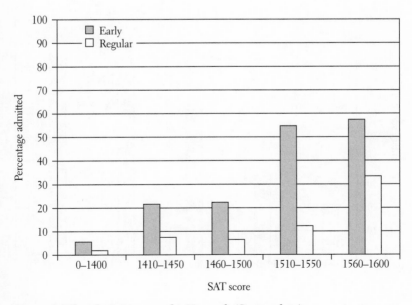

Figure 5.13b Admission rates for Harvard. (Survey data)

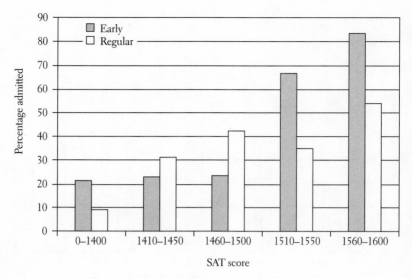

Figure 5.13c Admission rates for MIT. (Survey data)

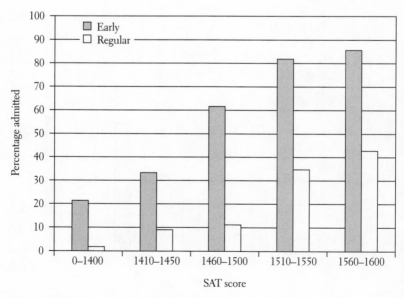

Figure 5.13d Admission rates for Princeton. (Survey data)

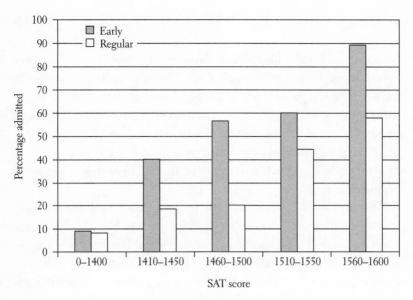

Figure 5.13e Admission rates for Stanford. (Survey data)

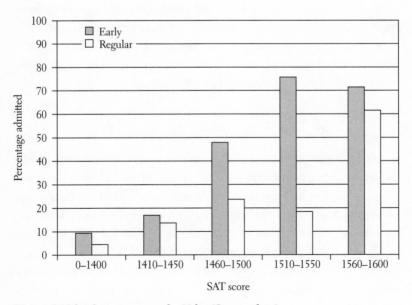

Figure 5.13f Admission rates for Yale. (Survey data)

Stanford, and Yale) also clearly favored early applicants. In every SAT-1 range above 1400, each Early Decision college admitted a higher percentage of early than regular applicants. Across these three schools, early applicants in any SAT-1 range were admitted at about the same rate as regular applicants with SAT-1 scores 100 points higher. In some cases, most notably at Princeton, the advantage for early applicants appears to be much larger than 100 points on the SAT-1.

The advantage of applying early to Princeton, Stanford, and Yale was especially strong for survey participants with SAT-1 scores from 1460 to 1500. These applicants are attractive but not truly exceptional candidates at these schools. At each of these three colleges, early applicants had double the chance of admission of regular applicants with the same SAT-1 scores.

MIT presents anomalous results in that it appeared to favor regular applicants with scores between 1410 and 1500, and early applicants with scores between 1510 and 1600. Thus, it is not clear from the survey information whether MIT favors early applicants over regular applicants in general. We would need information about a larger number of applicants to MIT to determine whether all applicants benefit from applying early to that school.

Regression Analysis for the Survey Data

Regression analysis estimates the separate effects of different factors in predicting an outcome—in this case, the admission decision. Thus, for example, regression analysis distinguishes the effect of applying as an alumni child from the effect of applying early, providing us with estimates of both effects. (See Appendix 5.3 for a more detailed description of regression analysis.)

Our main regression analysis included applications to the twenty-eight colleges that received at least ten early applications from survey participants.[17] The estimate from our regression analysis is that an Early Action application increases the chances of an average applicant by 18.9 percentage points. As expected, an Early Decision (binding) application has greater effect; it boosts the chances for an average applicant by 34.8 percentage points. These estimates correspond to an increase of 100 points on the SAT-1 for Early Action applicants, and an increase of 190 points on the SAT-1 for Early Decision applicants.

Just as there is no actual average family with 2.4 children, there is no actual "average applicant" in the comprehensive sample and no "average applicant" to Penn or any other college in the sample. The term "average applicant" simply refers to a hypothetical applicant with qualities equal to the average of the qualities of all the applicants in a given group. As shown in Table 5.2, the gain in admission chances varies with an applicant's qualifications. An early application has little or no effect for a student who is nearly certain to be admitted or nearly certain to be rejected as a regular applicant— this student is nearly equally certain to be admitted or to be rejected as an early applicant. The advantage of applying early is probably greatest for a student who is just at or below the admission standard as a regular applicant.

In subsequent regression analyses, we analyzed the results individually for each of the fourteen colleges that received more than thirty early applications from survey participants to secure a precise estimate of the effect of applying early at each of these colleges. Table 5.1 summarizes the results from these regressions, which indicate that an early application increases the average applicant's chances of admission by at least 15 percent at eleven of these fourteen colleges, and by at least 25 percent at each of the eight Early Decision colleges. These assessments are based on results for the survey participants, who are all particularly strong applicants, but they are consistent with the results from the admissions office data for a slightly different set of colleges (and half a million applicants).

These strong results may seem surprising given what the colleges say; Brown and Harvard, for example, clearly state on their websites that an early application has no effect on admissions chances:

Table 5.1   Estimating the admissions effect of applying early: separate regressions
for fourteen individual colleges

College	Average survey applicant's chance of admission: regular applicant	Average survey applicant's chance of admission: early applicant	Change in admissions chances	Number of applications
EARLY ACTION				
Boston College	76.9%	76.6%	- 0.3%	131
Brown	24.8%	45.4% ***	+ 20.6%	439
Chicago	92.3%	98.3%	+ 6.0%	116
Georgetown	44.3%	68.1% **	+ 21.8%	218
Harvard	10.5%	28.6% ***	+ 18.1%	513
MIT	25.4%	30.7%	+ 5.3%	188
EARLY DECISION				
Columbia	25.4%	85.3% ***	+ 59.9%	276
Cornell	55.6%	80.7% *	+ 25.1%	273
Dartmouth	27.6%	59.0% **	+ 31.4%	224
Duke	43.6%	81.3% ***	+ 37.7%	289
Penn	39.1%	83.6% ***	+ 44.5%	346
Princeton	9.6%	67.5% ***	+ 57.9%	305
Stanford	23.3%	44.9% **	+ 21.6%	417
Yale	17.9%	43.5% ***	+ 25.6%	389

* Statistically different from the results for regular applicants at the 5 percent significance level.

** Statistically different from the results for regular applicants at the 1 percent significance level.

*** Statistically different from the results for regular applicants at the 0.1 percent significance level.

Note: Results that are not starred are not statistically different from the results for regular applicants at the 5 percent significance level. See the "Note on Statistical Significance" at the end of the chapter for a description of statistical significance.

Source: Survey data.

Overall, as far as increasing chances for admission, there is not an advantage in applying to Brown early.[18]

For any individual student, the final admission decision [at Harvard] will be the same, whether the student applies early or regular.[19]

By contrast, our results estimate that an early application nearly triples the chances of admission for an average survey participant applying to Harvard and nearly doubles the chances of admission for an average survey participant applying to Brown.

The largest estimated effect in Table 5.1 is for an early applicant to Columbia. The average applicant to Columbia in the survey has an SAT-1 score of approximately 708 on each test. This applicant would have a 25 percent chance of being admitted as a regular applicant but an 85 percent chance of being admitted as an early applicant. That is, only one in four applicants with these scores would be admitted to Columbia from the regular pool, but more than eight out of ten would be admitted from the early pool. Penn and Princeton also appear to favor early applicants substantially. We estimate that the average applicant to these schools from the survey would increase her chances of admission by more than forty percentage points by applying early. Still these estimates are rough — some applicants will benefit more from an early application than others. A true shoo-in in December is a shoo-in in April as well.

To refine our figures, we estimated the chances of admission for a hypothetical male applicant who is approximately average within the survey in terms of activities and high school attended, and who has no other distinguishing characteristics. We assess the prospects of this average student four times, giving him four different sets of test scores varying from 650 to 800 on each of five SAT tests (the SAT-1 verbal and math, and three SAT-2 subject tests).

Applying early is estimated to double the chances of admission for this applicant at eleven of the fourteen colleges listed in Table 5.2, including all eight ED colleges, for at least one of the four sets of SAT scores. (The exceptions are Boston College and Chicago, where chances of admission are very high in all cases, along with MIT, where an early application only moderately increases admission chances.) At Columbia and Princeton, applying early increases the chances of admission more than fivefold for an applicant with a score of 700 on each of the five SAT tests. For Chicago, a hypotheti-

Table 5.2 Estimated chance of admission as a function of SAT score: male applicants in the survey data

College	SAT 1300, regular	SAT 1300, early	SAT 1300, change in chances	SAT 1400, regular	SAT 1400, early	SAT 1400, change in chances	SAT 1500, regular	SAT 1500, early	SAT 1500, change in chances	SAT 1600, regular	SAT 1600, early	SAT 1600, change in chances
EARLY ACTION												
Boston College	66.4%	66.0%	−0.4%	90.8%	90.6%	−0.2%	98.7%	98.7%	0.0%	99.9%	99.9%	0.0%
Brown	1.1%	4.4%	3.3%	4.9%	13.7%	8.8%	14.7%	31.4%	15.7%	32.9%	54.9%	22.0%
Chicago	69.8%	88.7%	18.9%	95.1%	99.0%	3.9%	99.7%	100%	0.3%	100%	100%	0.0%
Georgetown	3.4%	11.2%	7.8%	26.3%	49.1%	22.8%	71.2%	87.9%	16.7%	96.0%	99.1%	3.1%
Harvard	0.0%	0.0%	0.0%	0.1%	5.0%	4.9%	8.6%	24.9%	16.3%	34.6%	61.4%	26.8%
MIT	10.1%	13.1%	3.0%	35.4%	41.4%	6.0%	70.1%	75.4%	5.3%	92.4%	94.4%	2.0%
EARLY DECISION												
Columbia	0.1%	26.2%	26.1%	9.0%	64.4%	55.4%	36.8%	91.5%	54.3%	74.8%	99.1%	24.3%
Cornell	18.3%	42.8%	24.5%	42.7%	70.5%	27.8%	70.4%	89.6%	19.2%	89.5%	97.6%	8.1%
Dartmouth	3.7%	16.9%	12.5%	26.6%	57.8%	31.2%	70.3%	91.2%	20.9%	95.4%	99.4%	4.0%
Duke	0.1%	9.1%	9.0%	13.2%	47.4%	34.2%	56.1%	88.6%	32.5%	92.3%	99.3%	7.0%
Penn	10.8%	50.8%	40.0%	32.7%	79.0%	46.3%	63.2%	94.5%	31.3%	87.0%	99.1%	12.1%
Princeton	0.6%	21.7%	21.1%	5.5%	56.2%	50.7%	25.5%	86.4%	60.9%	61.0%	97.9%	36.9%
Stanford	1.5%	5.9%	4.4%	10.9%	26.5%	15.6%	38.2%	61.9%	23.7%	73.7%	89.2%	15.5%
Yale	0.5%	3.2%	2.7%	4.6%	17.5%	12.9%	21.8%	49.1%	27.3%	55.3%	81.3%	25.8%

Source: Survey data.

cal applicant would only reap a noticeable gain with an early application if he had an SAT score of 650 or below on each test. This is not surprising: the hypothetical applicant would be extremely likely to be admitted to Chicago with SAT scores of 700 or more.

Our data from more than 3,000 surveys of strong high school students, and from half a million college applications, tell a clear and consistent story. As logic would suggest, if admission is virtually assured, or nearly impossible, it does not matter when you apply. When a candidate has a modest to medium chance of admission as a regular applicant, however, the situations that matter, an early application increases those chances substantially.

Appendix 5.1: Two Objections to Our Results and Our Responses

We have discussed these results with many academic scholars, high school guidance counselors, and college admissions officers. A number have expressed some surprise at our findings, raising two common objections.

Statistical Analysis Is Not Relevant to Admissions Decisions

Some observers complain that we cannot capture all relevant factors about an applicant with a finite set of numerical variables. For this reason, some admissions deans have told us that they do not believe that any statistical analysis of admissions decisions can produce convincing results. We addressed this problem by including as many measures of each applicant's qualities as possible, refining our analysis with additional statistical tests, and replicating our results across two extensive and very different sources of data about applicants and their outcomes.

True, each candidate is unique, but this does not mean that statistics are unreliable. Statistics do not pretend to tell the future; instead, they tell us how likely a particular outcome is, on the basis of what we know about a situation. For example, if your blood pressure and cholesterol are high, your risk of heart attack surely is high. As the humorist Damon Runyan wrote, "It may be that the race is not always to the swift, nor the battle to the strong—but that is the way to bet." College applicants would do well to play the law of averages and apply when the chances of admission are high.

But maybe an early application indicates some additional positive information not captured in our analysis. For instance, early applicants at a particular college may be unusually well organized and also strongly enthusiastic about attending the college where they apply early. Such qualities could make them more successful if admitted early. The evidence to test this theory is limited and mixed. Russell Adair of Yale's Office of Institutional Research considered this possibility in an unpublished 1998 study. He found that students who were admitted early to Yale had statistically significantly higher grades and graduation rates than did students admitted from the regular pool, after controlling for test scores and demographic factors. In contrast, Michael Robinson and James Monks found that at Mount Holyoke, students admitted early had freshman grades very similar to those of students admitted from the regular pool, again controlling for test scores and demographic factors.[20] One possible explanation for the difference in the results between Mount Holyoke and Yale is that Yale's early applicants are unusually outstanding, even relative to Yale's regular applicants, in terms of hard-to-measure factors such as intellectual motivation and energy. It seems unlikely that Russell Adair's findings for Yale would hold at the many colleges where early applicants are similar to or weaker than regular applicants in test scores and grades (and thus probably in the hard-to-measure factors as well).

The many attributes of the 500,000 applicants in the admissions office data and the 3,000 survey participants that we could not incorporate into our analysis could throw off our analysis only if (1) early applicants systematically differ from regular applicants in qualities that we could not measure and include; and (2) those differences make the early applicants much more attractive than the regular applicants. How large could such differences be on average? It is implausible that they could be equivalent to a difference of 100 points on the SATs, the admissions advantage that we estimate for applying early.

Two of our measures of a student's attractiveness were included in response to the expected criticism that our measures could not capture the complete candidate. These were the admissions office ratings for applicants in the admissions data, and an activity rating based on extracurricular activities and accomplishments for applicants in the survey data.

If there are substantial differences between early and regular applicants beyond the measures that we have used in our statistical analysis, these qualities should be reflected in the admissions office ratings. We conducted our regression analysis of the admissions office data both with and without the admissions office ratings. Including these ratings slightly reduced the estimated effect of applying early at Early Action colleges, but it increased the effect by a similar amount at Early Decision colleges.[21]

One advantage of the survey data is that the participants are known to be fairly similar to one another because of the way they were chosen for the survey. They are all successful students at very good high schools. Thus they are not likely to be very different in motivation, organization, and other similar factors.

In addition to the academic information we used to compare early and regular applicants from the survey, we also gave them an "Activity Rating" of 1 to 5. An Activity Rating of 2 represents an ordinary level of activity in school activities, such as several years of participation in the debate club and the drama club. A rating of 4 represents superior achievement at the state level in some activity, such as a state championship in some event, performing in an all-state orchestra, or making the semifinals of the Westinghouse Science Competition.

An increase from 2 to 4 in the student activity rating, which should substantially enhance an applicant's attractiveness, is estimated to improve a student's admissions chances about half as much as an EA application and approximately one-quarter as much as an ED application. Once again, it seems quite unlikely that the unmeasured difference in the average quality of early and regular applicants could be as large as the difference between the students with activity ratings of 2 and the students with activity ratings of 4. And which is easier? To submit an early application? Or to master the trombone to the level of all-state orchestra or become a semifinalist in the Westinghouse Science Competition?

Some Early Applicants Are Deferred and Admitted in the Regular Pool

A second argument that has been made against our statistical findings is that if early applicants are given a considerable advantage in admissions decisions, then deferred applicants must be less qualified than any of the regular applicants who are admitted. Thus if early applicants gain an advantage in admissions decisions, very few deferred applicants should be admitted from the regular pool. The syllogism concludes with the observation that colleges that admit a number of deferred applicants cannot be favoring early applicants. Harvard's admissions deans advanced this argument in a 1998 editorial: "Further evidence of the high standard set for early admission is the fact that a considerable number of candidates deferred in Early Action are admitted in the spring. Last year, 222 Early Action defers were admitted to the Class of 2001."[22] This argument presumes that deferred applicants are considered on equal terms with regular applicants. But are they? If early applicants are favored to begin with, for whatever reason, then those who are deferred may well be favored later when competing with regular applicants.

Institutions may also opt to defer an applicant and then admit the student in regular decision for political reasons. At Wesleyan, for example, the admissions office would sometimes defer alumni children with the express intention of admitting them from the regular pool. It did this in cases where an alumni child attended a high school that sends many students to Wesleyan, and where the alumni child had somewhat lower-than-average credentials. A decision to admit the deferred application in regular decision or from the wait-list would reduce the risk of admitting an applicant who was perceived within his or her high school to be underqualified.

We have additional anecdotal evidence from two admissions offices that early applicants do receive special consideration even after they are deferred. One student who had worked in an admissions office at a highly ranked college (not Harvard) told us in an informal conversation that some early applicants were deferred with a notation that they should be admitted in the regular pool. Almost all such applicants were admitted. Similarly, in one of our formal interviews with a Harvard student, that student explained that her experience working in the Harvard Admissions Office convinced her that early applicants have an advantage in admissions decisions even after they are deferred:

> If you do not get in early, you're [still] better off when the regular pool rolls around. The admissions office does get excited about students, and individuals in the office take sides and lobby for particular students. Being in the early process improves your chances of getting selected out of the pools. (Megan, Harvard '00)

There are a number of additional reasons that acceptance of deferred early applicants need not imply equal or higher standards for the early pool: some applicants greatly improve their record from the early to the regular admissions season; the college, looking for a balanced class, may discover a shortfall in some types of applicants, and hence may accept them from the deferred pool; and some deferred candidates must be accepted to make the original deferral process legitimate. It is also possible in some cases, as several MIT students emphasized in our interviews, for a deferred applicant to call an admissions office to learn how to improve his or her application in the quest for admission.

Appendix 5.2: Notes on Statistical Significance

Suppose that you flip a coin four times and each time it comes up "heads." Can you declare that the coin must be "loaded"? No, because streaks like this happen all the time by chance. Even the worst baseball team occasionally has a winning streak. For example, the Pittsburgh Pirates won four consecutive games against the Milwaukee Brewers from June 26 through June 29, 2001. Judging just from those games alone, you might think that Pittsburgh was the better team. But Milwaukee had an above-average record before those games, while Pittsburgh was the second-worst team in the entire major leagues.

The key observation for these examples is that while these combinations of events are possible, they are unlikely. Standard statistical practice distinguishes between "four heads in a row" and "ten heads in a row." The former is unlikely, the latter nearly impossible. With a fair coin, there is an equal chance of "heads" and "tails" on a given coin toss. Thus if you flip a fair coin four times in a row, you have $(0.5 * 0.5 * 0.5 * 0.5) = 0.5^4 = 6.25$ percent chance of getting four heads in a row. If you flip a fair coin ten times in a row, you have $0.5^{10} = 0.1$ percent chance of getting ten heads in a row. That is, you expect to get ten heads in a row 1 time in 1,000 that you flip a fair coin ten times in a row. If in some future year Pittsburgh triumphs over Milwaukee in ten straight games, put your dollars on Pittsburgh thereafter.

Modern statistical practice distinguishes among relatively unlikely events by comparing their probabilities with standard "significance levels." The most commonly used significance level is 5 percent. With a 5 percent significance level, "ten heads in a row" would be deemed statistically significant evidence that a coin is not fair. There is 0.1 percent probability that "ten heads in a row" would occur with a fair coin, and 0.1 percent is far less than 5 percent. In contrast, "four heads in a row" would not be deemed statistically significant evidence that a coin is not fair. There is 6.25 percent probability that this outcome would occur with a fair coin, and 6.25 percent is greater than 5 percent.

This chapter raises the question, "Do we have statistically significant evidence that early applicants are treated differently than regular applicants in admissions decisions?" This appendix seeks to answer it. At almost all of the fourteen colleges that received more than thirty early applications from survey participants, early applicants had a sizeable advantage in the survey outcomes. Is that advantage great enough to be deemed statistically significant on the basis of the current evidence? As the coin-flipping examples suggest, statistical significance depends both on the disparity in results between early and regular applicants, and on the number of applications available in the survey.

In the admissions office data, we have exhaustive information on the treatment of applications for each participating college. Given this detailed information, the advantage given to early applicants is unquestionably statistically significant. The disparity in the results for early and regular applicants in the admissions office data, as shown in Figures 5.10 and 5.11, would occur by chance with probability less than 1 in a billion if early and regular applicants were evaluated on equal terms. This difference between admissions rates for early and regular applicants in the admissions office data soars beyond any traditional test of statistical significance.[23]

In the survey data, we observe similar disparities in results between early and regular applicants, but we have many fewer applicants to study than in the admissions office data. Still, the difference in admissions rates for early and regular applicants is significant at the 0.1 percent level for seven of the fourteen colleges, Brown, Columbia, Duke, Harvard, Penn, Princeton, and Yale. The difference in admissions rates is significant at the 1 percent significance level for Dartmouth, Georgetown, and Stanford, and at the traditional 5 percent level for Cornell.[24]

The difference in results for early and regular applicants is not statistically significant at the 5 percent level at four of the six Early Action colleges studied in the survey: Boston College, Chicago, Georgetown, and MIT. This should not be construed as evidence that early and regular applicants are treated equally at these colleges. In fact, the evidence in the survey suggests that Chicago and MIT also favor early applicants, but the numbers of applications to those colleges were limited; hence, this evidence does not leap over the hurdle of statistical significance.

Appendix 5.3: Notes on Regression Analysis

We presented results from numerous multiple regression analyses in this chapter. Such analyses are often simply referred to as regressions. In each regression, we are trying to predict the consequence for a single variable of changes in other variables that influence its value. In most instances, that single variable—called the dependent variable—is the probability that a student gets admitted to a college. Many independent variables are used to predict that probability. We used twenty-one independent variables in each regression for the survey data, where we were predicting admissions outcomes at a single college. (These results were presented in Table 5.1 and also used in Table 5.2). Regression analysis estimates a numerical coefficient for each independent variable. For each variable, regression analysis estimates a coefficient that indicates how much it influences the dependent variable. In our analysis, we are particularly interested in the coefficient on "Early Application," for that coefficient indicates the effect of an early application on the admissions outcome at each separate college.

Let's take a hypothetical example for a single college, using three independent variables: total SAT score, class rank (CR), and private school (PRIV). The first variable runs from 400 to 1600, the second is scored by percentile (the higher the better). The third just takes on two values: it is scored as 1 if the student is from a private school, and 0 otherwise. (In the language of statistics, this variable is an "indicator" or a "dummy variable.") The dependent variable is the likelihood of being admitted, denoted P(admission), and is measured as a percentage. We want to learn how much a change in each of the independent variables affects an applicant's chance of being admitted.

We run the regression on a computer. The program looks at each applicant's records to compute a relationship between the independent variables and the dependent variable, P(admission), the probability of being admitted. The output of a regression is a linear equation with a y-intercept and one term for each independent variable. For example, the regression result might be the following equation:

$$P(\text{admission}) = 0.05 \text{ SAT} + 0.1 \text{ CR} + 8 \text{ PRIV} - 40,$$

where this equation gives the percentage chance of admission as a function of SAT score, class rank (in percentile), and type of school (coded 1 for private and 0 for public). This (fictitious) equation indicates that a 1-point increase in SAT score gives, on average, a 0.05 percent increase in the probability of admission—meaning that a 100-point increase in SAT score gives an average increase of 5 percentage points in the chance of admission. Similarly, according to this equation, a jump of 10 percentiles in class rank would increase the chances of admission by 1 percentage point, while going to a private school instead of a public school would increase the chance of admission by 8 percentage points.[25]

To compute a single student's P(admission), we replace the variables with her SAT score, class rank, and value for the private school variable. For example, a student with 1400 SATs in the 80th percentile of her class who attended private school would have a

$$P(\text{admission}) = 0.05(1400) + 0.1(80) + 8(1) - 40 = 46$$

percent chance of being admitted.

Of course, the probability of admission can never be more than 100 percent or less than 0 percent. To allow for this fact, we use a slightly more complicated form of regression analysis known as a "Probit" analysis. A Probit analysis produces a nonlinear regression equation that only produces admission probabilities between 0 percent and 100 percent. An additional, realistic feature of a Probit analysis is that applicants who are very likely to be admitted gain little from an improvement in qualifications (or from applying early) because their chances of admission were already close to 100 percent and cannot increase by very much.

6

❧❦

The Game Revealed:
Strategies of Colleges,
Counselors, and Applicants

At first glance, college admissions may appear to be a straightforward process: students apply to their favorite institutions, and then the colleges and universities admit the applicants who are best qualified. Under the surface, however, the system is rich with Machiavellian machinations, transforming the admissions process into the strategic "Admissions Game." Colleges and universities must determine whether to set different standards for early and regular applicants, and if so whether to reveal that these standards are not the same. Students must make strategic decisions about whether to apply Early Action or Early Decision and, if so, to which institution. College counselors must make choices that can help some students at the expense of others when managing the application decisions of their respective graduating classes. This chapter highlights the strategies for each of these groups in turn. If you are going to play the game effectively, it is important to understand the strategies of each of the main players.

Incentives for Colleges

Colleges face two related decisions: whether to offer an early admissions program, and if so, whether that program should admit students at a lower standard than regular admissions. As Stanford's belated decision to adopt ED in 1995–96 indicates, colleges often feel that they need to institute and maintain early admissions programs to avoid losing applicants to their rivals (see Chapter 1 for details). Similarly, Michael Behnke, the vice president for enrollment at the University of Chicago, explained that competition gradually pushed his institution to adopt to a formal early admissions program: "Both Northwestern and Chicago put the plan into place because the Big Ten had such early dates, particularly for housing. Then NACAC encouraged us to get on board in some sort of formal plan, so we went with Early Action and Northwestern went with Early Decision. We never thought of it as a first-choice plan. It was a way to get word out to students early who were getting pressed from other places."[1]

Once a college has enacted an early admissions program, why might it favor early applicants given that admitting students early reduces the school's options? There are many incentives—especially for colleges that use Early Decision—to set lower standards for early than for regular admission. Some of these incentives are laudable; others are purely self-serving and collectively detrimental.

We sent a survey to the admissions offices at thirty-five colleges composing the membership of the Consortium on Financing Higher Education. Twelve colleges returned the survey, and we report some of their responses in this section.

Identifying Enthusiasts

Colleges want to admit students who are eager to attend because they believe enthusiasm will bolster performance and enhance a student's enjoyment of college life. As noted in Chapter 5, a study of Yale students found that those admitted early had higher grades and graduation rates at Yale than students with similar credentials who were admitted as regular applicants, though a study of Mount Holyoke students found that applicants with similar credentials had almost identical freshman-year grades.

Another reason that colleges might want to admit enthusiastic students is that, unlike Lake Wobegon, where "all the children are above average," at least some students in each college's entering class are below its average in academic ability. A theory attributed to Fred Glimp during his tenure as admissions dean at Harvard in the 1960s suggests that it is important to "search for the happy bottom quarter."[2] According to this theory, the enthusiasm of ED applicants for a particular college makes them attractive candidates. Robin Mamlet, then the dean of admissions at Swarthmore and now the dean of admissions at Stanford, observed that "some admissions offices use Early Decision to handpick the bottom of the entering class."[3]

An Early Decision application, which binds admitted students to attend a given college, is a more convincing signal of interest in a college than an Early Action application. But both convey information. As one admissions officer explained in response to our survey, ED is a "clean, honest way of using a student's interest [as a factor] in the decision-making process," enabling a college to build its entering class around a core set of committed students. Yet the signal conveyed by an early application is by no means perfect. Students may apply early to show enthusiasm even if they are uncertain of their preferences, or as a strategic measure to a school that is not their first choice, but that offers them the most net benefit from an early application. This dilutes or distorts the message conveyed by an early application. It also puts pressure on each student to apply early, the understanding being that a regular application to one school implies an early application somewhere else. (This problem of negative inference is a particular worry to students at a high school where it is known that students often apply early.)

Reducing Enrollment Uncertainty

Each early applicant admitted by a college provides insurance, a place likely filled. In our analysis of the admissions office data we found that 95.8 percent of early admits, but only 31.0 percent of regular admits, matriculated to the ten Early Decision colleges in our sample. Early Action admits are also much more likely to matriculate than are applicants from the regular pool. In our admissions office data, 67.9 percent of early admits and 42.5 percent of regular admits matriculated to the four Early Action colleges in our sample.

Each college's actual class size depends on its _yield, the percentage of admitted students who decide_ to matriculate to the college. A year with a surprisingly high or a surprisingly low yield can leave a college in an embarrassing situation. As explained in Chapter 2, Amherst instituted Early Decision "to minimize the uncertainties created by multiple applications" after it found itself with 306 freshmen in 1955, when its intended class size was 250—a 22 percent overenrollment.[4] Similarly, a Princeton student in the class of 1999 described the overenrollment problem from his freshman year, the last year that Princeton admitted students under Early Action:

> My class has 1,100 students and was the largest in Princeton's history. The college had to set up mobile homes on fields and build new dorms to accommodate everyone. I think that Early Decision helps to manage the enrollment process to avoid that predicament. (Edward, Princeton '99)

Two cases in 1995–96 (the first year that Princeton, Stanford, and Yale offered Early Decision) underscore the difficulty of enrollment planning. Yale admitted 415 students early and enrolled 401 of them. Instituting Early Decision gave Yale a more precise sense of the number of early admits who would matriculate to Yale. Ironically, the following fall, Yale found itself with 1,415 freshmen, thought to be its largest entering class in history, when it had been aiming for a class of 1,335. The problem was a surprising jump in the yield rate for regular admits—the admissions office anticipated a yield between 46 and 50 percent for the regular decision pool, but that number jumped to more than 52 percent. Such a large entering class requires special accommodations. Richard Brodhead, the Yale College dean, explained: "The first thing we did when we learned of the enrollment increase was to alert the departments . . . Already we have more sections planned than normal and if more are needed we'll take care of it."[5] That same year, the Cornell Medical School found itself with an excessively large incoming class. Cornell admitted 249 students, expecting 101 to 104 to enroll. When 119 students accepted the offer of admission, Cornell was in a bind. It offered free tuition for one year to the first fifteen students who agreed to defer admission by one year, and even allowed them to live in subsidized university housing during that year.[6]

As these stories indicate, overenrollment is costly to colleges. Presumably, empty seats are even less appealing to colleges than are overcrowded classrooms. Although highly selective schools can fill empty seats by turning to their waiting lists, most prefer to avoid the stigma of admitting students from the waiting list whenever possible.[7]

Why do colleges, which have years of experience in admissions, have so much trouble gauging how many students to admit? The problem is that when a college makes its admissions decisions it can only estimate the matriculation rate for regular admits. Although this estimate reflects past experience, it may not accurately reflect the current popularity of a college, particularly when the school has just changed its admissions rules and altered the composition of its regular applicant pool. Also, some colleges get "hot" in a particular year, while others turn "cold."

Suppose that a college admits 2,000 regular applicants, expecting 1,000 of them to enroll. If the college knew the true (average) matriculation rate would be 50 percent for a given year, there would still be a statistical probability that its freshman class would deviate significantly from 1,000, but that probability is not great. Say each of 2,000 students flipped a coin to decide whether to enroll. Then there is only about a 1 percent chance that 1,050 students or more would enroll.[8] Even a small amount of uncertainty about the matriculation rate can change matters decisively. Say the chance of each student's attending is either 52 percent or 48 percent (for an average of 50 percent) depending on whether the college is perceived as "hot" or "cold" that year, something it cannot predict at the time it sends out its acceptances. Then the chance that at least 1,050 students will enroll increases to 16 percent.[9]

By accepting students early, a college reduces uncertainty about its final class size, or over standards, should it have to adjust downward or upward to fill or limit the class. Indeed, most of the admissions offices that responded to our survey stated that Early Decision helps them to manage enrollment figures for the entering class. A common metaphor used in several surveys was that Early Decision "helps to build the base of the class." Locking in students through Early Decision acceptances also shields a college from the consequence of some unexpected springtime disaster that would discourage admitted candidates from attending the college. At Wesleyan, for example, the yield fell dramatically when the president's office was firebombed in the late 1980s. For several years after that, Wesleyan placed more emphasis than usual on Early Decision, in part to protect itself in case of another damaging incident.

Minimizing Financial Aid Commitments

Some critics assert that colleges give preference to early applicants to help limit their financial aid budgets. As Bruce Breimer, the college counselor at the Collegiate School in New York, notes, early applicants tend to be "well-heeled." The College Board makes a similar observation: "Some colleges find that they can stretch their limited financial aid budgets by admitting students [in Early Decision] who are not only bright and committed to their school, but who are also 'full pay students', i.e., ones who are not relying on financial aid."[10]

Vassar's admissions office amplified this point in responding to our survey: "Generally, ED applicants are a bit less needy than the overall pool (50–55% vs. 65%), which does allow for a greater share of the budget left for needy kids in regular decision.[11] But obviously the aid consequences of ED (for the institution) depend entirely on the Admission Committee's decisions—if you set out to admit a significantly less needy ED population, you can if you have the applicant pool. At Vassar, we don't really consider need in our ED committee discussions."

Many leading colleges announce a policy of need-blind admissions, which means that admissions officers do not examine financial aid applications to help decide which students to admit and which to reject. The wealthiest colleges may be able to implement need-blind admissions policies, but less well endowed colleges, which are concerned about tuition revenues, may find that admitting a large number of early applicants can reduce grant aid while preserving the trappings of need-blind admissions. Even some highly rated, well-endowed, and selective universities do not use need-blind policies.[12] Brown, for example, used a "need-aware" policy for a number of years. Under this policy, financial considerations played a role in admissions decisions for 5 to 10 percent of the class.[13] A public report of a 1999 meeting of Brown's advisory committee estimated that without this policy, Brown's financial aid commitments would have been as much as 30 percent higher.[14] A subsequent internal study estimated that adopting need-blind admissions would cost Brown anywhere from three to eight million dollars per year in increased financial aid.[15]

Before the 1990s, many highly selective colleges met to agree on financial aid need levels for incoming students through a process called Overlap, both to ensure equity for students and to avoid bidding wars. As discussed in Chapter 1, the eight Ivy League colleges agreed to stop this practice after the Justice Department charged that the Overlap process violated antitrust regulations.

Today, students who are admitted to several schools often receive financial aid packages that vary significantly from one college to the next, and they can then choose on the basis of their financial aid offers. William Fitzsimmons and Marlyn Lewis, who head Harvard's admissions office, explained that there "can be legitimate, defensible differences of opinion on levels of need-based aid."[16] As a result, many financial aid applicants are eager to compare financial aid packages from different colleges, and so tend not to apply early. This tendency reinforces the disparity in average wealth between early and regular applicants.

Whatever the composition of the applicant pool, admitting Early Decision applicants limits financial aid negotiations with accepted students. In 2000–01, after negotiations with 673 students, Carnegie Mellon increased financial aid offers to nearly half of them, with the revised offers averaging $4,000.[17] Since Early Decision admits cannot apply to other colleges, they forgo any leverage they would gain by documenting the financial aid offered by other schools. Each ED admit saves money for a college (on average), and also (according to many informal reports from admissions officers at various colleges) saves the college considerable headache by precluding the possibility of such negotiations over financial aid in the spring.

Some colleges may go one step further, exploiting their monopoly power by reducing the financial aid offers they would otherwise give to early admits, though many colleges state that need-blind admissions implies that all applicants are considered equally for financial aid awards. For example, one year Johns Hopkins offered smaller financial aid packages to students with a self-identified interest in science on the basis of data analysis demonstrating that the enrollment decisions of such students were the least sensitive to changes in financial aid.[18] A recent study by the National Association for College Admissions Counseling found that 45 percent of colleges use outside consultants to advise them on the admissions and recruiting process.[19] A college that hires admissions consultants or that utilizes detailed statistical analysis would surely be aware that financial aid demands would diminish if it admitted more Early Decision applicants.[20]

The guidance counselors we interviewed were divided over whether colleges offer systematically different aid packages to early and regular applicants, and over which group of applicants is favored in financial aid offers. Carlene Riccelli of Amherst Regional High School sees Early Decision as a "marketing tool" and notes that college financial aid officers have admitted to her that they are not as generous with early applicants as with regular applicants: "Financial aid administrators say they have to reserve money for negotiations (with regular applicants)."[21]

Nancy Beane of the Westminster School similarly observed that "scholarships, especially merit scholarships, are not as forthcoming" for early applicants as for regular applicants.[22] Colleges may subtly reduce financial aid by shifting money from grants to loans, while still fulfilling the literal requirement of meeting a student's demonstrated need; in our interviews, several guidance counselors said that they had observed this practice. The 2001 *Time/Princeton Review College Guide* quotes Bruce Hammond, a high school counselor in Albuquerque, N.M., to make this point: "Need can be met in a variety of ways. Will the loans be greater [for ED admits]?"

Still, a college's concern for its reputation may balance the incentive to trim the aid given to early applicants, particularly since financial aid offers can be more easily questioned than admissions decisions. No college wants to become known for chiseling. Whereas students only apply once, surely some experienced guidance counselors would catch on to conspicuous practices that take money

[handwritten margin note: hurts kids who want to apply ED, but need aid]

away from early admits. Princeton's reputation was clearly important to one applicant's decision to apply there in Early Decision:

> I knew that I would be bound to Princeton's financial aid package. Still, I heard that Princeton's policy was need-blind admission followed by need-based aid. I had also heard that Princeton tended to be more generous than comparable schools. (Akash, Princeton '00)

One counselor even mentioned several colleges that seem to offer unusually favorable aid packages to early admits. Some colleges make this practice explicit. For example, Franklin and Marshall offers a program called "Early Decision Advantage," which has, in some years, guaranteed early applicants the opportunity to enroll at the previous year's costs for tuition and room and board.[23] In its 1997 survey, the National Association for College Admission Counseling found that almost all colleges stated that "the admit status [Early Decision versus regular] had no bearing on the percentage of need met," though a small number of institutions (9.8 percent) "indicated they gave a more favorable ratio [of gift aid to self-help] to ED admits." Interestingly, NACAC adopted an additional guideline for Early Decision in September 2001 that discourages colleges from offering such advantages to Early Decision applicants: "An institution may not offer special incentives (such as scholarships, special financial aid, or special housing opportunities) to encourage students to apply under an Early Decision plan."[24]

Improving Selectivity Ratings

The *U.S. News* ranking of colleges has gained importance during the past fifteen years. One recent study finds that colleges lose applicants and bear heavy recruiting costs if their rankings decline.[25] Another study found that 79 percent of those attending "highest selectivity colleges" and 59 percent of those attending "high selectivity colleges" said that college rankings were at least "somewhat important" to their choice of college.[26] Thus each college has an incentive to adjust its admissions policies to improve its rating.

Each admissions office has some control over the measures that *U.S. News* uses to calculate the "student selectivity rating." Two of these measures, acceptance rate and yield, reward colleges for favoring early applicants. Colleges are ranked in selectivity on the basis of the proportion of applicants who are admitted. Colleges are ranked on yield according to the proportion of admitted students who enroll as freshmen.[27] Even though acceptance rate and yield together make up only a small part—less than 5 percent—of the overall rating for a college, our interviews suggest that administrators and admissions officers behave as though these measures are critical to a college's rating success. One of the reasons for this tendency may be the fact that yield and selectivity are two of the few variables that can be actively manipulated by the institution. According to Michael Behnke, the vice president for enrollment at the University of Chicago, "*U.S. News and World Report* has forced us to care much more about admit rates and yield. If we don't, other institutions will, and we'll be out of a job."[28]

Several college officials pointed out to us that colleges have always been aware that numerical selectivity conveys prestige. In their 1985 study, completed before the *U.S. News* rankings gained prominence, Peter Cookson and Caroline Persell already stressed the importance to a college of maximizing its yield: "Students lacking athletic ability may stand out because they are 'B for B,' meaning 'Burning for Brown.' One way a school raises its 'yield' figures is by accepting students who will definitely enroll . . . reliable evidence that a student really wants to attend a college may tip the balance in a candidate's favor."[29]

An obvious way for a college to improve its selectivity and yield is to accept more early applicants. This improves its yield because

Early Decision applicants are nearly certain to matriculate and Early Action applicants are more much more likely to do so than regular applicants. Pushed to the extreme, a college could accept its entire class from Early Decision applications, and yield would rise to a majestic 100 percent. With its yield increased, a college could reduce the total number of applicants it would need to admit to fill the incoming class. This would improve its selectivity ranking, unless the change in policy dramatically reduced applications. Worth David, the former dean of admissions at Yale, wittily underscored the connection between early applications and college rankings: "Ratings are detrimental to colleges because Presidents are interested in the rating. Now you have to pay an enormous amount of attention to promises of loyalty from seventeen-year-old kids [on the basis of their early applications]."[30]

But an early admissions program only improves a college's selectivity and yield statistics if that school favors early applicants, thereby changing the set of students who are admitted and who enroll. There are two ways that this can occur. First, by lowering the standards for early applicants, the college identifies and admits committed applicants who might have been denied admission otherwise. These admits take the place of regular admits, many of whom would not have enrolled even if accepted. Second, favoring early applicants may induce some applicants who are not fully committed to apply Early Decision. (If admitted, these new ED applicants will enroll, even though they might not have enrolled if admitted as regular applicants.)

It is widely reported that colleges can use early admissions programs to improve their selectivity and yield results. But the logical implication of that claim may not be so well appreciated. A college does not change its admissions rate or its yield if it only admits the same superior and highly committed applicants in ED that it would have admitted anyway if it did not have an early program. Therefore, if admission rates have declined and yield rates have increased because of early admissions programs, that implies that (1) colleges are favoring early applicants, or (2) applicants are being pressured into applying Early Decision when that is a premature action, or both.

In the early and mid-1990s, admissions officers at Wesleyan were quite candid with one another about the preference that would be given to Early Decision applicants, owing in part to a need to maintain the school's strong selectivity and yield statistics. While the admissions officers disliked policies that were influenced by these statistical factors rather than by the goal of admitting the most qualified class, they understood that the decisions of top students were, in turn, driven by yield, selectivity, and rankings. The admissions officers recognized to their chagrin that to attract top students in future years, they needed to defer to the importance of the rankings.

Compounding the problem were alumni and parents who were highly interested in and vocal about Wesleyan's ranking. As a result, the admissions office felt a responsibility to help fundraising efforts by doing what it could to increase Wesleyan's position in the rankings.

Although we can rely on firsthand experience at only one college, Wesleyan, we strongly suspect that admissions officers at other elite universities experienced similar pressures and spoke openly in their offices about the need to use early admissions programs as a mechanism for improving their school's ranking. Anecdotal evidence from former colleagues supports this view. Not surprisingly, however, admissions officers are reluctant to acknowledge publicly that they must sometimes bow to institutional pressures that lead them away from admitting the best-qualified applicants.

In a related ploy, more pernicious in appearance than admitting students early to increase ranking, colleges can improve their statistics by identifying very strong regular applicants who are particularly unlikely to enroll, and then either rejecting them or placing them on the waiting list. Several admissions directors confessed to such practices in interviews with the *Wall Street Journal*. There are several telltale signs that an applicant is unlikely to enroll: unusually strong qualifications relative to other applicants to that college, indicating that the applicant is likely to be admitted to a higher-ranked college; failure to visit the admissions office or to schedule an optional interview; listing another college first on standardized forms (such as a financial aid form), thereby suggesting that the student prefers another college. As the *Wall Street Journal* summarizes, "Over the years, predicting enrollment has evolved from guesswork into science . . . Many colleges rely on consulting firms to help them enhance yield by identifying prospective students on the basis of variables like zip code, religion, first-choice major, and extracurricular interests, as well as academic performance. In some of these models, if an applicant's test scores exceed the college's median, the probability of enrollment drops."[31]

In 2000–01 Franklin and Marshall, strategizing in this manner, placed 140 applicants with strong standardized test scores on the waiting list because they had not opted to interview with the college. On the basis of past history, the college expected only about 6 of those applicants to matriculate to Franklin and Marshall if all were admitted. Its assessments seem to have been proven correct, as only 16 of those applicants accepted spots on the waiting list. By eliminating its "unlikely-to-comes," Franklin and Marshall appeared more selective, admitting 51 percent instead of 53 percent of its applicants. Similarly, Connecticut College accepted only 18 percent of applicants in 2000–01 who did not interview or visit the college, though it admitted 34 percent of applicants overall.[32] The logical implication for applicants who view a particular college as a "safety school" is to make an official visit to that college even though it is not among their top choices.

In these cases, sophisticated statistical analysis has enabled colleges to adopt practices to boost their selectivity and yield. But no computer modeling is needed to indicate that early applicants, particularly Early Decision applicants, are the most likely to enroll. The same *Wall Street Journal* article observes, for instance, that Brown's decision to switch from Early Action to Early Decision was expected to improve its yield for 2001–02 by about 5 percent, from 53 percent to 58 percent.

Independent of early applications, another way for a school to increase its selectivity rating is to attract more applicants. One common complaint among high school counselors is that colleges encourage applications from students who are not likely to be admitted. As Carol Katz, the college counselor at Stuyvesant High School in New York, complained, "Admissions officers are too anxious to encourage students to apply. For a student with an 83 average, I would like them to say, 'You can apply, but your chances are limited.'"[33] Rachel Toor, the former admissions officer at Duke, also notes that there are strong pressures on admissions officers to encourage applications from both competitive and noncompetitive applicants:

> The job of admissions officers is to recruit, to boost application numbers. The more applications, the lower the admit rate, the higher the institutional ranking. Increasing application numbers is usually the No. 1 mandate of the recruiting season. Partly, that means trying to get the very best students to apply. But it also means trying to persuade those regular, old Bright Well-Rounded Kids (B.W.R.K.'s in admissionese) to apply—so that the college can reject them and bolster its selectivity rating. Reject them because there are so many of them, and because they're actually not as interesting as the "well-lopsided" kids—those who have shown real prowess and potential in a more focused manner.[34]

Competing for Applicants

Early admissions programs can serve as a valuable recruiting tool. A college that favors early applicants will attract early applicants—so long as its practices are known or suspected. Some students deciding between two similar colleges for their early applications will be drawn to the one that is perceived to tilt more in favor of early applicants. Similarly, applicants who are uncertain about a first-choice college may still be drawn to apply early, even if that requires a binding commitment through Early Decision. Applying early is a logical strategy for an applicant who believes that doing so is the most likely way to get admitted to a selective school.

Thus, a college that favors early applicants will draw applicants who would not have chosen that college at the end of the application process. The college gains overall if the new applicants it attracts are good enough to offset the loss of high-quality students who must be denied admission in the regular pool now that the college is favoring early applicants.

Steven Singer, the counselor at the Horace Mann School in New York, attributes much of the growth in early admissions to competition between colleges: "Whereas competition to [attend] elite schools used to be limited to pockets on both coasts, now it has become a 'mass phenomenon.' With these changes in competition, some schools are taking more students early as the best chance to attract talented students and improve their statistical performance."[35]

Several of the counselors we interviewed felt that college admissions officers were, in fact, using aggregate statistics about the difference in admissions rates for early and regular applicants to induce or pressure students to apply Early Decision. Larry Momo, the college counselor at Trinity School in New York, explains: "It used to be that colleges mentioned early admissions as an option. Now it is a real tool in their whole marketing package."[36] One college student described an information session at which this was obvious:

> The admission officer said that 33 percent of early applicants and 22 percent of regular applicants were admitted. He seemed to want to imply that you should apply early. (Scott, Yale '01)

Without changing the official rules, colleges make subtle refinements to early admissions policies so as to influence the decisions of applicants. Preferred deadlines are a splendid example. Harvard, for example, has a "Recommended Early Action Filing Date" of October 15, even though its deadline for Early Action is November 1. The benefits of applying by the earlier deadline are not made clear. It is possible that all early applications will be evaluated equally. Still, the mere delineation of applications into two groups could cause some applicants to conclude that it is advantageous to apply before October 15, rather than waiting until November 1 or applying as a regular applicant.

It is natural for admissions officers to use earlier deadlines to help induce students to make an early commitment. Leslie Miles, the counselor at New Canaan High School in Connecticut, explained that at information sessions in spring 2001, two Southern colleges asked students to submit Early Decision applications before the end of their junior year. That is, those students were asked to apply in June 2001 for the 2002–03 academic year, fifteen months before beginning college. Students came away from the information sessions with the impression that they would improve their chances of admission if they submitted an early application by June 2001.[37] Yet when we investigated the websites for those two colleges, we found that each lists an ordinary fall deadline for an Early Decision application, with no mention whatsoever of a June deadline in the junior year.

This discussion relies on the assumption that applicants may be influenced to apply Early Decision to a college because it is known to favor early applicants. We believe that applicants make these kinds of calculations and decisions almost routinely. For example, the 2001 *Time Guide* led off its article on early applications by telling the story of Tom Mayer, a student at Berkeley High School in California: "He decided he wanted to attend Columbia. His counselor told him he should apply early decision (ED) . . . A lot of his classmates were doing the same thing. 'Columbia has a rep for being an ED school, so no one wanted to risk it,' he says. The strategy worked—he got in." Clearly, Columbia benefited in this case from its reputation for favoring early applicants. Without his view of Columbia as "an ED school," Mayer might not have applied there early, leaving open the possibility of choosing another college.

The cases highlighted in this section beg the questions raised in Chapter 3: Why aren't these institutions more explicit in describing the differences in standards across their early and regular decision programs? These colleges do a strategic dance, trying simultaneously to attract early applicants without discouraging others from applying at the regular deadline. Each selective college also faces the challenge of convincing the most outstanding students that the school is sufficiently elite to make it their first choice, while simultaneously convincing middle-of-the-road students that the college is not out of reach and that they should still apply. Given all these conflicting goals, it is advantageous for colleges to take different positions about their standards for early applicants, depending on the audience.

The Politics of Deferral

Whether to defer or to reject early applicants has been a point of contention among colleges for two decades. Most colleges fear that whenever they reject an early applicant in December, that decision will deter other students from the same high school from applying to the college at the regular deadline: "Sometimes a student is deferred because he simply doesn't stand out that much, yet is too strong to be rejected outright without upsetting the high school or community. A valedictorian with low test scores will usually be deferred, not rejected, unless test results are extremely low."[38] For this reason, historically most colleges have rejected 5 percent or fewer of their early applicants in December. Some, such as Cornell, Georgetown, MIT, and Tufts, have automatically deferred to the regular pool all early applicants who were not admitted in December.[39]

Many counselors believe that it is best for colleges to reject early applicants immediately when the decision is obvious. Marybeth Kravetz, a guidance counselor and the president of the National Association for College Admission Counseling, explained: "Our main plea is for colleges not to let students linger and hang on a limb— kids are so vulnerable at that age. It's very hard for them—and their parents—to believe it's reality that they won't get in. Deferring them just doesn't let them concentrate on other options."[40]

In the early 1980s Yale was the only college to follow that recommended policy. It rejected 35 to 38 percent of its early applicants each year, a much larger percentage than any of its closest rivals.[41] But it was widely believed in admissions circles that Yale's policy hampered its ability to recruit students to apply.[42] Eventually, Yale started to defer a greater percentage of its early applicants: in 1995 and 1996, it rejected 17 percent of its early applicants in December.[43] Similarly, after Penn decided to reject rather than defer more of its early applicants in 1996, it found itself facing great discontent from applicants. Within a few years, Penn was already reversing its policy, as Lee Stetson, the admissions dean, explained: "We spent almost all January and February [of last year] talking to students who felt betrayed because we turned them down. So we cut down to let them stay in the pool as deferred applicants. We may back off even more next year."[44]

In general, deferred applicants are less likely than regular applicants to be admitted to the same college (see Figure 6.1). The differences in percentages are quite large in some instances. For example, Dartmouth admitted 19 percent of its regular applicants and only 5 percent of its deferred applicants, while Duke admitted 26 percent of its regular applicants and only 12 percent of its deferred applicants in 1999–2000.[45]

There is a clear connection between the percentage of students

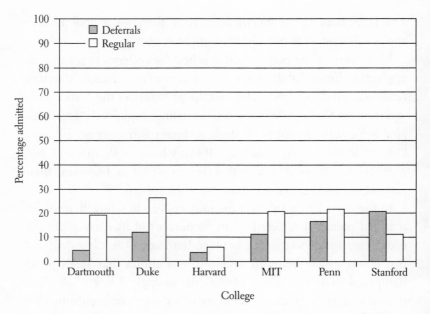

Figure 6.1 Admission rates for deferred and regular applicants. (College admissions offices, figures reported for 1999–2000)

who are rejected and the percentage of deferred applicants who are admitted in the spring. Among colleges that provided us with deferral figures, Stanford is the only one that admits a higher percentage of deferred than of regular applicants. But Stanford also rejects more than 60 percent of its early applicants in December. Lee Stetson of Penn explained this connection: "The students say they would rather have a chance than be denied early. But they have to know that the more we defer, the worse their chances."[46]

At Harvard and Stanford, only about 2 to 3 percent of early applicants are deferred and then admitted, but these two schools differ in their timing. Stanford rejects most unsuccessful early applicants immediately, whereas Harvard defers the majority and then rejects them in the spring. Only 3 percent of deferred applicants were admitted to Harvard in 1999–2000.

Incentives for Counselors

Parents once asked, "What kind of job can my child get after attending this college?" Now, their question is, "What kind of college can my child go to after attending this high school?" In one of our interviews, a New York City counselor recalled with horror a news article that compared New York's high schools in terms of the percentages of graduates admitted to particular elite colleges. Even without formal statistics for parents to use in comparing high schools, it is clear that placing students into desirable colleges is critical to a high school's reputation and to its ability to attract students. As one counselor stated bluntly, "Parents and others judge the success of the school by the admissions decisions of each year's students."

Several students felt pressure, both explicit and implicit, to apply and enroll at the most selective college possible in order to enhance the prestige of their school or counselor:

> The metric to the guidance counselor's job security was how many kids she got into Harvard . . . I was pushed extremely hard to do Early Action at Harvard. To get them to shut up, I thought that I would apply early to Harvard and regular to Princeton. If I got into Harvard, then at least they could have that statistic that I got in for their high school brochures. (George, Princeton '01)

> The counselors' reactions when I was admitted to Northwestern and Chicago was "Oh, really?" When I got into Harvard, it was champagne and cigars. (Kenneth, Harvard '00)

It is natural for an applicant and the applicant's family to conclude that a rejection would have been reversed had the applicant attended a different high school. In 1984, one parent complained in the *New York Times* that "to get into Harvard . . . you have to go to one of those prep schools."[47] One of the Needham High School students in our study echoed these sentiments:

> I think that private school students tend to be favored over public school students. I have friends from private schools who were admitted to Brown and Yale [the speaker was rejected at these schools] despite having SAT scores and extracurricular activities that were less than mine . . . In retrospect, maybe I should have gone to private school. [This last statement about going to a private school was intended as a bit of a joke; the student was laughing as he completed the sentence.] (Joey, Needham)

This view may well have some merit. In fact, David Karen's 1985 study of the Harvard admissions process found that students from certain boarding schools are favored over seemingly comparable applicants in admissions decisions.[48]

In 1985, Peter Cookson and Caroline Persell, drawing on their study of 1,035 preparatory students applying to college, wrote about the efforts that prep schools put into placing students. Given the explosion of applications since that time, such schools are probably under even more pressure today:

> Many students come to boarding school with the hope that it will enable them to get into a better college. The prep schools know that this promise poses certain problems for them, given the changes that have occurred in college admissions during the last twenty-five years. In the past most of their graduates could easily get into the college of their choice, but today it is not so easy. Prep schools have responded by honing their very professional college advisory operation and by exercising what political clout they can in relation to the colleges. The result is

a higher—though not perfect—payoff for the elite prep school graduates, compared to other applicants.[49]

Private school counselors have an advantage over public school counselors because they typically have many fewer students to advise, and because their schools devote considerable resources to help market their students to colleges.[50] Public school counselors generally advise as many as 400 students, while private school counselors advise fewer than 100.[51] Cookson and Persell explain: "Despite today's competitive admissions environment, the elite prep school advisors are still listened to more closely by college admissions officers than public school counselors, suggesting that the prep school advisor is known to consistently offer the colleges a steady supply of socially elite and academically prepared students."[52]

In addition, many private schools do not calculate class rank by GPA, at least not publicly. One widely reported statistic about the entering class at various colleges is the percentage of entering freshmen who ranked in the top 10 (or 25) percent of their graduating high school classes. Elite private high schools aim to send a significant proportion of their graduating classes to highly selective colleges. Naturally, not all of these students can be in the top 10 percent of the graduating class.[53] By eliminating official class rank, private schools reduce the cost to colleges of accepting those students who are not in the top decile of the class. The colleges happily comply.

An indication of the importance of college placement is the relatively new position of college counselor. Most high schools, especially private schools, have one counselor dedicated to helping students apply to college. Admissions officers cultivate relationships with college counselors at so-called feeder schools (the public and private secondary schools that provide large numbers of qualified applicants year-in and year-out to a particular college), recognizing that counselors strongly influence where their students apply. Many colleges and universities will hold formal meetings with counselors at feeder schools as they are reviewing applications. In these meetings, an admissions officer reveals to a counselor whether students from the counselor's school are likely to be admitted, rejected, or deferred. The counselor then has an opportunity to argue on behalf of some students.

College counselors play a dual role: they must act responsibly in the interests of each individual student, while also ensuring impressive outcomes for the graduating class as a whole. Since many counselors believe that their students are competing with one another, these goals may sometimes clash. Eileen Blattner, the counselor at Shaker Heights High School in Cleveland, explained: "My students are absolutely in competition. [College] representatives make comments that compare students in their debriefings."[54] Similarly, Rory Bled of Berkeley High in California complained that "schools do not admit that there are de facto quotas in terms of the number of students they'll admit from a given institution."[55]

Several counselors found that smaller colleges are more limited by regional constraints than their larger counterparts: if a liberal arts college admits a number of students from one high school, that means that there are fewer places for other students from the same region if the college wishes to maintain geographic diversity. Carol Katz, the counselor at Stuyvesant, believes that this phenomenon is important at larger colleges as well: the students at Stuyvesant compete not only with each other but also with other applicants from New York City for a limited number of places at Ivy League colleges.

Regardless of whether students from the same high school actually compete with each other for limited spots at selective colleges, they believe that they do. Steven Singer of the Horace Mann School views this as inevitable: "Going to school as an adolescent in the era of *U.S. News* . . . adolescents, who are by nature self-centered, don't see the world beyond their own school . . . All they see is the kid in their AP Physics class."[56]

College Counselors as Advocates and Matchmakers

Since experienced counselors get to know many of the college admissions officials with whom they deal on a yearly basis, they are able to advocate strongly for some students. First, as noted, they can pass on detailed information about the merits of some applicants—for example, explaining that one candidate is an outstanding citizen or a terrific actor—that probably did not stand out in their applications. Second, they can pass on information about college preferences and financial means. One counselor explained that it is common for certain colleges to contact him in March to ask if he can identify "full-pay" students for them to admit. Another stressed the connection between early applications and the ability to pay full tuition: "The ability to pay is now tied up with admissions chances, especially outside [the world of] top schools. At a less selective college, if you can pay and you apply Early Decision or write in February to convert your application [to ED], you can be admitted within ten days."

Few students are likely aware that they can write such a letter asking to convert an application to an Early Decision commitment in February. But those with well-connected counselors need not act so formally; their counselors can inform a college that it is a particular student's top choice. Sometimes these contacts are purely informational. For instance, Eileen Blattner of Shaker Heights High School explained that she will call a college in February or March to say that a student "was not ready to make a decision in time to apply ED, but is ready to make a decision now." As we described earlier in this chapter, such information is pertinent to colleges for enrollment planning.

The *Wall Street Journal* suggests that some colleges use these contacts as an important part of their strategy to improve yield statistics: "Admissions officers also often call a guidance counselor and simply ask whether their college is an applicant's first choice. If it isn't, the counselor may avoid answering the question—though evasion may be tantamount to confirmation."[57] Sometimes counselors act as more formal matchmakers: they ask a student to commit to attending a particular college and then turn to the college to request admission for that student. As one student summarized his situation,

> If I wanted to attend Yale, [the counselor] would get me in. (Dan, Yale '98)

Sometimes this bartering is initiated by the counselor, and sometimes it is initiated by the college, as in the following story told by a counselor: "In one instance this year, a college called and asked about a student who was admitted early to Harvard as a legacy. The other college did not want to admit him if he were certain to go to Harvard. I relayed this to the student and asked him to make a decision on March 25 rather than May 1." In these cases, the credibility of the information provided by a college counselor depends heavily on that counselor's reputation. And the reputation of the counselor depends in turn on the reliability of her guarantees that a student will attend a given college and that the student will perform well when he gets there. The guarantee that a student who applies Early Decision will matriculate is particularly important. Two counselors made this very clear in our interviews:

> Our reputation rides on what they do [after being admitted ED]. (Gail Roycroft, Marshfield High School, Mass.)

> If you don't get enough money [in aid as an Early Decision applicant], you can back out. We don't buy into that. We stand

behind our signature.[58] (Eileen Blattner, Shaker Heights High School)

The cost of a poor reputation is a disadvantage in future admissions decisions. At least two students felt that past history made it difficult for graduates from their schools to gain admission at particular Ivy League colleges:

[In her graduating class of sixty-five students], there are two students at Brown, two at Princeton, five at Yale, and none at Harvard . . . The reason why none went to Harvard is that my school has a bad history there: two students were expelled. No senior from [the name of her school] has been accepted since the second student was expelled. (Ellen, Yale '01)

My school definitely had a reputation among colleges. Penn, for instance, accepted few students from [the name of her school] because [its] students had turned down acceptances to Penn so often in the past. (Jessica, Yale '00)

At the same time, the benefit of a good reputation can be considerable. Over time, some counselors are able to build up credibility with college admissions offices.[59] Some students felt that their counselors were absolutely crucial to their outcomes:

My counselor has a good relationship with the Harvard admissions office. He handpicks people for admission and tells Harvard who to admit. (Mira, Harvard '98)

You have two meetings with the headmaster, and he is the critical one out of the college counselors because he is the one who sells you to colleges. It's a little scandalous because he does not support every student [equally]. (Ellen, Yale '00).

Limiting Applications and Slotting

Although matchmaking offers obvious advantages to students with well-placed college counselors, it may also hurt these students. If a counselor calls a college with the news that one particular student will matriculate if admitted, the college might rationally infer that other students from the same high school would not do so. The counselor also has to worry about placing a roster of students. If a student applies and is admitted to many prized colleges, each admissions offer that student turns down represents something of a missed opportunity for classmates.

Counselors and admissions officers alike decry the practice of "collecting scalps" (the same phenomenon that was once known as "ghost applications"), whereby some students apply frivolously to a wide variety of schools just to see where they can be admitted. This maximizes the competition within a particular high school and complicates the decisions of college admissions officers, not to mention the lives of college counselors: "It creates a tangle if students apply early all over the place. Some students are just eager to see where they can get in."[60]

We have heard tales of quite involved matchmaking by a counselor or the headmaster of a school. Some complicated arrangements amount to "slotting" a set of promising students into different schools. Many students from highly competitive schools recounted stories about such slotting:

> The counselors tried to slot students into schools they thought would be best for them. My counselor, for instance, tended to push Yale as my school. (Oren, Yale '98)

While that practice has obvious benefits when successful, it is also fraught with danger:

My friend was advised not to apply early to Harvard because there were a number of other people who were applying. It turned out that no one ended up applying early to Harvard. (Sunny, MIT '01)

The students who stand to lose in these games are those who are not viewed by their counselors as possibilities for top-tier colleges. One student who was eventually admitted to Harvard from a top New England prep school had to fight to apply there:

The counselor gave me a list of schools he thought I should consider. The list was B.C., B.U., Brandeis, and Simmons. I asked, "What about Brown, Harvard, or MIT?" He said this would be a major reach and said not to apply to Harvard. (Judy, Harvard '98)

One counselor, Bruce Breimer, argues that it is the responsibility of counselors to limit frivolous applications to help the system work smoothly: "Reciprocity among counselors demands that they discourage students from submitting needless applications." Early Decision caters to this interest, because students admitted early only apply to one college. In contrast, Early Action allows students who are admitted early to keep their options open and apply to other colleges. Early Action also allows a student to apply EA to a school that is not his absolute top choice in order to gain an advantage in admissions chances to at least one college. From the counselor's perspective, however, it is most desirable for a student admitted in Early Action to choose that college and not apply anywhere else. If that student applies elsewhere, it might reduce prospects for classmates, either by creating unfavorable comparisons or because colleges may not want to accept too many applicants from a single high school: "If [you apply] Early Action and you are not certain to go, you may knock out someone a little lower in the class."[61]

A regular applicant whose high school classmate was admitted in Early Action to a particular college may feel that she has lost her chance to be admitted to the same school, even if the two students were not truly in competition for a particular spot at the college. For example, students at Choate who were not admitted to Brown expressed discontent that several of their classmates who were admitted early to that school chose to go elsewhere in the end.

The counselors we interviewed took a range of approaches to Early Action. Bruce Breimer and Larry Momo have adopted a formal rule that EA applicants must commit to attending the college if admitted early.[62] In effect, Early Action is Early Decision for students at the Collegiate and Trinity Schools. Other schools have adopted the same rule or slight variants of it. For instance, Phillips Exeter Academy also converts Early Action into Early Decision for its students. In the years before Stanford had an early program, however, Exeter students with a preference for Stanford were allowed to apply Early Action to another school and then regular decision to Stanford.[63] The Buckingham Browne and Nichols School in Cambridge, Mass., allows students who were admitted in Early Action to apply to one other college at the regular deadline.

Usually counselors' efforts are more informal. Steven Singer says that he tries to convince students not to apply to other schools once they have been admitted in Early Action, but emphasized that he "does not muscle them" into withdrawing their other applications. Some counselors stated that it is important to allow students to apply to other colleges after being admitted in Early Action; they merely insist that students be serious about those additional applications.

Many counselors tell students that they must research colleges vigorously before considering an early application. Bruce Breimer asks students to make overnight visits to at least five schools while they are in session, and then to write an essay explaining the strength of their preferences if they want to apply early. Whatever a particular high school's policy, counselors make sure that the colleges understand its implications, assuming that they are favorable. At the end of one admissions cycle, Bruce Breimer wrote a letter to a number of colleges to remind them that relatively few Collegiate students apply early, indicating that a regular applicant from Collegiate generally did not apply early to another college and might very well be applying to a first-choice college as a regular applicant. Similarly, Steven Singer says that he calls Early Action colleges to explain to admissions officers that they need to continue recruiting an early admit from Horace Mann if that student is also applying to other schools.[64]

Providing Information and Guiding Decisions

A central responsibility of guidance counselors is to provide students with information helpful for their decision-making. Students are eager to know whether applying early will improve their chances of admission and, if so, at which colleges the gains from applying early will be the greatest. This puts counselors in a difficult position. If they believe that colleges favor early applicants and say so, then they may create an early admissions stampede. But if they do not report their true beliefs to students, they may lose credibility. One student whose counselors said that there was no advantage to applying early observed that it was

> the only politic thing that they can say to stop the college process from becoming the early process. (David, Harvard '01)

Larry Momo reports: "If students ask, 'Should I apply early?' I say, 'Yes.'" He asks additional questions of students who wish to apply early, and discourages those who do not seem to be settled in their choice by reminding them that the "worst thing is a premature decision." Unfortunately, he observes, "some people know how to give the right answers, but are still premature [in applying early]." Steven Singer concurs that he is "adamantly against a policy that says to 'apply to this one early because it is the smart choice.'" He admits to students that it might be a tactical error not to apply early, while emphasizing that the next four years of their lives are critical.

Alan Crocker of the Northampton School in New Hampshire noted that sometimes a college counselor is placed in the unfortunate role of playing Cassandra to a student who doesn't grasp the counselor's wisdom. In some instances, he says that he anticipates that a student will have a change of heart during the year, switching (say) from a preference for a small rural college to a preference for a school with a large urban campus. Yet nothing he can say will dissuade the student from applying Early Decision. And some counselors, in an attempt to sway a student's decision, may be less than forthcoming in pointing out the advantage of early applications.

Beyond informing students and helping to get them admitted, college counselors also have to manage expectations throughout the process, a difficult task when competition for admissions is at a historical peak, yet students have "a strong sense of entitlement about them."[65] The consensus among the counselors we interviewed is that it is important to inform students when the schools they are considering are beyond their reach, but then to let the students and their families make their own decisions about when and where to apply. Two of the Massachusetts public school counselors we interviewed indicated that one of their primary concerns about early applications is dealing with the psychology of rejection:

They [students who are deferred] think they're not getting in anywhere. (Gail Roycroft, Marshfield High School, Mass.)

Early Decision can also be the source of an early letdown, and that's one reason we tend to encourage [only] the strongest applicants [to apply early]. (Don Cranson, Oakmont High School, Mass.)

At the same time, and at the opposite extreme, some counselors are great advocates of early applications. Kathy Giles of the Groton School tells her students that there is a significant advantage to applying early and openly encourages them to do so. Almost all of them do. When a student is not certain of a first-choice school in November, Giles suggests applying Early Action or to a college with rolling admissions, possibly to a safety school. As a result, by mid-December 1997, for instance, more than half of the graduating class at Groton had received an offer of admission for the following year.

A student who is uncertain about applying early may be swayed by information about his chances of admission as a regular applicant. Kathy Giles described one such situation. A Groton student was particularly interested in Bowdoin, but she felt that his chances of admission were bleak. Instead, she directed him to Trinity (Conn.), a college closer to the student's home and with a strong program in his area of interest. She believed that Trinity would admit him as an early applicant but maybe not as a regular applicant.

Incentives for Students

Although students are the ones whose lives are most affected by college admissions, they have the least experience of those playing the game. Not surprisingly, there is a sizable and lucrative industry that helps them to win admission.[66] Some common strategies adopted by students include paying for standardized test-preparation courses, piling up Advanced Placement credits and tests, selecting activities with an eye toward improving their applications, and hiring editors to help with the crafting of application essays. According to all reports, applicants spend hours pondering the effect of each component of their applications:

You're told not to agonize over questions such as, "What is your favorite quotation?" but it is impossible not to agonize: "What will they think if I say that my favorite movie is *Star Wars?*" (Anthony, Princeton '99)

One student at Yale criticized the current admissions system for forcing applicants into "playing a game of chance," inducing "amazing meticulousness" on the part of applicants in a quest to figure out how to "play the system." Death and taxes may be inevitable, but so too is strategic behavior by those pursuing a goal that could greatly affect their lives. Witness the elaborate game-playing that evolves around courtship, whatever the norms of the era.

One cynical student argued that Early Decision is actually the last bastion of fairness in the system:

> The application process is broken because its elements do little to distinguish students. You can pay consultants to write your essays and to help you train for the SATs. Alumni interviews are not reliable—they serve more for alumni relations than anything else. Admissions office interviews would be helpful, but they are not required. As it stands, the only way to evaluate applicants is to determine if they have a singular passion [asking them to apply ED]. (Richard, Princeton '99)

Similarly, college administrators, who set the rules, are alarmed by the thought that students are following anything other than straightforward strategies, not unlike the way casinos are alarmed by the presence of card counters. In a 1999 editorial, the former Williams president Harry Payne wrote, "At a panel discussion on higher education, I was startled to hear a prominent educator indicate that, in the current era, the choice to apply early decision to college was a 'rational one' for students. I think I know what he meant—if college admissions is a game, then as a strategy, such a decision might well be rational."[67] The College Board, many college guides, and most college admissions officers contend that students should only apply early, particularly Early Decision, if they have a clear-cut first-choice college:

> Simply stated, early plans are wonderful options for students who have found a perfect fit between themselves and a particular college. (2001 *College Board Handbook*, p. 16)

> If you are absolutely positive about which school you want to attend, consider applying for an Early Decision. (2000 *Time/Princeton Review College Guide*)

Despite such advice, we found that many well-informed students see college admissions as a game to be played strategically. Thus, it is not surprising that of the college students we interviewed only two-thirds of those who applied Early Decision and less than half of those who applied Early Action applied early to a strong first-choice college (see Table 6.1).

Why had they chosen to apply early? Only a small percentage in-

Table 6.1 Preferences of early applicants[*]

Program	Applied to strong first choice	Applied to weak first choice	Had no clear favorite	Applied to a second-choice college
Early Action (181 applicants)	42%	33%	14%	12%**
Early Decision (48 applicants)	63%	35%	2%	0%

*We omit three Early Action applicants from the calculations in this table because we were unable to discern from our interview notes their ranking for the college where they applied early.

**The percentages in this table do not always add to 100 owing to rounding.

Source: Interviews with college students.

Table 6.2   Main reason for applying Early Action (183 applicants)

Applying to solid first-choice school	27%
Wanted to hear early	21%
Increase chance of admission	14%
Why not?	13%
Get a head start on applications	5%
Preferred ED college, did not want to apply ED	5%
Parents or counselor advised applying early	4%
Other	10%*

*The percentages in this table do not add up to 100 owing to rounding.
Source: Interviews with college students.

dicated that the main reason they applied early was that they had identified a first-choice college. There are many possible reasons for applying Early Action. Some applied EA to get a speedy evaluation and possibly security, since students who are admitted in Early Action need only apply to colleges they might prefer to the ones where they were admitted early. As one applicant commented, "Why would you not do this [apply Early Action]?" (See Table 6.2.)

Early Decision entails more of a commitment than Early Action, so to be worthwhile the possible gains must be greater. Thus, Early Decision applicants cited fewer reasons for applying early than did Early Action applicants—these are the few reasons that could provide sufficient motivation to warrant the commitment of Early Decision. Almost half the Early Decision applicants we interviewed applied early because they hoped to improve their chances of admission. Although many of them applied early to their favorite college, having a top choice was not the primary reason for applying early (see Table 6.3).

Applying Early as a Strategy to Get In

Nearly half the students who applied Early Decision and about one-seventh of those who applied Early Action did so to improve their chances of admission. This is a simple strategy for students with a

Table 6.3 Main reason for applying Early Decision (48 applicants)

Increase chance of admission	46%
Applying to solid first-choice school	31%
Attempt to end the process quickly	10%
Parents or counselor advised applying early	4%
Other	8%*

*The percentages in this table do not add up to 100 owing to rounding.
Source: Interviews with college students.

strong preference, but it is less attractive for students who don't know by October where they want to go. When does an advantage in the admissions process warrant the risk of committing to the wrong school? Students who are likely to need some help to be admitted have the most to gain by applying early. A number of students emphasized this point in our interviews:

> You should base your decision on the strength of your application. Some people have the power to wait, while others do not. (Robin, Princeton '00)

> Some people will get in no matter what—the ones with 1500 or more on the SAT, 4.0 GPA, and 10 AP credits. For someone like that, I would say to apply regular decision. (Jay, MIT '98)

> For Ivy colleges in particular, you should assess your chances realistically. If you are "on the bubble," then you should definitely plan to apply Early Decision. (Anthony, Princeton '00)

These comments demonstrate how much information students need if they are to play the Early Admissions Game skillfully. An applicant must be able to ascertain the chances of admission at a given college, and must also be informed about the logistical rules of the game and the likely advantages of applying early. Students who have this information generally come from competitive high schools, where counselors have enough experience and data to provide specific and relevant information:

> I was in the top 20 percent of the class (at Exeter) and had competitive test scores. Students with my record generally went to schools at the level of Brown and Columbia. (Jim, Princeton '99)

> There was a good and active counseling staff at Chicago Latin who met with students starting in April of the junior year. They gave students good advice about where they would be admitted. I was told I could apply anywhere. Everyone thought that the counselors were "insane" and overly optimistic at the start of the year. But, by and large, the assessments were on the mark. (Will, Princeton '99)

As this last quote underscores, it is difficult to be optimistic about the chances of admission to highly selective colleges even when an experienced counselor reports that the chances are very good. And for good reason, as evidenced by the story of one student, Scott, whom we interviewed at Yale.

Scott's counselors told him that he did not have to worry about applying Early Decision to Yale, probably his first-choice college, because they thought he would be admitted as a regular applicant. Six months later, he was on a train to the admissions offices at Columbia and Yale to express his continued interest after he was put on the waiting list at both colleges. Scott got a happy ending—he was still admitted to Yale from the waiting list. No doubt, some applicants can be absolutely certain of admission as a regular applicant to a particular highly selective college, but this is rare:

> My father is a trustee [of Princeton]. I knew that I would be accepted by Princeton under regular admissions due to my family connections. (Mary, Princeton, '00)

We asked the college students a series of scenario questions at the end of our interviews. The first was designed to find out if they would recommend Early Decision to an applicant who is a good candidate but not a superlative one:

1. *Your friend is considering only Early Decision schools. He says that his top choice is Stanford and his second choice is Amherst, but he thinks that he might change his mind. He is worried that applying ED to Stanford may be too committing, but he is also worried that not applying early may hurt his chances of admission. He is a strong candidate, but not one who is certain to be admitted to either school. Which of the following things would you recommend?*

    a. apply ED (binding) to Stanford (50.3 percent)
    b. apply ED (binding) to Amherst (0.3 percent)
    c. do not apply early (49.3 percent)[68]

That is, approximately half the students recommended an early application to Stanford, and approximately half recommended not applying early. There was no universal choice for early application strategies, but a (slight) majority of students were willing to be strategic by recommending Early Decision to a student who is clearly uncertain about his first-choice college.

Counselors often emphasize the importance of applying early to a college that will offer the greatest strategic advantage:

You must compare a realistic risk vs. a foolish gamble. An increase in chances from 2 percent to 3 percent is not much of an advantage.[69]

If you are willing to lower expectations one rung, you might be able to get better outcomes [by applying early].[70]

If that student blows his early application on Princeton [and he wasn't a good candidate for Princeton], then he will be sitting in the middle of the Wesleyan pool of regular applicants and he may have to go (down a level) to Connecticut College.[71]

Two of the high school students we interviewed concluded that they had mistakenly aimed too high, or too low, with their choice of early applications:

I jumped to apply Early Action to MIT, but competition was huge. I should have done ED to Tufts or Johns Hopkins, because then I would have gotten in [instead of being rejected as a regular applicant at those schools]. (Akshay, Needham student who is now attending Carnegie-Mellon)

My college counselor told me not to apply to Harvard early because he said I wouldn't get in. That was pretty discouraging. In the end, I really didn't want to go to Brown, so even when I got in [as an early applicant] it wasn't that relieving or exciting. If I had to do it over, I would shoot high and apply to Harvard or Yale early so I could be more decisive. (Chris, Choate student who is now attending Yale)

Regular applicants, in contrast, can take a diversified approach, such as applying to two "reach" schools, two "possible" schools, and two "probable," or "safety," schools. This strategy builds in a safety net at both extremes. A student who is overconfident will probably end up at one of the safety schools, and one who is underconfident will probably be admitted to the more selective colleges where she applied. But both types of students will end up with the best set of options possible given the strength of their applications. That is, applying to a range of schools with different levels of selectivity limits the need for assessing one's chances of admission *before deciding where to apply.*

But before deciding to apply early, students must juggle both their interest in various colleges with their differing chances of admission at those colleges. The choice of where to apply early can be a difficult strategic problem, one we provide help with in Chapter 7.

For applicants who are particularly unlikely to be admitted to their first-choice college, the best strategy may be to apply early to a second-choice college, where the early application will offer a greater benefit in increasing the chance of admission. But there are obvious dangers in a student's deciding to apply early to a second-choice college on the basis of his or her perceived chance of admission (or lack thereof) at the first-choice college. Several students told us that they were originally advised that they would not be admitted to the selective schools where they were eventually accepted:

> When I went over my list of possible colleges with my counselor, the counselor said that my chances were "slim to none" to be admitted to Princeton. (Meredith, Princeton '99)

Many students are overly pessimistic about their chances, and there is a very sound psychological reason for such negative feelings. You can lessen the blow of rejection by cushioning yourself to expect it in advance:

> Given the possibility of disappointment, I did not want to have my heart set on one school. (Joe, Princeton '99)

We suspect that students often convince themselves that a school that is likely to admit them is their first-choice college, when they actually prefer a more selective school. In a 1996 article about applicants to Harvard, the *New York Times Magazine* explained that all four of the profiled students became less enamored of Harvard as the notification day approached:

> Maybe it was the natural aversion to being judged, maybe teen-age insecurity, maybe an instinctive self-protection mechanism kicking in. (And then again, maybe it was the fact that they had all already been admitted to other colleges.) But for whatever reason, all four now seemed to think that acceptance to Harvard — the school that had at some point been the first choice of each — just didn't matter the way it once had . . . Further, more than half of this class was filled in December through Harvard's early-action program, which meant that 16 out of 17 of those waiting to hear from Harvard this month were going to be rejected. No wonder Parham, Mira, Anna and Maya were finding reasons to reject Harvard first.[72]

This strategy of rejecting a college before it rejects you may be psychologically sound, but it is disturbing in this age of Early Decision when students must select a single college before knowing its admission decision.

The choice of strategies becomes yet more complicated for students who are considering both Early Action and Early Decision colleges. An Early Action application offers the advantages of early notification and a possible gain in admissions chances, but without the cost of a binding commitment. In response to the question "Under what circumstances would you advise someone to apply early under Early Action [Early Decision]?" half of the college students we interviewed advocated a strategy that emphasized Early Action — apply early to your favorite EA college unless you are absolutely certain about your first choice and that school offers ED. Given the prevalence of that strategy, at least in conversation, it is not surprising that so many applicants applied to Brown, Harvard, MIT, and other Early Action schools once Princeton, Stanford, and

Yale moved to Early Decision in 1995–96. Most of the other students interviewed stated that a student should apply Early Action only to a school that was at least a weak first choice:

> Don't apply Early Action to a second choice because [then] you are screwing someone else over and abusing Early Action. (Jennifer, Yale '01)

> I would most likely tell a student to apply early under Early Action. But I would hold some reservations because it might be unfair to those who are sure they want to go to an Early Action school. (Monica, Harvard '01)

Two of our scenario questions looked at the decision to apply Early Action to Brown or Early Decision to Stanford:[73]

2. *Your friend says that his top choice is Stanford (which has Early Decision) and his second choice is Brown (which has Early Action), but he thinks that he might change his mind. He is worried that applying ED to Stanford may be too committing, but he is also worried that not applying early may hurt his chances of admission. He is a strong candidate, but not one who is certain to be admitted to either school. Which of the following things would you recommend?*

   a. apply ED (binding) to Stanford (19.9 percent)
   b. apply EA (non-binding) to Brown (68.8 percent)
   c. do not apply early (11.3 percent)

3. *How would you advise your friend in the same situation if his preferences were reversed so that Brown was his first choice and Stanford his second choice?*

a. apply ED (binding) to Stanford (1.1 percent)
b. apply EA (non-binding) to Brown (96.0 percent)
c. do not apply early (2.9 percent)

As these responses confirm, the college students were strongly oriented to Early Action. With Brown as a weak first-choice college in scenario 3, all but a few students recommended an Early Action application. With Stanford as a weak first-choice college in scenario 2, about two-thirds of the students still recommended applying Early Action to Brown, the second-choice college.

Secondary Consequences of Early Applications

Although the ultimate goal may be clear for students in the college admissions process—identifying a preferred college and gaining admission—the path to that goal may also have long-lasting consequences. For example, if you apply Early Decision to one college, you may always wonder where you would have been admitted, and what financial aid you might have been offered by other colleges, as the following story shows:

> Back in the fall of 1987, this writer was the Darva Conger of college admissions—willing to marry an elite college I'd never met if it would have me. I applied ED to the University of Pennsylvania . . . I though it was my best shot at the Ivy League. In retrospect, it might have been nice to see how much financial aid I might have been granted otherwise.[74]

Financial aid is only one of a host of other factors, both anticipated and unanticipated, that complicate the decision to apply early.

A number of students decided to apply early to shorten the admissions process. For some, early admission provides an escape from the drudgery of applications and irksome essay questions:

In my view, one college application is enough. (Yael, Princeton '00)

For others, early admission represents relief from the stress of waiting for a decision, checking the mailbox every day, dreading the possible arrival of a thin envelope containing a rejection letter from one's dream college:

Why postpone hell for four months? (Susan, Harvard '00)

It was a relief to know that I was admitted on December 14, when everyone else was sweating out their decisions in April. (Justin, Princeton '01)

These quotes underscore one reason that Harvard, Princeton, and Yale originally changed from Early Evaluation to Early Action and Early Decision in 1976–77: they wanted to relieve the stress for students who worried that they might be rejected despite an early evaluation that they were "likely" to be admitted. But some students we interviewed said that they had the opposite reaction to early admission—the usual letdown after achieving a long-anticipated goal:

When I got in [early to Princeton], I was extremely relieved. The pressure was off and I didn't have to worry as much. But . . . I felt a kind of emptiness once I had been accepted. It felt as if my fate had been sealed and once everything was done, it was almost too good . . . Getting into college wasn't all that it was cracked up to be. Moving towards that goal was better than actually achieving it. (Raj, Princeton '00)

Once admitted in December, students no longer have an incentive to continue working hard for the rest of senior year. In our interviews, exactly half of the 182 college students who were admitted early reported that early admission had a noticeable effect on the remainder of their senior year. Of the 91 students who said that early admission affected their work for the rest of senior year, 38 (41.8 percent) reported that they slacked off after being admitted early:

> After I was admitted to MIT, I started skipping school and going to the beach. (Lisa, MIT '00)

Still, a majority of the students who were accepted early said that they worked just as hard after being admitted. Some reported that they still had obvious reasons to continue performing well, often to prepare for Advanced Placement exams or to compete for a high rank at graduation:

> I was in the lead for valedictorian and I had to keep that lead. GPA counted until the last day of class. (Eduardo, Princeton '01)

Further motivation is provided by the veiled threat that a college can rescind its offer of admission to students whose grades fall off precipitously. Michele Hernandez, the former assistant director of admissions at Dartmouth, summarized her institution's policy: "Schools always reserve the right to revoke an acceptance, so once you are accepted, it is wise to continue to have a strong senior year and to avoid trouble of any kind. At Dartmouth, usually two or three students a year have their acceptances revoked for academic reasons, while the same number have theirs revoked for disciplinary reasons."[75] But for some students we interviewed, getting admitted early provided the freedom to pursue their own goals. A significant percentage, 20 of the 91 students who said that early admission affected their work senior year (22.0 percent), felt that they became more productive after they were admitted early:

After I was admitted my grades went up. I don't think that I worked harder by intent. It was just the result of the beauty of doing work for work's sake rather than to get into college. (Meredith, Princeton '99)

Getting in early relieved a lot of stress from academics. Now I could throw myself into the activities that really interested me without worrying about grades. (Jessica, Yale '01)

Some students reported that early admission to an elite college put them in a favored position among their classmates and teachers, while others said that it made them vulnerable to attack:

I found myself getting special treatment from my teachers for the rest of the year [after early admission to Princeton]. When I performed well, they would say, "This is a Tiger quality exam." When I performed badly, they would say, "They'll fix this at Princeton." (Mark, Princeton '01)

Being admitted early to Harvard made me a target. My swim coach said that I was too smart, and started announcing my name as "Harvard" at swim meets. (Jim, Princeton '01)

Applying early, especially Early Action, enables students to learn something about their outcome at one school (or more, if applying to multiple colleges in Early Action), before deciding whether to apply to other schools. Most students who apply early intend, at least implicitly, to make use of this flexibility. If admitted, they need not apply to as many schools as they would have otherwise.

Even a negative outcome for an early application, such as a deferral, can provide useful information. It may tell a student to apply to some less selective colleges. Further, it helps to identify weaknesses in the student's application. For some of the students we interviewed, the extra time provided by a deferral was useful—a time when a decision could be further influenced:

> [After being deferred from MIT] I contacted the admissions office and they told me to improve "everything" on my application to make it stronger. I worked harder and raised my grades. I also sent in two extra recommendations and a scientific paper I wrote for a Westinghouse competition. (Paul, MIT '00)

> When I was deferred, the president of the Yale Club of D.C. wrote a letter to the admissions office saying that the admissions committee must not value his opinion because his recommendation (for me) was very strong. (Kate, Yale '00)

These two applicants—both of whom received an extra push when they needed it—were eventually admitted to the schools where they applied early.

A counterweight to the informational value of an early decision from an admissions office is the psychological cost of a negative decision. An outright rejection would be a devastating blow, but many applicants find even a deferral to be quite depressing:

> I was deferred from Princeton. This was a blow. I had hoped and expected to be admitted early. You question your whole worth as a human being when things don't happen as planned. (Amanda, Princeton '99)

> My reaction to being deferred was to consider postponing college for one year and to try out for Ice Capades and Disney on Ice. (Holly, Harvard '00)

But only 6.4 percent of the college students we interviewed said that the psychological costs of deferral were so great that they might constitute a reason for some applicants not to apply early.

The Psychology of Commitment

By definition, an Early Decision application requires a commitment by the applicant to attend a given college. One would expect that students with a strong preference would apply Early Decision, and they usually do so. But the need to make a commitment may also attract students with particular personality traits.

Of the thirty-nine students who were admitted Early Decision to Princeton or Yale, fifteen (38.5 percent) said they liked the fact that they did not have to choose a college in the spring. If admitted in Early Action, they would feel compelled to explore options by applying to other schools, and then to agonize over a choice among colleges:

> I would have filled out more applications after an Early Action application, and I am glad that I wasn't able to do that. (Jill, Princeton '00)

> If Princeton had Early Action . . . I probably would have applied to Williams [as a regular applicant] and then chosen Princeton later. This would simply have postponed my decision by six months. In fact, I liked the idea of not having to make a choice among schools as my sister did. (Carrie, Princeton '01)

The idea that an option can be a burden is quite familiar to psychologists but unthinkable to economists. The latter ignore the possible emotional difficulties inherent in choosing between pleasant options, and instead emphasize that a binding commitment can only be a disadvantage because it reduces flexibility. Some of the students in our interviews took exactly this view. A number of them argued that even if an applicant has done enough research to identify a college as the best match for him or her by October of senior year, that student cannot be certain that it will still be the best match six months later:

> What if you're a different person by the end of the senior year and you don't want to go to that school? (Emily, Harvard '98)

> In high school, two years is the approximate equivalent of infinity. So even the six-month difference in the deadlines is a long time. (Will, Princeton '99)

Another student argued that it is very hard, perhaps impossible, to choose a college before you know if you have been admitted there. (Similarly, job applicants often find that some jobs become more attractive and others less so after they receive their offers.):

> When you apply, you are focused on whether you can get into a particular school. Afterwards, you can focus on whether you want to go there. Therefore, it's important to visit a college after you have been admitted in order to facilitate your final decision. (Jim, Princeton '01)

A number of students could not bring themselves to apply Early Decision even when they felt certain of a first-choice college. For these students the binding commitment of Early Decision was incompatible with their personalities:

> Early Decision makes applicants bitter because no one wants to be forced into not having a choice of where he wants to go to college. (Charles, Yale '01)

Binding yourself early is too Faustian for me. (Thuy, Harvard '00)

One applicant considered applying Early Decision, but her parents convinced her that she would come to regret it if she did:

If I applied Early Decision, I would probably change my mind 1,000 times and find myself frantic to get out of the commitment. (Courtney, Princeton '01)

Although Early Action explicitly offers options to students, many found that it was more binding than they had expected:

Even Early Action limits your choices. Once you get in, you start to picture yourself at that school. You get it in your mind; you have a mindset—"These are the things I have to do. I have to go to this school." (Megan, Harvard '00)

I was sort of socially obligated to go [after being admitted Early Action to Harvard]. I had told everyone, and how could I refuse Harvard? It would be really snobby. (Tom, Harvard '00)

Among applicants who were admitted through Early Action, 33.9 percent did not apply to any other schools. Within that group of forty-three students, thirty-six had planned to end the process immediately if admitted EA, but the other seven had not:

I felt parental pressure to apply early to Harvard. They pulled a "bait and switch" on me by emphasizing the flexibility of Early Action when I applied, but then arguing that I should not apply anywhere else after I was admitted. (Magnus, Harvard '99)

My mother said I was holding someone else's spot at the other places [after being admitted Early Action to Princeton], so I felt

compelled to pull my applications before I found out if I'd gotten into Duke or Dartmouth. (Francine, Princeton '98)

My teacher didn't want to write any more recommendations
[after the speaker was admitted Early Action to Yale]. He said,
"I know you'll go to Yale anyway." (Beth, Yale '99)

The remaining thirty-six students in this group treated Early Action
as though it were Early Decision (and some were required to do so
by their high schools). Most of these students were overjoyed to be
admitted to their favorite school early, but some still felt in retrospect
that they should have considered other colleges:

It would have been healthier and safer if I'd given more schools
a look. (Rebecca, Harvard '98)

A student from the Westridge School in Pasadena, which sent her
and four of her classmates to Yale, stated:

For students who do not know much about colleges [including
herself] Early Action is an implicit choice. (Clara, Yale '98)

Presumably, Early Action schools do not find this surprising.

Strategies for Financial Aid Applicants

As noted earlier, admitting early applicants saves money for a college because those applicants tend not to qualify for financial aid. In
addition, Early Decision applicants cannot compare the packages
from several colleges to help in negotiations.[76] Every dollar the college thus saves in financial aid is one less dollar in the pocket of a
student and her parents. So if early admissions programs help colleges to reduce their budgets, they do so at the expense of financial

aid applicants. High school counselors have long advised financial aid applicants not to apply early. As discussed in Chapter 2, of the college students in our interviews who were not worried about financial aid, 78.0 percent applied early to some college. Among the college students who reported that financial aid was important to their choice of college, only 48.0 percent applied early somewhere.

Furthermore, among the college students we interviewed who did not apply early, 15.2 percent cited concern about financial aid as at least one of the reasons they did not do so. Bruce Breimer supports this traditional view for minority applicants: "I counsel strong minority candidates who qualify for financial aid not to apply early. Private colleges will maintain a policy of inclusivity regardless of any Supreme Court decision. So long as a strong student has a hook, he will do well in regular admissions [and then be able to compare several financial aid packages from different colleges]."[77]

One "unhooked" nonminority applicant explained that applying early was never a possibility, because she was anxious about financial aid:

> I never considered applying early because I wanted to compare my financial aid offers. My family is solidly middle class, and they have been saving for a long time. (Karen, Princeton '01)

Yet Bill Matthews, the former college counselor at the St. Paul's School (N.H.), wrote that the value of waiting to compare financial packages has been eroded by the seeming advantage given to early applicants: "Unless you are one of the top applicants in the regular applicant pool, you might never receive the offer and never be able to compare. I no longer discourage financial-aid applicants from applying early."[78]

Although no one we interviewed was certain how applying early might affect the financial aid package that was offered, those who applied early tended to be optimistic:

My thinking was that by applying early, the money was still there and not all handed out. Since the money gets distributed from a pie, there might be a better package if you apply early. (Barbara, Harvard '01)

Others took the opposite view and so did not apply early:

They figure they've already convinced this guy to go if he's applying early. "Why sweeten the deal if we don't have to?" (Kenneth, Harvard '00)

Only rich kids who don't care about aid can apply early. Early Action gives you a worse [financial aid] package, and Early Decision binds you to it. (Gary, Harvard '99)

Princeton took a positive step to enable financial aid applicants to apply early by providing an "Early Estimator for Financial Aid."[79] This allows each applicant to receive an estimate of his or her financial aid offer if admitted to Princeton. Although the estimate is not a guarantee, it is unlikely that Princeton would make a financial aid offer that is substantially lower than this estimate. The estimate provides reassurance of fair treatment to Early Decision applicants, particularly since Princeton does not offer merit scholarships.[80] A problem remains, though, because Princeton's early admits still do not know what financial aid offers they would receive from other colleges.

The Rush to Apply Early

In response to our survey, one admissions officer wrote, "It bothers me when I hear a student say, 'I'm applying early, but I don't know where.'" This statement sticks in the craw of admissions officers and counselors everywhere, and was often repeated and decried in our interviews with them. The statement gets under the skin because it is so brazen in dismissing the ideal that early applications are appropriate only for those students with strong preferences. Yet, it should be expected that applicants will seize upon every morsel of advantage in the admissions process, and the advantage of an early application can be sizeable. Many students who are not certain of their top-choice college are willing to accept the tradeoff of applying early, making a somewhat premature commitment to one college in exchange for an increase in chances of admission. It may in fact be to lure these very students that colleges are most willing to favor early applicants.

Indeed, many students responded to the scenario questions described earlier in the chapter by questioning the premise that the student could not identify a clear first-choice college:

> This guy needs to make up his mind—it's hurting his chances. (Bonnie, Harvard '99)

> Figure it out. Certain schools call for certain measures to really indicate interest, and if you want to go, you should be willing to apply to whatever system they have. (Nelson, Harvard '00)

Larry Momo explained that sophisticated applicants may feel it is necessary to apply early: "When 40–60 percent of the class is admitted early, that leaves the impression of astronomical odds in Regular Decision and may force some students to make an early commitment. It would be hard for students aiming at such schools not to anticipate this."[81] The pressure to apply early is worrisome to many participants, such as the former Williams president Harry Payne: "Often the process forces students to convince themselves that they have an unequivocal first choice when that is just not so."[82] Consistent with that critique, our interviews suggest that the definition of a "favorite" college is itself an elastic concept for some students:

Princeton was my first choice, but it was only a clear first choice by convenience. I thought that it was possible that there could be a better match for me, but that it could not be very much better. (Akash, Princeton '00)

As this comment indicates, the fear of not being admitted may push some students away from finding their ideal college and toward finding an acceptable college for an Early Decision application. Ironically, a system designed to identify students with strong preferences for individual colleges may also select students who are relatively indifferent among a variety of colleges, but eager to play the game to gain admission to one of them:

Yale, Harvard, and Princeton are all so similar that Early Decision is no big deal. (Cameron, Yale '01)

In such a competitive environment, applicants who are taking the traditional route of considering and applying to many colleges may find themselves labeled impractical. One student at a well-known New York City private school felt that he stood out among classmates who were rushing to apply early:

Getting the right college is more important than getting into a big name. I had the "romantic notion" that you should try to identify the best school for you. (David, Harvard '01)

This chapter detailed the incentives for the prime players in the early admissions game—colleges, counselors, and students—and the nature of their strategies. With the incentives well understood, the behaviors identified in this book make good sense. It is readily understandable why colleges substantially favor early applicants, and why well-informed students often apply early to other than their first-choice college.

The game is a subtle one, and it keeps changing. As for playing it well, between colleges and applicants, the colleges have the advantage. They play the game repeatedly with thousands of applicants. The students play the game but once, and only for a single applicant. Moreover, the colleges set the rules. Chapter 7 is intended to right the balance a bit, by explaining how applicants can effectively approach college admissions.

7

❧

Advice to Applicants

So you land on Mars, ready to visit the casinos. You've never been here before, but in your back pocket you have an undercover agent's report on how each casino runs its operation. So you can easily decide which casino would be your best bet. Or can you? As you visit the casinos for a first look, you notice that each one pays its winners in a different coin.

This book is like the private eye's report—it provides the information that applicants and their families need to understand the decisions they face. In the next few years, our descriptions of different programs and our statistical analyses will remain fairly precise as a guide to the admissions process. As years pass, the names and features of early application programs will change, and so will the admissions statistics for different colleges. But the general insights will remain much the same, as they have for the past fifty years. For example, colleges will always be eager to identify the applicants who are most likely to enroll, so applicants who convey their interest in, or who make a commitment to, a college will gain an advantage in admissions decisions.

We summarize our insights in ten guidelines to help applicants play "the Early Admissions Game" wisely. The students who face the most difficult choices are those who have no clear favorite colleges and no Early Action colleges among their likely top choices. In the Technical Appendix to this chapter, we assess the tradeoffs that two such hypothetical students face, and we show how the two could reach different decisions after carefully considering their prospects and preferences.

1. Take the decision seriously.

Your college decision needs to be taken seriously for two reasons. First, it is of great importance. Second, the workings of college admissions are difficult to understand, involve many subtleties, and may call for strategic behavior on your part. This book has explained how the system works, highlighting the motivations behind other players' actions and the rationales behind their words. In such a complex game, an understanding of the strategies of other players can be an important guide for one's own decision.

The early application decision—"Should I apply early, and if so, where?"—looks simple, but in fact it is quite intricate. Before deciding to apply early, you may have to balance your interest in different colleges with your likely admission chances and then decide whether the commitment required by Early Decision suits your prospects, your personality, and your purse. The remaining guidelines can help you through this process.

2. Start the process early.

If you do not start learning about colleges and meeting test deadlines early, the later steps are virtually impossible. You won't have enough time to digest information, to reflect on your preferences, and to do any further research you may need.

Early application deadlines now fall in mid-October to early November of the senior year in high school. It is important to work backward from those deadlines to plan your schedule. Most selective colleges require the SAT-1 (or the ACT) and the SAT-2 tests. It is possible to take one or both of these tests in the fall of senior year, but it makes sense to start or even finish taking them in the spring of junior year. This allows you to retake a test early in senior year to try to improve your score. Most colleges and universities consider your SAT score to be the sum of your best verbal score and your best math score, even if they were received in different sessions, so taking the test more than one time tends to help your chances of admission.[1] This can only be accomplished if you begin the college admission process before the start of senior year.

You should begin researching and visiting colleges in your junior year. Colleges are not in session during the summer, and there isn't enough time for thorough visits in the fall of senior year, particularly to distant campuses. The college students we interviewed were virtually unanimous in saying that college visits were a valuable influence on their decisions, especially if they were able to stay overnight at a school while it was in session. Talking to older friends and relatives may also give you a good sense of life at different colleges, and may help you to pinpoint what to look for on your visits.

Getting an early start in these ways does not commit you to applying early, but it gives you the chance to do so intelligently should you wish.

3. Look for a good match.

Much of the buzz about college admissions, and much of this book, is about getting into a prestigious college. But getting into a prestigious college is much less important than getting into the college that is right for you, both academically and socially. Colleges differ in their environments and their approach to academics and social life, and they appeal to widely different types of students. There is no

single rank ordering of colleges that would ring true for every applicant, just as there is no single rank ordering of jobs or cities on
which every adult could agree.

Make sure to apply to the college or colleges where you would be
happiest and learn the most. When decision time comes, do not be
afraid to turn down a higher-ranked college if you would prefer going elsewhere. Similarly, do not commit early to a highly ranked college if you are not sure that you would be happy there—even if you
think you could get in by applying Early Decision.

If you start early, you will have time to resolve important concerns about the match. Consider a young woman who is contemplating an Early Decision application at either Brown or Bryn Mawr.
She greatly enjoyed her visits to both schools in the spring of junior
year, and she knows that both colleges are highly rated. One strategy would be to apply early to the college that would give her the
best chance of admission. This would be a mistake, since the colleges are extremely different. Brown is relatively large, coed, and academically progressive (for example, it offers many pass-fail courses),
whereas Bryn Mawr is a small women's college with rigorous distribution requirements. This applicant should identify and reflect on
such differences, and perhaps revisit one or both colleges. A moderate admissions advantage at one of them is unlikely to outweigh a
better match at the other, given their considerable differences. If she
is a competitive applicant at both colleges, she should apply early to
the school that best fits her preferences, or she should wait until the
regular process and apply to both schools.

*4. Be honest with yourself about your qualifications and learn as
much as possible about your chances of admission at various colleges.*

Your college aspirations should reflect your qualifications. Start by
developing an accurate assessment of yourself as a prospective applicant, not as a human being or a friend. Colleges care about charac-

ter and compassion, but C students—however noble their characters—should not expect to be admitted to Columbia or Cal Tech.
Grades, extracurricular activities, and SATs are easy to convey and
assess; dignity and human worth, alas, are not. Thus, you should
look at the readily observable qualities in yourself: Do they give you
a good chance of admission to the colleges you are considering?

How can you tell your admissions prospects? What you should *not*
do is rely on anecdotal information or single data points. What happened to Cousin Joe, or to a particular schoolmate who applied a
year ago, is but a single piece of evidence, and not a very reliable
piece at that, since you are unlikely to have accurate information
about someone else's qualifications.

Unfortunately, applicants rarely get an honest assessment from
the institutions to which they are considering applying. Admissions
officers are hesitant to discourage students from applying for both
noble reasons (they do not want to tell a person not to apply without
seeing all the information on the case) and self-interested reasons (a
desire to boost total number of applications). Consequently, a student who asks an admissions officer the straightforward question—
"What are my chances of being admitted"—is unlikely to get a candid answer.

Much more reliable sources of data about college admissions are
your high school, college guidebooks, and this book. Data on the
high school grades and SATs of admitted or entering students can
tell you whether you are broadly in the ballpark. If your school keeps
detailed records of past applicants, you may be able to get a good
picture of what constitutes a qualified student, at least for the colleges that attract many applications from your school.[2] You might
also consult your college counselor, experienced friends, and others
to get their assessments. But keep in mind that even the most experienced observers may not assess your chances accurately—we have
quoted several stories from college students whose counselors were
grossly in error.

Table 7.1 is a good place to start the assessment process (the tables in Chapter 5 are even more valuable if you are considering one of the fourteen colleges studied in detail there). It should be useful for several years. You can judge your chances of admission as a regular applicant to the most selective schools on the basis of your SAT-1 score and the average SAT-1 score for incoming freshmen at the college, as shown in Table 7.2.[3] For example, suppose that your SAT-1 score is 1350 and that you are considering applying to the University of Notre Dame. According to the list of colleges and scores in Appendix A, the median SAT-1 score for freshmen at Notre Dame is also 1350.[4] (The median is the fiftieth percentile, meaning that at Notre Dame there are an equal number of students with SAT-1 scores above 1350 and students with SAT-1 scores below 1350.) Then Table 7.1 shows that your chance of admission as a regular applicant to Notre Dame is approximately 59 percent.

Table 7.1 applies to students in the top of their class at prominent high schools (the top 10 percent of good public high schools and the top 20 percent of good private high schools) who also have a reasonably strong extracurricular record, such as the captain of a high school team or the officer in a school club. If you have even more outstanding achievements, you stand at the very top of your class in grades, or if your SAT-1 scores fall toward the top of a range of scores (for example, 1490 falls toward the top of the range 1400–1490), then your chances will be somewhat better than Table 7.1 indicates; conversely, alas, if you fall below these standards, your chances are somewhat worse. Once again, if you are a priority applicant (a targeted minority, alumni child, or recruited athlete), your chances are probably significantly greater than Table 7.1 indicates. Finally, if you live far away, you would bring the college geographic diversity, and that would also help your chances. But if you bring none of these extra benefits, your chances are somewhat worse.[7]

We emphasize one important caveat in using Table 7.1 to assess your likelihood of being admitted to a given institution: the table ap-

Table 7.1   Admission rates for unhooked regular applicants, College Admissions
            Project (1999–2000)

Applicant's SAT score	College's average SAT score				
	400–1090	1100–1190	1200–1290	1300–1390	1400–1600
400–1090	91%	69%	41%	18%	0%
1100–1190	98%	88%	67%	28%	6%
1200–1290	99%	90%	81%	44%	9%
1300–1390	100%	94%	90%	59%	16%
1400–1490	100%	97%	95%	75%	28%
1500–1600	100%	100%	99%	87%	54%

Note: These tabulations are based on the results from the College Admissions Project for
applications to the 274 colleges that received at least 5 applications from survey participants
(including the 14 colleges studied in detail in Chapter 5) and that also reported SAT scores for
entering freshmen to the College Board for the 1999–2000 database.
    Source: Survey data.

plies to white, unhooked applicants. Other studies have demonstrated that the average academic credentials for underrepresented
minorities may vary significantly. One study, for example, found that
African-American applicants receive an advantage equivalent to an
increase of 400 points on the SAT-1 at selective colleges (those
whose students have an average SAT-1 score of 1100 or better).[5] Similarly, the academic standards for legacies, recruited athletes, performing artists, and other institutional priorities tend to be lower
than those of the rest of the applicant pool.[6] Users of the table
should adjust their projected admission rates accordingly (see also
guideline 5).

    Our analysis in Chapter 5 suggests that applying early has an ef-
fect on admissions chances similar to a 100-point increase in SAT-1
score. To get a sense of your chance of admission as an early applicant, simply add 100 points to your SAT-1 score before turning to
Table 7.1. In this case, you would conclude that your chance of admission as an early applicant to Notre Dame with an SAT-1 score of
1350 is similar to your chance of admission as a regular applicant
with an SAT-1 score of 1450. That is, Table 7.1 suggests that apply-

ing early to Notre Dame increases your chances of admission from 67 percent to 81 percent.

The key insight in Table 7.1 is that applicants stand to gain most from applying early when they have moderate chances of admission in the regular process. In particular, applicants who have a chance of admission of 80 percent or more increase their chance of admission only marginally by applying early.

Table 7.2 presents a list of 200 colleges grouped by median SAT-1 score; these are the colleges that received at least 10 applications from participants in the College Admissions Project. You can use Table 7.2 to identify a group of colleges with similar selectivity. Once you determine (say) that you are a competitive applicant at Notre Dame, you should also consider yourself to be a competitive applicant at all other colleges with median SAT-1 scores in the same range—in this case, 1300–1399. (Appendix A at the end of the book provides a comprehensive list of colleges, the average SAT scores of their students, and their early admissions programs, if any.)

The groupings in Tables 7.1 and 7.2 are crude—they rely on just one measure, but a fairly unequivocal one. Some of the colleges in one particular category will be more selective than the table suggests, and others will be less so. For example, our analysis in Chapter 5 indicates that Brown is more selective than either Dartmouth or Penn, yet Dartmouth and Penn fall into the highest category of SAT scores, whereas Brown does not.

In addition, colleges with higher median SAT-1 scores within a particular range of scores will be more selective than others in the same category, while colleges with lower median SAT-1 scores within that same range of scores will be relatively less selective. For example, Claremont McKenna College has a median SAT-1 score of 1390, while Wake Forest University has a median SAT-1 score of 1300. Although Table 7.2 groups these colleges in the 1300–1399 category, Claremont McKenna is probably more selective than Wake Forest. In this case, we would estimate that the chances of admission at Claremont McKenna are slightly worse than the percent-

Table 7.2   Colleges classified by SAT-1 score for incoming freshmen

Median SAT-1 score for 1999–2000	Colleges
400 to 1099	Arizona, Arizona State, Cal. State–Long Beach, George Mason, Hartford, Hofstra, Indiana University (Bloomington), Louisiana State**, New Mexico, Rhode Island, UC-Riverside, U. Illinois at Chicago**, Utah**
1100 to 1199	Alabama, American, Auburn, Baylor, Bradley, Brigham Young**, Cal. Poly–San Luis Obispo, Catholic U., Clark, Clemson, Colorado State, Conn. College, Dayton, Delaware, DePaul, Drexel, Fairfield, Florida State, Fordham, Goucher, Hobart, Iowa, Ithaca, James Madison, Lake Forest, Loyola of Chicago, Loyola Marymount, Loyola–New Orleans, Marquette, Miami (Fla.), Michigan State, Missouri (Columbia)**, New Hampshire, North Carolina State, Northeastern, Ohio State, Oklahoma**, Oregon, Penn State, Pitt, Providence, Purdue, Rochester Inst. of Tech., Rutgers, SMU, St. Lawrence, Stonehill, SUNY–Albany, SUNY–Buffalo, SUNY–Stony Brook, Tennessee, Texas A & M, TCU, UC–Davis, UC–Irvine, UC–San Diego, UC–Santa Barbara, UC–Santa Cruz, U. Colorado, U. Connecticut, UMass-Amherst, U. San Diego, UTexas-Austin, U. Washington, Vermont, Virginia Tech
1200 to 1299	Bard, Boston U., Bucknell, College of New Jersey, Colorado College, Denison, Dickinson, Drew, Florida, Franklin and Marshall, Furman, George Washington, Georgia, Gettysburg, Hamilton, Hampshire, Holy Cross, Illinois, Illinois Wesleyan, Kenyon, Lafayette, Lehigh, Lewis and Clark, Maryland, Mary Washington, Miami (Ohio), Michigan, Minnesota, Mt. Holyoke, Muhlenberg, North Carolina, Occidental, Pepperdine, Pitzer, Puget Sound, Rhodes, Rose Hulman*, RPI, Santa Clara, Sarah Lawrence, Scripps, Skidmore, Smith, St. Olaf, SUNY-Binghamton, SUNY-Geneseo, Syracuse, Trinity (Conn.), Trinity (Tex.), Tulane, UCLA, Union, University of the South, Villanova, Wheaton (Mass.), Wisconsin, Worcester Polytechnic

Table 7.2   (continued)

Median SAT-1 score for 1999–2000	Colleges
1300 to 1399	Barnard, Bates, Boston College, Bowdoin, Brandeis, Brown, Bryn Mawr, Carleton, Carnegie Mellon, Case Western, Chicago, Claremont McKenna, Colby, Colgate, Cornell, Davidson, Emory, Georgetown, Georgia Tech, Grinnell, Haverford, Illinois Institute of Technology, Johns Hopkins, Macalester, Northwestern, Notre Dame, NYU, Oberlin, Reed, Rochester, Tufts, UC-Berkeley, USC, Vanderbilt, Vassar, Virginia, Wake Forest, Washington U. (St. Louis), Washington and Lee, Wellesley, Wesleyan, Wheaton (Ill.), Whitman, William and Mary
1400 to 1600	Amherst, Cal Tech, Columbia, Dartmouth, Duke, Harvard, Harvey Mudd, MIT, Middlebury, Penn, Pomona, Princeton, Rice, Stanford, Swarthmore, Williams, Yale

* This SAT information was taken from the 2003 *U.S. News* database (data were based on applicants submitted in 2001–02), since the college's SAT information is missing from the 1999–2000 College Board database.

** This SAT information was converted from the composite ACT scores for the college in the 2003 *U.S. News* database (using a standard conversion chart for ACT-SAT scores), since the college's SAT information is missing from both the 1999–2000 College Board database and the 2003 *U.S. News* database.

Source: College Board database for 1999–2000.

ages given in Table 7.1 and that the chances of admission at Wake Forest are slightly better than the percentages in Table 7.1.

Since Table 7.1 gives just a broad estimate of your admission chances, you may wish to use calibrations from college guides, or from your counselor, to get alternative comparisons. You might also want to adjust the percentages from Table 7.1 on the basis of a careful assessment of the strengths and weaknesses of your application.

Table 7.1, together with the material in Chapter 5, provides a ballpark estimate of your admission chances at most leading colleges. Another way to gauge your chances is by comparing your record to the other numbers published for each college in the various college guides. The two numbers that are usually published are the "interquartile range" for SAT scores and the percentage of students in the top 10 percent of their high school graduating classes. The interquartile range lists a lower score, the twenty-fifth percentile on the SAT-1 for entering students at a college, and a higher score, the seventy-fifth percentile on the SAT-1 for entering students. In other words, 25 percent of the freshmen scored below the lower of the two scores, and 25 percent of the freshmen scored above the larger of the two scores on the SAT-1.[8] Half of the freshmen scored in the range between the two scores. Table 7.1 relies on the average of the inter-quartile numbers to classify colleges by their approximate (median) SAT-1 scores. But you can still use the original numbers given by the interquartile range to assess separately whether your academic quali-fications make you a competitive applicant at a given school.

If your SAT-1 scores are below the twenty-fifth percentile for a col-lege, then unless something stands out in your application, you are not likely to be admitted. Of course, some students at each col-lege fall into the college's bottom quartile in scores and grades, but they are often admitted because of an extra hook: at top colleges these students are often alumni children, star athletes, or under-represented minorities. By contrast, if your SAT scores are above the seventy-fifth percentile for a college, then your chances for admis-sion look bright, assuming that the rest of your record is on par with the expectations of that college.

5. Understand your "hooks" and their potential affects on your likeli-hood of being admitted at each of the colleges to which you are inter-ested in applying.

Each applicant has different strengths and weaknesses, and each col-lege has different institutional priorities. The key is to find those in-stitutions that are seeking the strengths that you have to offer. For example, if you are a good but not great high school football player, a top Division III school, such as Williams, may see you as a potential star student-athlete, whereas a top Division I school, such as Northwestern, may not consider you a viable candidate for its football program. In this case, Williams might admit you and Northwestern might reject you, even though the academic standards for admission at Williams are generally thought to be more stringent than those for Northwestern. Similarly, a significant talent in the trombone will likely be of more help in your candidacy at a school with a marching band than at a school that lacks a significant music presence.

Develop a list of your skills and attributes that a college would find appealing. Do some research into your target institutions' commitment to these areas. If you find a match, contact a person such as a coach, an advisor, or a faculty member who has oversight of your area of interest. These people often have influence in the admissions process. An impressive musical audition, art portfolio, interview with a faculty member, science project abstract, or athletic record can often make a difference between rejection and acceptance at particular colleges.

Similarly, family connections can make a difference. If you have a family member who attended a given institution, or if you have a close family friend who is active at your target institution, then you should mobilize your resources and ask that person to contact the alumni office or submit a letter of support to your admission file advocating your candidacy.

After going through this process, you might find that one institution in particular appears interested in your skills and talents. If that is true, the college could be a good candidate for an early admission application. In applying there, you get to play two trump cards—one for applying early and one for having an advocate within the institution. The value of the advocacy trump card may be greater in early admission than it would be if you waited to apply in regular decision. But the value of applying early in these situations may vary across colleges and also across notable characteristics. In some but not all sports, coaches who are particularly eager to recruit scholar-athletes in the fall may place great emphasis on Early Decision. Michele Hernandez, the former assistant dean of admissions at Dartmouth, explained this connection: "probably the most impor-tant benefit of early decision has to do with athletics. Coaches have lists of those candidates they wish to have admitted and they want to get as many as possible . . . accepted early so they don't have to worry about yield later on. With some early-decision admits, they are guar-anteed a certain number of students for their teams without having to fight with other colleges over them."[9] By contrast, if you know that you are an institutional priority, you may have a large enough advan-tage in the admissions process that it is not necessary to apply early. Once again, we recommend using Table 7.1 as a starting point for assessing whether you are a competitive applicant. But if you recog-nize that a college has a particular interest in admitting you, add the appropriate number of points to your SAT-1 score when you look up your chances of admission in Table 7.1.

6. *Determine if you have a preference for a particular school where you are a competitive applicant. If you do, then make that your target school, and plan to apply early there.*

Once you have identified the colleges that fit you best, and have as-sessed your rough chances of admission at each, you are ready to consider your options and their possible consequences. For some the choice is easy. If you discover that you have a strong preference for one college, and have at least moderate prospects for admission there, say, 20 percent, make that your target school and apply to it early. Once your early application is complete, you should begin to think about where to apply if you are rejected or deferred.

Make sure that you are a competitive applicant at your target school. College admissions is all about reaching for something that may not be available, but could be with reasonable luck, appropriate effort, and clear thinking. Say, for instance, that you want to go to Vanderbilt, where the interquartile range for SAT-1 scores is 1220 to 1400 and the average high school grade-point-average (GPA) is 3.5, but your SAT-1 score is 1200 and your GPA is 3.4. One danger is that you might convince yourself that you actually prefer Virginia Tech, where the average high school GPA and test scores for freshmen are somewhat lower, simply because you fear that Vanderbilt will not take you. But you might have a reasonable chance at Vanderbilt, particularly as an Early Decision applicant. (In fact, Table 7.1 indicates that you have a 44 percent chance of admission to Vanderbilt as a regular applicant and a 90 percent chance of admission to Virginia Tech as a regular applicant, though these numbers are based on the results for applicants with very high grades.)[10]

In Chapter 4, we explained that Chrissy, a student from Needham, applied Early Action to Brown and only discovered that it was not her first choice when she was admitted as a regular applicant to Yale. She was very fortunate that she was a strong enough candidate to be admitted as a regular applicant, so she got to choose between the two colleges in the end. But this isn't the case for everyone:

> If I had applied under the regular decision process, I wouldn't have been admitted [to Yale]. (Sam, Yale '01)

In the early admissions game, you need to decide separately where you want to go to college and where you think you can get in. Difficult as it may be, you will make better decisions even if you have to admit: "I want to go to Vanderbilt, even though I realize that my prospects are only moderate." The advantages of applying early are sufficiently great that you should at least consider applying early to a first-choice college where you would be a long shot for regular admission.

There is a danger of the opposite sort, which is equally important:

you can easily convince yourself that you actually have a chance of being admitted as an early applicant to a school that is well out of reach. As counselors and students emphasized repeatedly in our interviews, and as our statistics reveal, an early application will not help you at a college where you are not close to being a competitive applicant. Once again, honesty with yourself, however painful, is the best policy. Say you visited Emory in Atlanta and thought it would be just right for you. However, your SAT-1 score is 1100 and you are in the middle of the graduating class at your high school. You check the statistics and find that at Emory the interquartile range for SAT-1 scores is 1280 to 1430 (for an average of 1355) and 90 percent of entering freshmen (in both early and regular pools) graduated in the top 10 percent of their class. It is time to turn your attention elsewhere. If you apply Early Decision to Emory, it will cost time and emotional energy, it will take away the opportunity to apply early to a college that is within reach, and you are exceedingly unlikely to be admitted. (Similarly, Table 7.1 would tell you that you would have an 18 percent chance of admission to Emory as a regular applicant in this case, but only if your grades were significantly higher than the middle of the graduating class. Thus, your chances of admission as a regular applicant to Emory are probably significantly less than 18 percent, suggesting that applying early is not going to improve your chances very much.)

7. *If you do not have a target school for an early application, then lay out your options carefully, including the possibility of applying Early Action or Early Decision. You should determine whether the advantages of applying early outweigh the disadvantages of doing so for you.*

Since early applications, whether Early Decision or Early Action, provide a significant admissions advantage, you might want to apply early even if you do not have a strongly preferred college. Your choices are to apply Early Decision to one college, Early Action to another college or colleges, or to make all applications at the regular deadline.[11] We present four strategies—one for each of four reasons you might not have a target school.

A. If one or more of your current top colleges offers Early Action, you should *probably* apply Early Action to all of them. The primary costs of an Early Action application are psychological. The act of applying early may create an artificial commitment to that college, and you may also have to deal with deferral or rejection. The advantage of an EA application is that it substantially improves your admissions chances and preserves all your options.[12] If you are admitted in Early Action, even if only to a college that proves to be your third choice or worse, that still simplifies the rest of the process for you. If the psychological costs do not loom large to you, apply early.

B. If you are relatively indifferent among two or more Early Decision colleges at the early application deadline, then the reason for your indifference is critical to your decision. If you have researched the colleges closely and find that you would be happy at either one and simply want to give yourself the best chance of attending one of them, then you should apply early. You should use Table 7.1 and the tables in Chapter 5 and Appendix A to see which school would provide the greatest benefit from an early application. Then apply early to that school.

C. If you cannot choose among colleges because you don't know that much about them, or if you expect to develop a strong preference between them by the end of the year, then you should *not* apply Early Decision. You may be committing yourself to the wrong college if you do so. Your preferences may become clear after a second campus visit, from differences in financial aid packages the colleges ultimately offer, or because you tend to develop strong preferences as a decision comes closer.

D. If you are only considering Early Decision colleges, and you think that it will be particularly difficult to gain admission to your favorite college, then consider applying Early Decision to one of the others. In particular, if your second- or third-choice college will give you a much larger admissions gain than your first-choice college, you have a strategic choice between admissions gain and preference.

We urge you to look at the formal scoring procedure that we use in the Technical Appendix to this chapter. Many of you will not wish to use such an analysis. Even without making any calculations, however, we suggest you look at your options one at a time. Howard Raiffa, a professor at Harvard and a trailblazer in decision analysis, likes to point out that even the process of thinking systematically about the structure of a decision and its possible outcomes can make the right choice seem obvious. The key is to be honest with yourself about your preferences.

Consider each option in turn—this will clarify the benefits and the costs of each one. A specific alternative may emerge as the obvious or preferred choice. Reviewing the options individually can also help you to refine your sense of your preferences. You may not be able to decide how you feel about going to Vanderbilt until you think specifically about applying Early Decision to Virginia Tech, which would rule out the possibility of applying to Vanderbilt if admitted.

As you think about these strategies, you should also consider your own personality. Just as there is no right college for everyone, there is also no single strategy for the Early Admissions Game that is best for all applicants. Some people enjoy taking risks more than others, some people prefer to be locked into a choice, and some people can't abide rejection of any kind. Take such factors into account when you decide whether or not to apply early.

If applying Early Decision will leave you feeling that you were coerced into making a premature decision, then the emotional cost will probably outweigh the admissions advantage of applying early. For example, one Princeton student we interviewed seemed to be haunted by her decision to apply Early Decision to Princeton when she had a significant interest in going to Stanford. If you think that you may have strong regrets if you don't apply to each of two schools that offer Early Decision, then you should apply to both of them, which means you will have to apply in regular admissions. There may be other reasons for you not to apply early. If you expect senior year achievements and first semester grades to strengthen your application considerably, then wait until the regular deadline to apply. Similarly, if you are under time pressure and are not satisfied with your application by the early deadline—for example, you could write much better essays with a month or so of extra contemplation and rewriting—by all means submit your application at the regular deadline.

8. The guidelines above apply to financial aid applicants as well. Our unequivocal advice is to research the financial aid policies of your top-choice colleges before making any decision on applying early. Your need to know about financial aid options, or a desire to bargain with colleges, may prevent you from having a target college. If it does, you should only consider applying early to one or more Early Action colleges.

Managing financial aid considerations alongside the desire to reap an early application advantage can be extremely complicated. It is widely reported that students receive very different offers from several colleges after being admitted as regular applicants, but these claims are based mostly on anecdote and speculation. Similarly, many informed observers believe that colleges may limit the aid awards they give to Early Decision admits. We were not able to investigate either of these possibilities in our research for this book. Colleges have not admitted that financial aid applicants may suffer by applying Early Decision. But then again, few colleges are straightforward about how they treat early applications.

If you are a financial aid applicant, you can research the financial aid programs at the colleges where you might apply early. Perhaps one college offers specific guarantees that make it more palatable for financial aid applicants to apply Early Decision than regular decision. At Princeton, for instance, a new policy guarantees that all financial aid will be given in grants rather than in loans. This rules out a practice that sends fear into the hearts of Early Decision applicants—that a college will meet a given level of need with a package that is heavy with loans—effectively a much worse package than one that meets much of the same need with grants. Similarly, New York University promises Early Decision admits "first consideration for all NYU merit scholarships."[13] (Interestingly, as we described in Chapter 2, NYU's stated practice contradicts the NACAC guideline that colleges should not favor Early Decision admits over others in financial aid decisions, because this added inducement could be seen as pressuring students to apply ED.)

The best policy is to study the websites for the colleges you are considering and then contact their financial aid offices if you have any questions about their practices. You might determine that the financial risk of applying early is very small.

9. *If you decide not to apply early, try to find other ways to demonstrate interest in a college. If you do apply early and are deferred, do the same.*

Chapter 5 shows that you gain a substantial advantage in admissions chances if you apply early. But you should not feel that you absolutely must apply early to be successful. A major reason a college gives preference to early applicants is that they have shown enthusiasm for the college and are likely or certain to attend. You can still indicate your enthusiasm by writing a letter to your preferred college once you have firmly decided that it is your first choice. It would be even better if you could also submit a companion letter from your guidance counselor to verify the strength of your interest:

I didn't apply early because I still had to take the SATs . . . I called the Yale admissions office and told them that I would have applied Early Decision if I could have. I was told to do that by a friend who was an admissions officer at Yale. (Jared, Yale '01)

In effect, a concise letter stating your interest gives your application the strong flavor of an early application.[14] We emphasize that a single letter is preferable to bombarding an admissions office with many letters, phone calls, and other contacts. There are further ways to convey your interest in a school without calling undue attention to yourself. Respond to mailings from the college promptly, visit the campus and spend a day and a night there, and learn about the college in preparation for an on-campus interview, even if you are told interviews do not count. In short, treat the college as you would a good friend or favorite relative: pay attention and be interested. (You may even wish to make an effort to demonstrate interest in a single safety school to ensure that you do not lose out if it attempts to finagle its admission decisions—as we revealed in Chapter 6, some colleges such as Franklin and Marshall put strong applicants on a wait list if they think that those applicants are likely to go to another college.)

Such advice carries over if you are deferred or put on a wait list. In her book on the Dartmouth admissions process, Michele Hernandez provided common-sense suggestions for early applicants who have been deferred: "After speaking to an admissions officer, reaffirm your interest by writing a brief letter to the college saying that you are still considering that school as your top choice . . . Then update your file by having the guidance counselor send updated grades and any new awards or accomplishments (or you can include those in your letter). What you should avoid is sending reams of new material, because the officers do not have time to read copious amounts of new information."[15] These suggestions are consistent

with our discussions with admissions officers, as well as with our inti-
mate knowledge of the admissions process at Wesleyan, and they apply equally to regular applicants.

Finally, understand that each college's primary goal in admissions
is to recruit strong students. If you are a strong applicant relative
to the average qualifications of entering students at your preferred
college, you are likely to be admitted in the regular admissions
process.

*10. Compile sufficient information and then make your application
decisions with confidence. In the end, although some students are disappointed, the vast majority end up happy with their college choices.*

Some applicants are in the fortunate position of having a clear
choice for an early application, whether Early Decision or Early Action. These include students who have a target college, one that is
both their first choice and a school at which they have reasonable
prospects. Also in this group are students without a clear first choice,
but whose top choices include an Early Action college or colleges.
Such students should apply Early Action where they can, since
there is no commitment involved. These two groups of students get
all the benefits of applying early without cost to themselves.

For everyone else, playing the early application game involves
tradeoffs. You can either apply Early Decision and make a commitment you would rather not make, or wait until regular admissions
and accept a dash of disadvantage in acceptance chances. We have
discussed at length above how to choose between these two options.

Whatever your decision, the admissions process remains fickle.
Some applicants are admitted, while seemingly similar, if not more
qualified, applicants are rejected. No matter how much time you
spend planning, there is no guarantee of success. Even if you are a
strong applicant and you apply early, you may not be admitted. We
recommend that you at least contemplate the worst possibility—you

might be rejected by your preferred college—and try to find a way to limit your bitterness and disappointment if that should happen. You should begin by recognizing that the college is judging you not as a person but rather as a student, and that it is judging you overwhelmingly from a written record, not from personal experience. Moreover, you knew from the beginning that the school's admissions process was competitive.

Before embarking on this journey, we urge you to turn back to the conclusion of Chapter 4, where we found that the overwhelming majority of high school students in our interviews were happy with the college they ultimately attended. Your college admissions process, if approached effectively, will take a lot of work. The payoff of attending a strong college that fits you well makes it all worthwhile.

Technical Appendix: Albert and Barry—Using Decision Analysis to Help Make a Tough Choice

At the end of Chapter 5, we estimated the probabilities of admission at certain schools for early and regular applicants. Consider two high school classmates: Albert and Barry, who are both interested in attending Penn and Stanford. Albert has test scores of 700 on each section of the SAT-1 and SAT-2, and Barry has test scores of 750 on each section. Table 7.3 shows their estimated chances of admission if both have solid extracurricular records at a good high school and

Table 7.3 Admission probabilities for Albert and Barry

	Albert's chances of admission regular	Albert's chances of admission early	Barry's chances of admission regular	Barry's chances of admission early
Penn	32.7%	79.0%	63.2%	94.5%
Stanford	10.9%	26.5%	38.2%	61.9%

Source: Survey data.

neither is an alumni child, a recruited athlete, nor a targeted minority. These estimates of admission chances are taken from Table 5.2.

Neither student is a shoo-in as a regular applicant to either Penn or Stanford; both may wonder whether they should apply Early Decision to one of the two colleges.

Penn and Stanford are the most selective colleges that Albert and Barry are considering. If they are not admitted to either college, then they will attend a less selective local public college, where each is certain to be admitted. That is, the third college is the "safety school" for each of them.

If Albert (or Barry) had a very strong preference for Penn or for Stanford, then it would be simple to decide to apply Early Decision to that college. Neither student, however, has such an overpowering preference. They both slightly prefer Stanford to Penn, but each is unsure whether he would rather attend an Eastern or a Western college.

What should they do? We explore this question using a fair dose of calculation, for the numbers do a particularly good job of showing how difficult some of Albert and Barry's decisions are. (We are not suggesting that all readers follow such an approach.)

Table 7.4 shows the chances of admission for Albert depending on what strategy he follows. These calculations are based on the assumption that Albert's chances at one school are not influenced by the other school. In statistical terms, the admissions outcomes at the

Table 7.4 Albert's strategies and outcomes

Strategy	Admitted only to Penn	Admitted only to Stanford	Admitted to Penn and to Stanford	Admitted to neither college
Apply ED to Penn	79.0%	2.3%	0%	18.7%
Apply ED to Stanford	24.0%	26.5%	0%	49.5%
Do not apply early	29.1%	7.3%	3.6%	60.0%

Source: Survey data.

two schools are "independent" once we know Albert's SAT-1 score.[16] This means that we can multiply the probability of a given outcome at one school by the probability of the outcome at the other school to determine the overall probability for the combination of outcomes at both schools. For instance, if Albert applies as a regular applicant to both colleges, he has a 32.7 percent chance of admission to Penn and a 10.9 percent chance of admission to Stanford. His chance of being admitted to both Penn and Stanford is simply 32.7 percent × 10.9 percent = 3.6 percent. Similarly, his chance of being admitted to Penn but not to Stanford is simply 32.7 percent × 89.1 percent = 29.1 percent. (Note that if Albert has a 10.9 percent chance of admission to Stanford, he has an 89.1 percent chance of not being admitted to Stanford.)

The calculation is a bit more involved if Albert applies Early Decision to one of the colleges. If he is admitted ED, then he never applies to the other college. So if Albert applies Early Decision to Penn, where he has a 79.0 percent chance of admission as an early applicant, he has a 79.0 percent chance of being admitted to Penn and not being admitted to Stanford because he would not then apply to Stanford.[17] In this case, Albert has no chance of being admitted to both colleges; his chance of not being admitted to Penn and then admitted to Stanford is 21.0 percent × 10.9 percent = 2.3 percent. The remaining numbers in Tables 7.4 and 7.5 are computed from similar formulas.

One possibility, naturally, is to wait and apply to both colleges as a regular applicant. This strategy has substantial costs. If Albert does not apply early, then there is a 60 percent chance that he will not be admitted to either of his preferred colleges, and only an 11 percent chance that he will be admitted to Stanford. He is right on the cusp of being admitted to Penn at the regular date. Still, chances are that he would end up at his safety school if he chose not to apply early (see Table 7.4).

Unfortunately, neither of the early application strategies is a clear choice for Albert. If he applies Early Decision to Penn, he is very likely to get admitted there, but that all but closes the door on his chances of going to Stanford, which he probably prefers. If he applies ED to Stanford, Albert gives himself the best chance of admission to his favorite school, but then he may well be rejected by both Penn and Stanford. And applying Early Decision to either college could lock him into a school that is not ultimately his favorite one.

Barry's test scores put him in a stronger position than Albert (see Table 7.5). He is likely to be admitted as an early applicant to Stanford and just about certain to be admitted as an early applicant to Penn, but he faces broadly the same tradeoffs as Albert. If he is willing to "settle" for going to Penn, he can simply apply Early Decision to Penn. An early application to Stanford would almost double his chance of admission (from 36 percent as a regular applicant to 64 percent as an early applicant), but then Barry might end up at his safety school. Finally, if Barry simply applies to Penn and Stanford at the regular date—so that he might get admitted to both and then get to choose between them—there is a larger chance of being rejected by both Penn and Stanford.

Depending on how each of the two students weighs these tradeoffs, any of the three strategies could be best. For example, if either of them is solely focused on avoiding the safety school, then he should apply early to Penn. If either only values the option of choos-

Table 7.5 Barry's strategies and outcomes

Strategy	Admitted only to Penn	Admitted only to Stanford	Admitted to Penn and to Stanford	Admitted to neither college
Apply ED to Penn	94.5%	2.1%	0%	3.4%
Apply ED to Stanford	24.1%	61.9%	0%	14.0%
Do not apply early	39.1%	14.1%	24.1%	22.7%

Source: Survey data.

ing between Penn and Stanford if at all possible, then he should apply to both as a regular applicant.

But in most cases, the tradeoff will not be so obvious. To show how much one student's best strategy might differ from another's, we had the hypothetical Albert and Barry follow a scoring procedure that weights the risks and benefits of each strategy. (The field of decision analysis has well-developed methods for making such decisions under uncertainty. We illustrate the method without discussing its underpinnings.)[18]

Albert's most preferred option is to be admitted to both colleges: he gives that a score of 10. His least preferred option is to be rejected by both of them: he gave that a score of 0. Then he would have to determine his values for the other options on a scale between 0 and 10. Suppose that he gives the other two options scores of 8 (admitted to Stanford only) and 6 (admitted to Penn only).[19]

Albert can use these scores to calculate the average result for each strategy. He multiplies the probabilities of each admissions outcome by the scores that he assigned to that outcome. For instance, applying Early Decision to Penn gives Albert a 79.0 percent chance of a score of 6 (admitted to Penn only), a 2.3 percent chance of a score of 8 (admitted to Stanford only), and an 18.7 percent chance of a score of 0 (admitted to neither). His total score across these options is then

$$.790 \times 6 + .023 \times 8 + .187 \times 0 = 4.92.$$

That is, applying Early Decision to Penn gives Albert an expected score of 4.92. Further calculations show that applying Early Decision to Stanford gives him a score of 3.56, and not applying early gives him a score of 2.69. The comparison among these three options is not close for Albert. He should apply early to Penn. But a similar calculation shows that Barry, assuming that he has the same preferences as Albert, gets scores of 5.84 for Early Decision to Penn, 6.40 for Early Decision to Stanford, and 5.88 for not applying early.

For these particular scores, Albert should apply Early Decision to Penn, but Barry should apply Early Decision to Stanford. Even though they place the same values on the four possible outcomes, their decisions could be different since their prospects for admission are different. For Albert, there is a much larger increase in his chances of admission to Penn than to Stanford as an early applicant (from 32 percent as a regular applicant to nearly 80 percent as an early applicant to Penn, a jump of almost 50 percentage points). That advantage pushes him toward applying Early Decision to Penn. For Barry, applying early to either school offers a similar increase in chances of admission, so preference for Stanford tips the calculation.

Conclusion:
The Essence of the Game
and Some Possible Reforms

College admissions is a grand two-sided courtship, with colleges seeking the best students and students aspiring to their most-preferred colleges. Together their strategies—programs for the colleges, ploys for the applicants—have produced "the Early Admissions Game," the most rapidly growing and swiftly changing element of admissions at selective colleges. The game has a number of consequences, some favorable, others disturbing. In this concluding chapter we discuss the advantages and disadvantages of the game, as well as some possible reforms.

Favorable Features of Early Admissions

Early Action and Early Decision offer important advantages to both colleges and students. A mundane but important advantage is that these programs help to spread out and limit the workload for admissions offices in two ways. First, they allow colleges to get a head start on evaluating applications, relieving the crush of applications arriving at the regular deadline. Second, they limit the number of applications submitted, since applicants who are admitted Early Decision apply to only one college, and applicants who are admitted Early Action apply to significantly fewer colleges than they otherwise would.[1]

For applicants, the critical advantage of early admissions programs—Early Decision in particular—is that they provide a way to declare a special interest in one college. This is called signaling. Fred Hargadon of Princeton has been a consistent advocate for the value of Early Decision, focusing on its signaling advantages:

It's the only way in the process you can allow students to say how important Princeton is to them—you can't ask them straight out. I don't know how many times we've come to the end of March trying to make hairline decisions, being completely uninformed if a person really wants to go to Princeton. We wind up making offers to some who don't even want us, and turn down other talented kids who do. Early Decision introduces a little more rationality into the process.[2] (December 1996)

Early Decision seems to me to be the most "rational" part of the admissions process these days. To be able to admit precisely the kinds of students we seek from among those who have decided that Princeton is where they want to be is far more "rational" than the weeks we spend in late March making hairline decisions among terrific kids without the slightest knowledge of who among them really wants the particular opportunities provided by Princeton and who among them could care less or, worse, who among them is simply collecting trophies.[3] (September 2001)

To Hargadon, a major additional benefit of Early Decision is that it unclogs the pipeline. He would like to see all his major competitors adopt his preferred system: "If everybody—including Brown and Harvard—were Early Decision, it would clear the pipeline of about 4,000 multiple applications" (October 1995).[4] Lee Stetson, the admissions dean at the University of Pennsylvania, reinforces Hargadon's remarks: "Early Decision has served us well. It allows students who really want to be at Penn to apply early and finish the process early, and has brought more students to Penn for whom Penn is the first choice. Our data tells us that students who are admitted earlier tend to be happier here because they made an early commitment."[5] Hargadon and Stetson, distinguished figures in the admissions world, along with many others, see no reason to change the early admissions system. They see strong merits in the current scheme.

Disturbing Features of Early Admissions

There are equally distinguished attackers of early admissions; we quote some of them below. They cite a number of disturbing elements of the system: (1) Early admissions programs put students under extreme pressure to choose a favorite college early in the fall of their senior year. (2) The combination of two admissions cycles at virtually every selective college, with standards and practices that vary significantly from college to college, introduces a considerable degree of randomness and confusion into a process that is critical for tens of thousands of students. (3) Colleges are pulled strongly in opposite directions. They gain competitive advantage by favoring early applicants in admissions decisions, yet they are supposed to be bastions of fairness, considering all students equally for admission. As a consequence, colleges often dissemble about early admissions practices, sometimes stretching the truth, and other times making purposefully incomprehensible statements. (4) The Early Admissions Game may magnify the advantages of the wealthy and the well connected. Since few colleges provide accurate information about the advantages of applying early, only students with sophisticated counselors, family, or friends can understand the game they are playing. In addition, Early Decision programs require financial aid applicants to make one of the most significant investments of their lives without knowing what the alternatives cost, since Early Decision admits only learn their aid award at the college where they are admitted. The aid applicant is in the same position as the homebuyer who is required to commit to a specific house without being able to negotiate with other owners. (5) From the standpoint of colleges, students, or both, there may be other systems with other rules that would be superior to the current Early Admissions Game.

A 2001 article by James Fallows in the *Atlantic Magazine* quoted two admissions directors of highly ranked colleges who contend that everyone would be better off without early applications:

> In an ideal world we would do away with all early programs. We'd go back to the days when everyone could look at all their options over the senior year. Students, parents, and high schools would be very grateful. Philosophically and in every other way it would be so much better if we all could make the change.[6] (William Fitzsimmons, Harvard University)

> The whole Early Decision thing is so preposterous, transparent, and demeaning to the profession that it is bound to go bust. I can't think of one secondary school counselor who sees the benefit of the program.[7] (Tom Parker, Amherst College)

The Game among Colleges

Before discussing the possible effectiveness of reforms, we must consider the underlying nature of the Early Admissions Game. A cosmetic change that fails to alter the nature of the game will not succeed. Even worse are piously proposed reforms that colleges really would not welcome. We start by looking at the game between colleges, since they are the actors who make the rules.

If it would indeed be better to "do away with all early programs," and if the "whole Early Decision thing is so preposterous, transparent, and demeaning," why does Harvard maintain Early Action and Amherst stick with Early Decision? The answer has to do with what economists call "externalities." Externalities occur whenever one person's actions affect the well-being of another. Industrial waste, for example, conveys an externality. Suppose that Company A's waste products hurt company B, and vice versa. Acting on its own, Company A will not change its polluting practices because they hurt B but not A itself. Company B will continue polluting as well. So without some collective arrangement, both firms get too much pollution. Similarly, at least according to critics of early admissions, when each college acts on its own, we get too much reliance on early programs in college admissions.

The decisions of colleges to use early application programs may represent a case of the Prisoners' Dilemma. The Prisoners' Dilemma can explain many failures of cooperation in everyday life, both large and small—from the failure to end a bloody civil war to a massive accumulation of dirty dishes in a sink shared by several roommates. In each case, there is an outcome that would be better for everyone, such as resolving the war without further bloodshed, or establishing a rotation to wash the dishes on a regular basis. The Prisoners' Dilemma explains our fifth disturbing element of early admissions, that current practices may produce inferior results for colleges as a group and also for students as a group: William Fitzsimmons, Tom Parker, and many other college administrators would welcome some of the reforms discussed in this Conclusion, but only if they were established at all colleges, or at least at all with whom they regularly compete.

The Prisoners' Dilemma was first introduced as a story: the police arrest two criminals, Arthur (A) and Benjamin (B), after finding them lurking suspiciously in an alley near some recently burgled houses. The police place them in separate rooms at headquarters to pressure them individually to confess. Each culprit is promised lenient treatment if he confesses. If neither confesses, then they can only be convicted of possession of burglar tools, leading to a minor sentence of one year in prison. If only one confesses, he is granted immunity to testify against the other, who can expect a full sentence of five years in prison. If both confess, they will each get a moderate sentence of three years in prison.

This is a "game" because the outcome depends on the actions of both suspects. Each must decide whether to sit tight or confess. In Figure C.1, Arthur's strategy determines the row; Benjamin's strategy determines the column. The entries in the four boxes tell the sentences that Arthur and Benjamin receive.

What should Arthur do? He should consider how he would fare given each possible action by Benjamin. If Benjamin sits tight, then Arthur gets a sentence of 1 year by sitting tight, but full immunity (0 years) by confessing. And if Benjamin confesses, then Arthur gets the maximum sentence (5 years) if he sits tight, but only 3 years if he

	Benjamin	
	Sit tight	Confess
Arthur Sit tight	1 year, 1 year	5 years, 0 years
Confess	0 years, 5 years	3 years, 3 years

Figure C.1 The Prisoners' Dilemma for Arthur and Benjamin. Outcomes: Arthur, Benjamin.

too confesses. Thus, whatever Benjamin does, Arthur gets a lighter sentence by confessing. Similarly, whatever Arthur does, Benjamin gets a lighter sentence by confessing. If both players follow their own self-interest, both will confess. They will end up in the lower right box, getting 3 years each. But if both sit tight, they will each get a sentence of only 1 year. (The code of "honor among thieves" is designed precisely for this kind of situation.)

The use of early admissions appears to be a Prisoners' Dilemma, at least to those, like Fitzsimmons and Parker, who want to see the system abolished. With early admissions, the colleges can choose either to "offer" an early program or "not offer" it. Suppose that two colleges are close and equally matched rivals. College 1 offers Early Decision and favors early applicants, but college 2 chooses not to offer an early program. Then college 1 will attract many early applicants who are uncertain between the two schools, yet eager to apply early to improve their chances of admission (or to end the admissions process early). Although college 1 would then be admitting some early applicants in favor of yet stronger regular applicants, it might still gain overall because of the increased strength of its applicant pool. Under these circumstances, college 2 might prefer to offer Early Decision and favor early applicants as well so that it would not lose so many attractive candidates to college 1's early program. Figure C.2 shows the Prisoners' Dilemma that can arise from the choice of whether to offer Early Decision. The numerical payoffs might represent the average quality of students enrolled. Once again, each college does best by offering Early Decision, regardless of the action chosen by its rival. But if both offer Early Decision, each does worse than if neither offered ED.

The reason this example is a Prisoners' Dilemma is that if both colleges offer Early Decision, neither can lure any wonderful students away from its rival. Yet by favoring early applicants, they both must sacrifice quality by employing a lower standard for early admits so as to attract applicants.[8] Fred Hargadon and Lee Stetson see the

College 2

	Don't offer ED	Offer ED
Don't offer ED	90, 90	50, 100
Offer ED	100, 50	70, 70

College 1

Figure C.2 The Early Admissions Game between colleges. Outcomes (average quality of enrollees): College 1, College 2.

game differently. They believe that early admission programs are collectively good for colleges. In effect, they see a payoff of 95 for each college when both offer Early Decision. These deans may consider benefits other than overall quality of matriculants, such as reducing the total number of applications that must be read or reducing the number of admitted students who choose to attend another institution, in assigning their value of 95.

In the world of admissions, of course, there are many colleges in the game, and clusters of colleges compete against one another. The game is further complicated by the option of offering Early Action. But whatever the choices of other colleges, each will do best for itself by offering an early program. It is not surprising that competitive pressures led Stanford to depart from its longstanding "don't offer" policy in 1995–96. Brown considered many options in 2000–01, when it decided that its Early Action program was becoming untenable. But it never considered dropping its early program completely, because that would put it at a considerable disadvantage in recruiting applicants. Brown chose to move to Early Decision.

Game theory predicts that every selective college will offer an early admissions program if the situation is indeed a Prisoners' Dilemma. If no one is offering a program, any college can gain by introducing Early Decision (or Early Action), and when it does, that will only increase the benefit other colleges will reap by adopting early admissions programs too. With many players, the situation is not unlike people standing up in a baseball game at a critical moment. The view doesn't improve, but the legs get tired.

The Game among Students

The Prisoners' Dilemma can also occur among students in a game in which each student chooses to "apply early" or to "wait." Since most selective colleges offer Early Decision and favor early applicants in admissions decisions, some students may choose to apply ED as a defensive strategy, even though they would prefer not to make such an early commitment.

Some students know their preferences very early and have a clear-cut college choice. They might be "Passionate for Pomona" or "Crazy for Carleton." We refer to such individuals as "Partisans." Partisans always benefit by applying early, no matter what other students do. Applying early enables Partisans to improve their chances of admission by announcing their first-choice colleges.

The Prisoners' Dilemma arises among "Nonpartisans." After colleges admit (or deny) the Partisans, only a certain number of places remain at each college for Nonpartisans. The Nonpartisans understand that applying early will provide an admissions advantage, but they do not have a clear first-choice college. As our interviews with college students reveal, many of the Nonpartisans will choose to apply Early Decision to improve their chance of admission to at least one highly selective college. As more of these Nonpartisans get admitted early, they reduce the number of spots left for the regular process, thus increasing the pressure for other Nonpartisans to apply early.

In this way Early Decision places unnecessary stress upon Nonpartisans who do not really know where they want to go, and it may create bad outcomes by inducing premature commitments. If Non-partisans lose overall when they all apply early, then Early Decision presents them with a Prisoners' Dilemma. Any one of them gains at the expense of the others by applying early, but they would all prefer to wait on their applications.[9]

The Future of the Game

Each year, the interaction of college and student strategies transforms the environment for future years. The major effect is that the process moves earlier and earlier. Larry Momo of the Trinity School explains: "Early programs force the process earlier—to January of the Junior Year—as students say, 'I might want to apply early and there aren't a lot of test dates in the fall.' Conversations about colleges, planning, and testing begin earlier. It's too early for tenth-graders to be taking the writing test."[10]

Our interviews with high school students tell much the same story and show how far the process has moved, particularly for the admissions-savvy students at Choate. In the summer before their senior year, 75 percent of the Choate students (twenty-one of the twenty-eight) were already preparing to apply early. These students had visited colleges and taken most of the required standardized tests. Given the current prevalence of early applications, every moment of the calendar year from January of junior year to December of senior year can be crucial as a part of the college process.[11]

This acceleration affects colleges as well. William Fitzsimmons and Marlyn McGrath Lewis, who lead Harvard's admissions office, told us that they have shifted their schedule to make more recruiting trips to meet with juniors in the spring rather than with seniors in the fall. By meeting with the juniors, they hope to forestall their rivals who are attempting to induce those same students to apply Early Decision to them rather than apply to Harvard, early or regular. Interestingly, the Harvard website now states plainly that the process has moved forward in time: "Since more of our top candidates now apply early, Harvard has, in effect, been admitting its students on a slightly different timetable in recent years."[12]

Alvin Roth, a scholar of game theory, has documented the phenomenon of "time creep" in competitive selection processes ranging from Rush Week for college fraternities, to invitations to colleges to play in football bowl games, to the job markets for graduates of professional schools. In fact, Rush Week gets its name because each fraternity wants to rush to complete its selection of pledges before any of its rivals can begin to woo them. Over time, with each fraternity trying to sneak ahead of the others, pledge week moved from the senior year of college to the very first week of freshman year. Similarly, hospitals, judges, and businesses now recruit students well in advance of graduation from professional schools, sometimes considerably more than a year before they have finished.[13]

In all these markets, one recruiter (an admissions office, fraternity, football bowl game, or corporation) is competing with others to sign up high-quality applicants. Each recruiter wishes to make offers ahead of the others, for the first mover will attract candidates who are eager to accept an offer. But once one recruiter moves early, the others will have to follow suit, and many may well try to jump still further ahead. With such a process, the timing of each market moves inexorably forward. Meanwhile, the candidates put pressure on one another to move earlier as well. If everyone else is accepting offers on Monday, one can hardly wait until Wednesday to make a decision, since the most attractive positions will have already been filled before that.

Although the details of the strategies vary in these different markets, the central result is that the timing of selection inches forward. The college admissions market is likely to continue its forward movement in two ways: volume and timing. The volume effect would arise if more students applied early, leading colleges to fill larger portions of their entering classes with early applicants. Another possibility is that colleges without early programs could add them, though almost all of the selective private colleges already have them. The timing effect would arise if due dates and notification dates of early applications advanced. In the two decades since the Ivy League colleges adopted formal early programs and the first *U.S. News* rankings were published, much of the admissions process has moved up from May 1, the deadline for regular applicants to choose colleges, to mid-December of the senior year in high school, when Early Decision applicants are notified of admission. Without some collective action by colleges, the average time of application will continue to advance. The junior year of high school may no longer be an application-free zone.

We do not believe that early applications provide an immediate threat to American college admissions as a whole. The creep forward in timing tends to be slow; the tip toward early applications has been gradual rather than precipitous. But the pressures to move the recruiting process earlier have proved inexorable in other realms, much like the gradual loss of fitness and gain of weight for adults in the decades after college graduation. In time, the threat becomes real.

Can the System Be Changed?

Can the movement toward early applications be checked? In this section we discuss reforms that would limit early applications or change the system dramatically. Most of these reforms would require considerable collective action by colleges. We also consider whether any of these reforms could actually be implemented and what effects they might have in practice.

Limiting or Eliminating Early Applications

Several commonly proposed reforms take a direct approach by placing formal limits on the number of early applications, or by introducing an entirely new system of applications. We discuss four such reforms, and then consider whether they could be enacted and whether they could be successful.

Restrict the Number of Early Admits. It is frequently suggested that colleges limit early applications in some way, perhaps by capping the number of early admits that they allow themselves. This would prevent further erosion of the regular application process, as colleges would be limited in how much they can favor early applicants lest they exceed their self-imposed limits. But there is little reason for any one college to cap its own program if its rivals are not doing so. When Yale's admissions committee changed its program from Early Action to Early Decision in fall 2002, it also considered limiting the number of students admitted under the new Early Action program, but chose not to do so. Richard Levin, Yale's president, elaborated the reasons for maintaining the (approximate) size of Yale's current program: "Our sense was that the quality of the applicant pool—early—was very strong and if we deferred a great many students, we might discourage them or somehow make them feel less positive about Yale."[14]

Prohibit Early Action and Early Decision or Call for a Moratorium. Selective colleges could simply reach an agreement to prohibit early admissions. For example, James Fallows recently suggested a five-year moratorium on Early Action and Early Decision.[15] Such a moratorium would allow a reasonable period of time for study, so that colleges could compare their results with and without early applications to see which system produces better outcomes. Prohibition proposals have been heard before. At a meeting of the College Board in 1998, Joseph Allen, then the director of admissions at the University of Southern California, suggested that member colleges should give up their early programs permanently.[16]

Eliminate Early Decision. One major concern about early admissions pertains only to Early Decision, not to Early Action. Because Early Decision is binding, it prevents applicants from gathering more information during their senior year, and possibly changing their minds. It also prevents financial aid applicants from seeing, much less bargaining over, aid packages at other colleges. Officials at both Stanford and Yale cited these related concerns in explaining their decisions to change from Early Decision to Early Action in 2003–04. Yale's admissions dean, Richard Shaw, explained: "I think that the [early] applicant pool will probably be more diverse because students from all levels of socioeconomic status will apply . . . We think it also doesn't force them into making a decision, locking them in when they're not prepared to do that."[17]

The simplest way to address these concerns would be to abolish Early Decision programs but allow Early Action to continue. In this model, if students were only allowed to apply Early Action to one college, they could still signal a top choice by applying early, and they would still be allowed to apply to other schools if admitted early. This would allow applicants and their families to make an informed choice based on the quality of colleges to which they were accepted, their match with the student's interests, and the net prices, after accounting for different aid offers, of each college. (In the alternate model of Early Action, as specified by the rules of the National Association for College Admissions Counseling, students would be allowed to submit Early Action applications to more than one college. If all colleges offered such a system, this would give even more flexibility to students, but it would limit their ability to signal a preference for a particular college by simply applying early.)

In addition to these obvious advantages, a universal system of Early Action would likely lead to a further proliferation in early applications, particularly if students were allowed to apply early to more than one college. Some observers, like Fred Hargadon and Richard Shaw, the admissions deans of Princeton and Yale, see this proliferation as a disadvantage:

> Absent any quid pro quo for seeking an early decision from colleges, I have no doubt that more and more students will be ap-

plying Early Action. I don't happen to think that's a good idea, [but] I recognize that some colleges would simply welcome the resulting increase in their applications, regardless of how serious or well-thought-through such applications may be. (Fred Hargadon)

[When all colleges offered Early Action, trophy-hunting students would] collect a lot of admissions from places that were not their first choice, and would take up the space that might have gone to other students.[18] (Richard Shaw)

One danger, emphasized by Hargadon, is the possibility that students might feel even more pressure to apply early if all colleges offer Early Action than if all offer Early Decision. For this reason, Shaw explained that Yale is choosing to limit students to applying early to only one college in order to check the growth in early applications: "We're hopeful that it doesn't go out of control. Even under early decision we've seen our numbers rising. We think it may not be as significant an increase as if students could apply all over the place."[19]

Use a Centralized Matching System. Early admissions, indeed college admissions more generally, could be supplanted by a centralized matching system like that used for American medical school graduates seeking internships. In the early 1950s, after years of chaotic competition, hospitals agreed to introduce a voluntary medical match that remains in force today. The American system has worked successfully for more than fifty years. Although enrollment in the match system is voluntary, the vast majority of students and hospitals participate. Today, students submit their preferences for hospital positions, and hospitals submit rank-order lists of the students they want to fill those positions. The National Medical Review Board collects this information and matches the students to hospital positions with a well-known computer algorithm. The centralized match system is widely credited for pushing the timing of medical internship agreements back from the first year of medical school to the fourth year.[20]

Could a similar system work for colleges? The answer from England seems to be yes. In England, college admissions for 338 colleges, including Cambridge and Oxford, is conducted through a centralized agency, the University and College Admissions Services (UCAS).[21] But there would be two major and likely insurmountable barriers to the introduction of centralized matching for college admissions in the United States. First, it would be difficult to get all colleges to agree to such a significant change in the system, and centralized matching would not work smoothly unless the vast majority of colleges participated. Second, it would be hard to incorporate financial aid into the system. Since financial aid is determined on an individual basis by colleges and other entities, and not by the government, as it is in England, both students and colleges would have to state preferences contingent on financial aid.[22] Thus, one student might state that she prefers Macalester to Grinnell so long as Macalester gives her at least $4,000 more (in grants or loans) per year, while colleges would have to make similar comparisons between students, contingent on financial aid levels. The added complexity of this system would probably make it unworkable.[23]

Could Major Reform Be Enacted?

Implementation of any reforms that change the system itself would require concerted and monumental effort, an effort hardly observed to date. Dan Murphy, the counselor at the Urban School in San Francisco, spoke at the 2000 National Association for College Admissions Counselors meeting about his frustration at the lack of change in the system:

> Years ago at NACAC, I took heart when I heard deans lamenting the "madness." Perhaps, I thought, someone will take the

lead and pull the plug. But as I see this spinning off in ever more variations, I think of how the citizens of small Eastern European countries felt when Germany and Russia spoke grandly about peace: time to head for the bomb shelters. Something dangerous is coming our way. Now when I hear a college dean stand up and criticize Early Decision, I worry that the enrollment managers are back on campus designing Early Decision III.[24]

This is a cynical view, to be sure, but the colleges have provided no evidence to contravene such cynicism. The effort required for a major reform to limit the emphasis on early admissions is probably beyond the reach of most colleges, and beyond the interest of a number of them. It is no surprise that despite many years of discussion, colleges have done virtually nothing to rein in or eliminate their early admissions programs. The Prisoners' Dilemma structure vastly complicates the problem. Any college that made a serious effort to cut back its use of Early Decision (or Early Action) would simply lose applicants to rivals who maintained or expanded their programs.

Some collective action or agreement would be required to bring about any major change. Most discussions, both in our interviews and in the article by Fallows, suggest that the Ivy League colleges would have to take the initiative for any systematic reform to succeed:

> It will take an act of God or a change of policy by Harvard to change the system, and I don't know which one is more powerful.[25]

I realize that your project is much broader than Harvard, but I do think that whatever they do often determines what other institutions do. If they take over 50 percent of their students early, others seem to take steps to position themselves in a better light. If they ultimately go to the wait list (obviously that's long after EA and ED are over), others feel the trickle-down effect and do the same . . . Harvard is in the driver's seat. It's why Yale and Princeton went to ED.[26]

The places that would have to change are Harvard, Princeton, Columbia, Penn. Those are the four. If they were to drastically reduce the percentage they take early, this would all change in a heartbeat.[27]

Even if Harvard and a few of its influential compatriots tried to rouse support to prohibit early programs in general (both Early Action and Early Decision) or to limit the number of students admitted early at each school, they would quickly encounter a brick wall. As we described earlier in this chapter, not everyone agrees that the system is working badly. Colleges that perceive the current system to be beneficial to them would not join a reform effort of their own free will. If not all colleges joined in a reform effort, then, as suggested by the Prisoners' Dilemma, the colleges that kept their early programs would simply gain at the expense of their public-spirited rivals.

William Fitzsimmons of Harvard sums up the difficulties of abandoning early admissions: "If we gave it up, other institutions inside and outside the Ivy League would carve up our class and our faculty would carve us up."[28] Yale's admissions director, Margit Dahl, concurs: "You couldn't possibly have a national mandate to put a cap on [early] admissions."[29]

Although it seems impossible to eliminate or limit early applications, it may be possible to limit the emphasis on Early Decision in favor of Early Action. As of fall 2002, the efforts of Richard Levin, the president of Yale, have helped to induce four colleges to switch from Early Decision to Early Action and led others to question the value of their Early Decision programs as well.

At the top of the pecking order of colleges, there is relatively little difference between Early Action and Early Decision; these colleges are sufficiently popular that they can count on the majority of early applicants to matriculate even if they do not make a formal commitment to do so (with Early Decision). Among the 61 institutions with at least 250 freshmen and an average SAT score in the entering class of at least 1300, only 4 have a yield rate of at least 60 percent: Harvard, Princeton, Stanford, and Yale.[30] Thus, it is no surprise that Stanford and Yale were the two colleges that switched from Early Decision to Early Action for 2003–04. (It is also no surprise that these colleges insisted on enacting an Early Action rule that prohibits their early applicants from also applying early to Harvard.) Similarly, it can be argued that many of the prominent colleges that already offer Early Action, such as Cal. Tech, Georgetown, MIT, Notre Dame, and the University of Chicago, have a very strong appeal for students with particular interests. These colleges likely have the least to lose by offering Early Action rather than Early Decision, as their Early Action applicants are very likely to matriculate.

By contrast, colleges with less unique appeal have more to lose by adopting Early Action, and they will be more likely to retain Early Decision. Consider a college that believes that Early Decision enables it to identify keenly enthusiastic applicants, and that this enthusiasm makes it worthwhile to reduce the admissions standard for those early applicants. Under Early Action, these same enthusiastic applicants would still apply early, but many other applicants with similar credentials and less interest in the college would also apply early. This would leave the college with two relatively unpalatable choices: (1) reduce the advantage given to early applicants in admissions decisions and give up on the possibility of using early applications to enroll so many enthusiastic students; or (2) maintain the advantage given to early applicants, understanding that this will lead to enrolling some additional early applicants who are not committed to the college, would not have been admitted as regular applicants, and are only enrolling because they were not admitted to their more preferred colleges.

Early Decision also fulfills different purposes for different types of colleges. As described in Chapter 1, liberal arts colleges such as Amherst, Wesleyan, and Williams place particular value on Early Decision because it helps them to maintain class size. Today, at least partly for this reason, the vast majority of the most selective liberal arts colleges offer Early Decision.[31]

It is certainly possible that the movement toward Early Action will gain momentum beyond 2002, but it is also likely that many colleges with a particular interest in Early Decision will retain these programs. In fact, Yale's unilateral decision to switch from Early Action to Early Decision reflects something of a defeat for Richard Levin's initiative. Levin encountered two significant obstacles to his goal of establishing collective action by colleges to change their early programs. First, his preliminary discussions with the Justice Department indicated that he would have to request a formal review to receive antitrust clearance before he could form a coalition of colleges to act in concert.[32] Second, he concluded that it would be difficult to achieve consensus among selective colleges to enact Early Action. As Levin commented, "First of all, it would be unlikely to get everyone in the Ivy League to agree, and second, the process of getting antitrust clearance would have taken a couple of months and effort. So we decided back in the spring that we would have to do this on our own."[33]

But what would happen if, by some magic, a curb on early admissions were enacted? Suppose that America's elite colleges overcame antitrust problems and reached a consensus to enact a formal agreement to give up their early programs, or to impose a moratorium on them. Would such an agreement alleviate the problems created by the Early Admissions Game? Unfortunately, no.

Lessons from Other Arenas

Given sufficient incentives, organizations can be very clever in devising methods that meet the letter of the law but violate its spirit. That is, it is relatively easy to produce formal restrictions on early admissions, but nearly impossible to rule out informal agreements that produce equivalent results. Three selection processes that failed suggest that formal rules alone may not be sufficient to limit early agreements.

Legal Clerkships. In 1999–2000 the top American law schools agreed not to send out transcripts or recommendations until after February 1 of the second year in law school for their students who were applying for legal clerkships with judges for the year after graduation. But so many professors and law schools provided informal information and recommendations that many of the prestigious positions were filled before February 1, the nominal date at which interviewing might start.[34] The system had swiftly unraveled.

College Football Bowl Games. For many years American college football bowl games were governed by an invitation date that fell near the end of the season, usually in mid-November. No bowl game could issue an official invitation to a college before that date, which came to be known as Pick-Em Day. The National College Athletic Association (NCAA) had introduced the rule to guarantee that the teams with the best records would play in the most important bowl games. But the bowls went around the rules by making under-the-table deals with colleges. These violations were so rampant that newspapers routinely published lists of teams playing in particular bowls several weeks before Pick-Em Day. In one extreme case, Penn State agreed to play in the Blockbuster Bowl before the season started.[35] Eventually, the NCAA gave up on the idea of Pick-Em Day, adopting instead a qualifying system that matches teams to bowls on the basis of their records for the entire season.[36]

British Medical Positions. British regional hospitals require medical students to apply for postgraduate hospital positions through a centralized government organization that does not assign positions until the last year of medical school. Each region uses a separate centralized matching rule to match graduating students to hospitals in that region. On the surface, those arrangements seemed to prevent the possibility of early agreements. But some regions, such as

Newcastle, unwittingly adopted flawed rules for assigning positions; it was common for a student to get matched to her third-choice hospital even though her second-choice hospital ranked her higher than some who got positions there. Once students and hospitals came to distrust the match system, they found ways to get around it. Most hospitals in Newcastle (and in other regions with inferior matching rules) would reach informal agreements with students before the centralized match. The student and hospital would then submit information to the government to guarantee that the student would be assigned the position. Usually, the student would apply only for the position that she had already agreed to take, and the hospital would state that she was the only student qualified for the spot. The government was forced to abandon the system in Newcastle after it discovered that 80 percent of the positions had been agreed upon in advance.[37]

What lessons do these examples hold for college admissions? First, the trend toward earlier agreements is a general problem that arises despite the best intentions of those who designed the system. As Richard Brodhead, the dean of Yale's undergraduate college, commented, "We adopted early decision for the sake of the rare student who knows exactly where he or she wants to go by mid-fall of the senior year of high school. We never meant the early cycle to become the normal cycle."[38] But it can be extremely difficult to reduce the trend and restore the original timing of the system. Second, an agreement prohibiting early admissions—both Early Action and Early Decision—though helpful, would not address the roots of the problem. The incentives for colleges to identify applicants who are most likely to enroll, and to secure commitments from them as early as possible, would still remain. Similarly, many students would be willing to commit to a selective college that is not their certain first choice in order to enhance their chances of admission. When both parties have an interest in reaching an agreement, they can often work around formal rules to enact that agreement. For example, a student could still apply in November and a college could still notify that student of an admission decision in December, before the January deadline for most applications, in effect replicating Early Action.

Although a prohibition on early admissions would limit the ability of students to make a formal commitment to a college, a student could still write a letter to a college with her application to say that she would commit to attending that school if admitted. Or the college could initiate the transaction by contacting the student to say that it will admit her, but only if she agrees to withdraw applications to all other colleges.[39] (This type of offer, known as an "Exploding Offer"—an offer that must be accepted by a particular date—is common in some job-recruitment areas.)[40] Williams used a form of this practice in the 1960s when it sent an early notification of its admission decisions and gave admitted students a deadline that required them to respond to the offer before they learned if they were accepted to other colleges.

Unintended Consequences of a Prohibition

Even if an effective prohibition could be put in place, there might be unfortunate consequences. We discuss two. First, the prohibition could enhance the role of high school counselors as matchmakers, and thereby exacerbate the discrepancy in outcomes between haves and have-nots. Suppose that an admissions officer calls a student's counselor and says, "We want to admit your student Lisa, but we will only admit her if we know that she will enroll. Please notify us once she has withdrawn her other applications." The counselor might understand that this practice violates the spirit of the prohibition, but he might also realize that he needs to go along to help Lisa gain admission to that college.

Our interviews revealed that very experienced counselors are quite adept at pushing for their students within the confines of the existing system. For example, relatively few of Bruce Breimer's students at Collegiate School in New York apply early. Instead, he helps them by communicating their preferences to admissions offices during the course of the year. As a result, he thinks that the outcomes of his students are just as good, if not better (because they have more time to identify a favorite college), than if all of them applied early. He explains: "Someone is being hurt [by early applications], but it is not my students."[41]

Students with a counselor like Bruce Breimer will always be able to get the best possible results, regardless of the system that is in place. But without early applications, students without such capable advisers may not even know that it is appropriate or important to tell a college that it is their first choice.

Second, in the absence of early applications, colleges might start asking students for expensive demonstrations of interest, just as King Lear asked his daughters to proclaim their love for him as a condition for receiving their inheritances. In the absence of Early Decision, colleges could develop elaborate quid pro quo arrangements to improve their yield statistics: anyone who makes a special effort to arrange an on-campus interview and attend other events for prospective students will get special consideration in the admissions decision. The more expensive the action, the more convincing would be the student's indication of interest in the college, and the greater the boost in prospects.

Admissions offices already employ complicated models to gauge a student's interest in the college. They also scrutinize SAT score reports and financial aid forms to try to identify the other colleges to which a student is applying. But some schools have gone further still. For instance, Carnegie Mellon requires a $400 deposit for students on the waiting list to join a "priority waiting list." A student on that list who turns down a subsequent offer of admission forfeits the deposit.

Emory University has mastered the commitment game:

Emory University in Atlanta is credited by other schools with popularizing the yield game. A longtime safety school for would-be Ivy Leaguers, it has boosted its yield to 33% from 23% a decade ago by favoring strong applicants who, all other things being equal, make the most contacts with the school—interviews, campus visits, and the like. Daniel Walls, Emory's dean of admissions, describes contacts as a "tip factor" that makes the difference between a student's being accepted or wait-listed.[42]

Although this strategy improves Emory's yield, and thus its college ranking, it can take a toll on applicants and their bank accounts. Leslie Miles, the counselor at New Canaan High School (Conn.), tells a story of one of her students who applied to Emory as a regular applicant in 2000–01. After the student had visited the campus once, Emory sent him an invitation to visit a second time. While Emory never stated it explicitly, the student (and Leslie Miles) got the sense that its admission decision might well be contingent on whether the student accepted the invitation and made a second trip to Georgia. After some thought, the student decided that the plane fare was too expensive to warrant the flight. He was rejected.[43]

These practices are disturbing, because they favor applicants with the most financial resources and the greatest willingness to "play the game." Such practices might well expand if early applications are eliminated. If the application fee for a college implicitly jumps to include the price of one or more plane tickets (and several days of travel during the academic year), some students will not be able to afford to participate.

Could Other Reforms Improve the System?

Another set of reforms take a different approach, working to improve the existing system of Early Action and Early Decision by changing incentives for colleges or providing better information or additional options to applicants. These reforms would still require some collective action to enact, but they would not require the vast majority of selective colleges to agree on them in advance in order to be successful.

Improving Incentives or Information

Change the Rating System. Ratings are so important to a college's competitiveness that the *U.S. News College Guide* significantly affects how colleges behave. The current system allows colleges to improve their rankings by admitting more early applicants, a practice that a number of recent articles have decried.[44] In the current system used by *U.S. News*, "lowest acceptance rate" and "yield" are two of the measures used to compute a college's "student selectivity" rating, which in turn counts 15 percent toward the overall rating of a college. The acceptance rate counts only 15 percent and yield only 10 percent toward the student selectivity rating, so that these two measures together count for less than 5 percent of a college's overall rating (they count for 25 percent in a category that counts for 15 percent, and 25 percent × 15 percent = 3.75 percent).[45]

Still, admissions rate and yield have become watchwords to colleges because they are among the easiest rating categories for schools to manipulate. Colleges go to extreme lengths to identify and admit students who are most likely to enroll, and to encourage noncompetitive students to apply even though they have little chance of being admitted. These practices are natural responses to the pernicious incentives created by the current rating system.

Since acceptance rate and yield count relatively little toward the student selectivity rating, we recommend eliminating them altogether.[46] This would be very easy to adopt, and it would make it very clear to colleges that there is no longer any reward for trying to pump up their yield numbers. Colleges would still have an incentive to play other games to try to improve their rankings, but at least they would no longer have as much reason to overemphasize their early programs.[47] Michael Behnke, the vice president for enrollment at the University of Chicago, summarized the argument for eliminating these measures entirely from the ratings: "This is popularity contest data, which is too easily manipulated. It's not quality data."[48]

A second approach would be to change the methods used to calculate a college's admission rate and yield so that they do not reward colleges so much for admitting early applicants. Ideally, the adjusted rating system would reflect the popularity of each college and the difficulty of being admitted, but would steer clear of current incentives for colleges to admit early applicants. Richard Levin, the president of Yale University, suggested the simple adjustment of using only the results of regular applicants to compare colleges:

> *U.S. News and World Report* could do us all a big favor by changing the way they compute the yield on admissions. It is true that schools can manipulate their yields and make it higher by taking more students early; it's almost definitional. If *U.S. News* measured only the competitive yield, that is the yield in the second round, the yield that occurs with April offers of admission, that would be a much more direct measure of the nonmanipulable part of the schools' competitive performance. That would eliminate part of the reason that schools take so many students early.[49]

There is still a loophole in Levin's suggested method, because a college can still improve its regular admissions numbers by admitting more early applicants. The more early applicants a college admits, the fewer regular applicants it must admit to fill the class. That is, admitting early applicants reduces the admission rate for regular applicants and might also increase the yield for regular admits if the college focuses on admitting those regular applicants who are most likely to attend. But it may be most important just to adjust the rating formula to reduce the perception that colleges stand to gain by admitting early applicants. Thus, any well-publicized revision that limits the reward for admitting early applicants would be welcome.

A third approach is to attack directly the misperception that ratings are strongly influenced by selectivity and yield. This would leave the rating system unchanged but would emphasize that colleges do not gain much in the ratings by altering their admissions practices to improve their statistics. If colleges conclude that they have little to gain from slight improvements in their yield numbers, they would presumably feel less pressure to admit early applicants.

As noted above, a college's acceptance rate counts for only 2.25 percent (15 percent × 15 percent) and yield for only 1.5 percent (15 percent × 10 percent) of the overall rating. Franklin and Marshall sought to improve its yield by placing attractive regular applicants on the waiting list if they seemed unlikely to enroll. This practice also reduced the school's acceptance rate. How much could this improve its overall rating? The actual reduction of 2 percent in acceptance rate would move Franklin and Marshall from a tie for twenty-ninth to a tie for twenty-seventh in "lowest acceptance rate" among the Top 50 Liberal Arts Colleges in *U.S. News.*[50] This small improvement in a category that accounts for only 2.25 percent overall is unlikely to have much effect, if any, on Franklin and Marshall's total ranking. Ann McGrath, the special projects editor for education for *U.S. News and World Report,* highlighted this point in a recent radio commentary: "I . . . think that it's important for schools and college presidents who might be making these kinds of policy decisions to have a real sense of how the yield and acceptance rate actually play into our formula. I think that there's maybe a misconception that changing these numbers has a bigger and more dramatic impact than it actually does . . . To suggest that just changing these numbers is going to have a big effect is really wrong."[51] Of course, larger changes in a college's yield and acceptance statistics could have a more significant effect. Connecticut College reportedly reduced its acceptance rate from 50 percent to 33 percent, and a change of this magnitude undoubtedly improved its rating.

Eliminating or adjusting the student selectivity measure would improve the accuracy of the *U.S. News* rating system without requiring *U.S. News* to collect additional data. *U.S. News* reviews its system every year, so it seems realistic to hope that the magazine might adopt such a change. As Peter Cary, who preceded Ann McGrath as special projects editor for education at *U.S. News*, wrote in an open letter responding to a *Washington Monthly* article that criticized the rating methodology,

> Ever since 1983, when *U.S. News & World Report* first published its college rankings, the magazine has striven to improve its methodology . . . We continually seek guidance from educators and education experts on how to improve our rankings, and most of the additions and changes we've made over the years have come at the suggestion of outsiders . . . we maintain an advisory council of admissions deans who meet with us for two days every year. We have added an advisory group of high school guidance counselors, with whom we meet annually, and we hold regular meetings with institutional researchers during the year. In addition, we meet with representatives from 50 to 100 colleges who visit us each year [and we] listen to their suggestions.[52]

Create an Independent Verification Agency. One of the greatest problems in college admissions, and especially early admissions, is that there is little reliable information about the process. College admissions offices are generally the sole source for statistics and details about their criteria for admissions and financial aid decisions, and they are notoriously closed-mouthed. They also have considerable discretion in how they compute or report statistics. Naturally, whenever they can, colleges will report statistics in a way that makes them look more selective. We cite two disparate examples: 1. When most colleges calculate their admission rates, they include any partially completed application in the count of applications. 2. When colleges report interquartile ranges for SAT scores, they compute the

SAT score of each student on the basis of his or her maximum score on each section of the SAT-1.[53]

In the college world, there is no equivalent to the accounting system of the corporate world, in which outside professional firms conduct yearly audits according to uniform standards overseen by a national board.[54] Instead, the admissions process is surrounded by an atmosphere of ignorance, misinformation, and distrust. Many applicants do not believe the statements that colleges make about their admissions rules, and this book shows that they should not believe many of the claims that colleges make about their early applications programs.

The best way to build credibility about the process, and to allow students to make informed decisions about where to apply and whether to apply early, is to create an independent agency that verifies statistical information and other statements by colleges. Such an agency could issue a yearly report detailing the number of early and regular applications at each college, tallied according to some uniform standard, along with information about deferred applicants and the academic qualifications of both applicants and admitted students. The agency could also evaluate broader statements, such as, "All of our decisions are need-blind," or, "We give early applicants a benefit equivalent to 50 points on the SAT in our admissions decisions." The affiliation or profit status of the agency would matter little, so long as it is clearly separate from the colleges that it evaluates. Even if the agency only provided uniform standards and reporting requirements, without direct verification, that too would be valuable. Today many colleges are happy to make misleading statements about their admission practices. Murkiness facilitates distortion. If, however, the reporting standards were clearly defined, we expect that virtually all colleges would tell the truth.

Newly available and accurate information about early applications would not keep colleges from favoring early applicants. It might conceivably increase the number of students applying early, because all applicants would be able to learn about the likely advantages of early applications. But accurate information would enable all students to make better decisions. For example, accurate information about financial aid offers to applicants admitted early, if available, could ease fears at some colleges but confirm them at others. Where offers are trimmed, many financial aid applicants might decide not to apply Early Decision, but at least they would be informed about what they stand to gain and lose by applying ED. Knowing that information would be reported honestly might also change the practices of colleges. For example, a college that was currently favoring regular applicants in aid decisions might find the threat of exposure sufficiently embarrassing that it might changes its practices and offer uniform financial aid packages to early and regular admits.

Adding Additional Options to Existing Early Programs

A final set of reforms would maintain the early programs but provide further options to level the playing field among applicants, or to reduce the pressure on applicants to apply early. We address two such options in detail.

Increase the Number of Early Decision Rounds. The current Early Decision system allows students to signal their preference for a single institution. Since they have only one chance to signal enthusiasm, students will at times bypass their true top choices and make a commitment to their second-, third-, or even fourth-choice school to maximize the likelihood of getting into a highly ranked institution. The outcome can be disadvantageous for both colleges and students. Colleges are accepting early applicants on the (possibly mistaken) premise that they have a passion for the institution, while students are going to second- and third-choice institutions when they might have been admitted to their first choices.

A reform that would address some of these concerns would be to enrich students' signaling capabilities, that is, their ability to indicate their preferences, while maintaining the essential structure of the current system. As we described in Chapter 2, some colleges already offer more than one Early Decision deadline. At these colleges, the Early Decision 1 deadline is typically in October and November, and the Early Decision 2 deadline is typically at the same time as the regular application deadline.

Early Decision 2 allows students who could not select a first-choice school or complete a strong application by the Early Decision 1 deadline to still indicate a preference for a college. It also opens the possibility of signaling interest to more than one school. Consider a student whose first choice is Macalester, second choice is Wesleyan, and third choice is Emory, all highly ranked colleges that could easily be concerned that the student ranks its competitors higher. With Early Decision 2 in effect at Wesleyan, the student can play two trump cards. She can signal her preference for Macalester by applying Early Decision there. If the student learns in December that she has been deferred or rejected, she can then apply Early Decision 2 to Wesleyan by the January 15 deadline. This hypothetical student could make a clear set of choices that optimized her chances of being admitted to one of her top two choices. She would be willing to apply to Macalester first because she would still get an advantage at Wesleyan in Early Decision 2 if she were not admitted early to Macalester.

Only forty-eight colleges offer Early Decision 2. One possible reform would be for all Early Decision colleges to offer Early Decision 2, so that all students would have the option of applying Early Decision 2 to a second-choice college if not admitted in the first early round. It would even be possible to expand early programs to more than two rounds, thus enhancing the possibility for students to signal interest to more than two colleges. For example, it would be possible to have a system with four rounds of Early Decision and consistent deadlines and notification dates across colleges.

Table C.1 Possible deadlines for a multiround Early Decision system

Round	Application deadline	Notification date
1	July 1	September 1
2	September 15	November 1
3	November 15	January 1
4	January 15	February 15
Regular Decision	March 1	April 1

Table C.1 lists the deadlines for one possible system with multiple rounds of Early Decision. Here, the application deadline for round 1 of Early Decision would be July 1 and applicants would be notified by September 1. This would enable students to submit final junior year transcripts with their Early Decision 1 applications. Given the expected volume of round 1 submissions, the period for reading applications would be longer than for other rounds. There would then be a fifteen-day period between round 1 notification and the round 2 application deadline. This gap would give people who were deferred or denied admission in round 1 the opportunity to submit a new early application to their second-choice school. Since the programs are binding, we would expect schools to give significant advantages to applicants in round 2.[55] This same cycle would continue through three or four rounds of Early Decision. For students who were not admitted to one of their first four choices, or who just couldn't decide on colleges or get their applications completed in time, there would be one final Regular Decision round to fill institutions' classes.

We believe that such a system would bring three significant advantages. First, offering students more opportunities to signal interest to colleges may reduce the pressure toward strategic behavior. With a single round of Early Decision, as we discussed in Chapter 7, a student who prefers Vanderbilt to Tulane might decide that it is prudent to apply ED to Tulane, where his chances of admission are better. With multiple rounds of Early Decision, that same student could apply Early Decision 1 to Vanderbilt, while maintaining the option of applying Early Decision 2 to Tulane if deferred or rejected by Vanderbilt. The general point is that it is less of a risk to apply Early Decision 1 to a most preferred college when there are more rounds of Early Decision beyond that. Second, a multiround system would save applicants time and money by significantly reducing the average number of applications that students submit. Third, the system would spread out the reading load for the institutions across the whole calendar year.

But this is not a perfect solution. Indeed, it would continue to pose problems for applicants who did not have a favorite college at which they had reasonable prospects. Such students would include those who might gather valuable information during their senior year that could push them to one college or another, those who were likely to strengthen their applications in senior year, and those who felt a need to compare financial aid packages. In fact, the multiple rounds of Early Decision could exacerbate the advantages of wealthy students over financial aid candidates, who might not be able to apply Early Decision at all.

Furthermore, although the multiple rounds of Early Decision would reduce strategic behavior, they would not eliminate it. Colleges could interpret Early Decision 2 applications as indicating a second choice, Early Decision 3 applications as indicating a third choice, and so on; they might then decide to favor Early Decision 1 applicants over later Early Decision applicants. Thus, there could still be reason for some applicants to apply strategically to a second-choice instead of a first-choice college in round one. In addition, a student who is deferred by one college in Early Decision 1 would have to give up the possibility of admission to that college in order to apply Early Decision 2 to another school—still not an easy decision even though the chances of admission after deferral tend to be poor.

Given that few colleges have adopted Early Decision 2 to date, it is unlikely that many schools would agree that it is valuable to offer more than one round of early applications. We also suspect that high school counselors like Dan Murphy, quoted earlier in this chapter, would tend to oppose a system that appears more complicated than the current one. The complexities—with multiple deadlines, the possibility of applying to multiple colleges early, and the need for a sequential approach—could overwhelm some students. Michael Behnke notes: "When I was Dean of Admissions at Tufts, I was one of the first people to do Early Decision 2. It seemed like a great idea at the time, but it seems to have confused the waters a great deal, and maybe it's time to go back to a single date."[56]

Implement an Independent "Gold Star" System for Signaling Preferences. A major advantage of early admissions is that it allows applicants to indicate their enthusiasm for a particular college by applying early. Colleges learn who is eager (and who is committed, if the college offers Early Decision) to attend, while students get a boost in admissions chances at their supposedly favorite college. A simple reform, the Gold Star system, would allow Regular Decision applicants to indicate preferences among colleges when they apply. To implement this reform, Regular Decision applicants would submit information naming a single preferred college. In effect, each student would be given a single gold star to be placed on one college application.

In practice, the system would probably work through an independent clearinghouse that would share the information with colleges. Each college would receive the same information about the preferences of each applicant. Students would be able to submit more extensive information, such as a rank ordering of their top colleges.

The primary advantage of this approach is that it lets regular applicants signal their preferences cheaply and convincingly without having to make a formal commitment. Colleges could then identify the regular applicants who are most likely to enroll, and favor them in admissions decisions if they so choose. For a small number of privileged students, such a system is already at work through other mechanisms, such as back-channel communications from counselors.

One problem with the current system is that colleges only learn about the preferences of students who work with a small number of well-established counselors. It is possible for any regular applicant to contact college admissions offices by letter or phone to pledge interest in a given institution, but few do so. Nor can the institutions be confident that a particular student is not making a similar pledge to five other universities. Consequently, such pledges hold little value for most students.

With an independent clearinghouse, all students could submit believable preferences to colleges. The key is to have applicants list their preferences only once, with the information checked by a third party. Such information would have value, since applicants would be eager to send a signal to their top choice, and institutions would be eager to use that information in their admissions decisions. In the age of the Internet, the costs of operation would not be great. The clearinghouse could be funded by an independent third party such as NACAC, the College Board, or a private foundation, by a consortium of universities, or even by a private firm that would cover its costs through fees paid by students or colleges.

Many colleges and universities have invested hundreds of thousands of dollars in enrollment-management models designed to distill applicant preferences from the limited information produced during the application process. These models estimate the chances that each applicant will enroll at a given college on the basis of the applicant's zip code, SAT scores, class rank, number of visits to campus, response rates to mailings, and attendance at school visits or college fairs. Clearly these colleges should prefer more reliable information on applicants' preferences.

An independent clearinghouse for preference information would also benefit students significantly. Since all students could count on the ability to identify a preferred college without applying early, there would be less pressure to apply early. Colleges would presumably favor regular applicants who indicated interest through the clearinghouse. Even if those regular applicants were not favored as much as early applicants, the clearinghouse would still reduce the pressure to apply early. Furthermore, the clearinghouse would allow financial aid applicants to identify a preferred college yet still compare financial packages.

The clearinghouse concept could be implemented in many variations. One possibility is a "Gold-Star-Only" model, with each student identifying a single preferred college through the clearinghouse. This simple rule combines features of Early Action and Early Decision. As in Early Decision, the student singles out one college and declares a preference for that college. As in Early Action, the student can apply to other colleges with no commitment attached to the Gold-Star application. At the same time, the Gold-Star system has two obvious advantages over the current early application system. First, it relieves the pressure of applying early by allowing each student to apply at the regular deadline and still indicate a preference for a particular college. Second, it reduces the degree to which students are beholden to the idiosyncratic nature of the early programs of different colleges, offering a unified system that does not require consensus or collective action on the part of the colleges.

We stop short of endorsing a particular structure for the clearinghouse. The details would have to be negotiated by a governing body and then approved by colleges and guidance counselors. The details would be important; there are always possibilities for students to try to gain by reporting their preferences strategically rather than honestly, and those possibilities would depend on the clearinghouse's specific procedures. But the essential nature and advantages of the clearinghouse would be the same, regardless of the details of implementation.

The Path to Reform

We have considered seven reforms to address the main disadvantages of the current early application system. All have significant potential benefits, but many have drawbacks as well. Only a few seem both feasible and clearly advantageous. Ideally, *U.S. News* would improve its rating system and colleges would agree to limit or eliminate early applications. But the history of early applications indicates that colleges will always take pains to identify interested students—through the application process or information provided by counselors—and then favor those applicants in admissions decisions.

Table C.2 summarizes the likely results for the reforms that we have discussed in this concluding chapter. The reforms that seem most feasible and promising are those that promote opportunities for colleges and students to provide accurate information to each other, with colleges providing information about their early application practices and students providing information about their preferences. This information, if verified by an objective outside organization or clearinghouse, would help both sides make better decisions. Information about students' preferences would reduce the advantage of applying early. If colleges are forced to provide accurate information about their decisions, they might be shamed into reducing the advantages given to early applicants as well. In either case, students would no longer feel coerced into applying early, at least not as much as they are under the current system.

For those who are eager to impose a moratorium on early applications, assuming that the colleges want to agree and the Justice Department does not prevent them from doing so, we urge that the moratorium be combined with a preference clearinghouse. As described, if early applications were banned, colleges would have reason to re-create them informally by asking students to make commitments through their counselors. In effect, the counselors would act as brokers, matching students to colleges. The preference clearing-

Table C.2   The likely results of possible reforms to the system

Reform	Could it be implemented?	Likely effect
Change *U.S. News* rating system	Yes	Less incentive to favor early applicants
Better information on timing and statistics by college	Yes	Better decisions, still lots of early applications
Size limits	Superficially, at best	Minimal
Moratorium	Only by some colleges	Free riding
Central match	No	Chaos
More rounds of ED	Only by some colleges	Confusion
Gold star	Yes	Reduces early applications; less incentive to favor early applicants
Eliminate ED, retain EA	Probably only by some colleges	Less pressure to commit early, more early applications

house would reduce the importance of counselors, and it would also level the playing field by giving the same opportunities to students whose counselors are not well known to college admissions offices.

The most promising path to reform, we believe, lies with providing better information to applicants. In praising openness, Supreme Court Justice Louis Brandeis famously remarked: "Sunlight is the best disinfectant."[57] We hope that this book has helped explain the mystery of early applications and, until a more open and equitable system is established, provided valuable advice for playing the Early Admissions Game.

Early Admissions 2004

Several significant changes in the early admissions system have occurred since the first edition of this book was published in March 2003. At that time, Stanford and Yale had already announced their plans to switch from Early Decision to Early Action. Both colleges emphasized that their Early Action programs would require students to agree not to apply early to any other college, thereby introducing a new term, "Single-Choice Early Action," to the world of early admissions. In April 2003, Harvard stated that it would also change the provisions of its Early Action program to match the rules at Stanford and Yale.

As a result of these jolts to the system, early applications to Stanford and Yale skyrocketed in 2003–04 and early applications to their competitors Harvard and Princeton fell substantially. Aftershocks will be felt for a number of years, as the system settles down. For example, the colleges that changed their rules are highly uncertain about the percentage of this year's early admits who will enroll. To protect themselves, they may have accepted a few more students than usual. But some may still be forced to go heavily to the wait list.

For applicants, the system is more complicated than ever. This year's applicants had no idea of how many students would apply to the colleges that switched their systems or of the magnitude of the advantage in admissions chances of applying Single-Choice Early Action. Next year, applicants will be responding to this year's results. Single-Choice Early Action also complicates the choices of students, who now have to contend with multiple varieties of both Early Action and Early Decision. One article in *USA Today* described the decision of one student who "considered [applying early to] Yale, but went with the University of Chicago, whose less restrictive policy allowed him to apply to two other less expensive schools [early]," leaving Bill McClintick, the student's counselor at Mercersburg Academy, Pennsylvania, to lament, "It used to be that it was all about finding the right fit for the kid."[1]

Table 1 depicts four separate sets of changes in the early application programs of six prominent colleges in the past decade. In 1994–95, five of these colleges (Brown, Georgetown, Harvard, Princeton, and Yale) offered Single-Choice Early Action[2] and Stanford had no program. By 2001–02, four had switched to Early Decision and the other two allowed multiple Early Action applications. Thus, the changes of 2003–04 only partly reversed an earlier trend among these colleges towards Early Decision.

A second significant development occurred in the summer of 2003 when *U.S. News* announced that it would eliminate yield as a component of its college rankings, a change advocated forcefully in our first edition, and by others. This change reduced one well-known incentive for colleges to favor early applicants, but did not eliminate it entirely.[3] As the magazine explains on its website: "*U.S. News* had been told that schools felt they could manipulate their ranking by manipulating the yield number through early decision or early action admissions programs . . . Since yield played such a small part of the ranking model and was unlikely to affect the standing of any college, it was eliminated from the ranking model."[4]

The debate about early application policies even got tossed into

Table 1 Changes in early application programs, 1994–2004

	Existing Program, 1994–95	Changes in 1995–96	Changes in 1999–00	Changes in 2001–02	Changes in 2003–04
Brown	Early Action*		Early Action**	Early Decision	
Georgetown	Early Action*		Early Action**		
Harvard	Early Action*		Early Action**		Early Action*
Princeton	Early Action*	Early Decision			
Stanford	No Program	Early Decision			Early Action*
Yale	Early Action*	Early Decision			Early Action*

* = Single Choice Early Action – an EA applicant can only submit one early application.

** = Multiple Choice Early Action – an EA applicant can submit multiple early applications.

the mainstream political arena in 2003. During his presidential campaign, John Edwards called for the elimination of Early Decision programs.[5] Senator Edward Kennedy of Massachusetts, normally a strong supporter of the practices of higher education institutions, was extremely vocal in his criticism of Early Decision. Indeed, several educational organizations, including the American Council on Education, wrote open letters to Kennedy asking him not to introduce legislation that would punish colleges that offered Early Decision programs.[6] The thrust of their argument in these letters—following on the heels of the University of Michigan affirmative action decision—was that the federal government should not legislate the details of admissions practices of private colleges and, to some degree, it defended existing Early Decision programs.

In the end, Senator Kennedy introduced into committee a watered-down bill titled the "College Quality, Affordability, and Diversity Improvement Act of 2003" (S.1793) in October 2003. The bill, associated with the 2004 reauthorization of the Higher Education Act, includes a measure that calls for colleges to make a formal report including "the percentage of freshman students enrolled at the institution in the previous academic year who were admitted to the institution through binding early decision, disaggregated by race and eligibility for Federal Pell Grants" (S. 1793, Section 420M, (a2)).

One aspect of this bill is consistent with one of the recommendations from our concluding chapter: "Create an independent verification agency." Given the vast uncertainties about how the system operates (see Chapter 3, "Martian Blackjack"), an organization that independently verifies the admissions practices of various colleges would benefit applicants who have no choice but to participate in the admissions game. We are agnostic as to whether the federal government should be involved with that effort.

Early Applications in 2003–04

As remarked, early application patterns changed conspicuously in response to the change in application rules in 2003–04. Early applications to Stanford and Yale increased by 70 percent and 56 percent, respectively, while early applications to Harvard fell by approximately 50 percent.[7] While the magnitude of these changes may seem startling, the directions were completely predictable. The world will beat a path to leading colleges that relax the strictures on their early admissions programs (e.g., by switching from Early Decision to Early Action), and their competitors' paths will be less traveled as a result.

These magnitudes are less startling in the light of recent history. Harvard gained 30 percent in early applications when its three main rivals (Princeton, Stanford, and Yale) adopted Early Decision in 1994–95. Harvard gained another 30 percent in early applications when it agreed to allow its Early Action applicants to submit early applications to multiple colleges in 1999–2000. Because both of these factors, which noticeably favored early applications to Harvard, were eliminated in 2003–04, the drop in early applications to Harvard could be seen as a simple reversal of the two earlier jumps. Similarly, when Yale switched to Early Decision, it lost some 40 percent of its early applications—approximately the same percentage of early applications that it regained when it switched back to Early Action.

Several institutions that did not change their rules were jostled by the changes at Stanford, Yale, and Harvard. Prominent Early Action colleges such as Georgetown, MIT, and the University of Chicago saw their early applications fall by 15 percent or more. Charles Deacon, dean of admissions at Georgetown, attributed the 25 percent decline in early applications at his institution to the fact that early applicants to Harvard could no longer submit early applications to other colleges. "We share a huge overlap with Harvard in that early action pool . . . We anticipated that [decline in applications]."[8]

Princeton, which did not change its Early Decision program at all, also suffered a decline of 23 percent in early applications. The most obvious explanation was that Princeton lost early applicants because Stanford and Yale changed their programs to Early Action. Janet Rapelye, dean of admission at Princeton, took a sanguine view by suggesting that applicants who were lured away from Princeton by Early Action programs elsewhere probably did not view Princeton as a true first-choice college.[9] If so, this shift in applications would confirm that Early Decision applicants have been acting strategically.

Despite these large swings in early applications to certain colleges in 2003–04, the overall import of early admissions for many other elite colleges remained much the same as in the previous year. Figure 1 compares early applications in 2002–03 to those in 2003–04 for eight highly selective colleges. Brown, Dartmouth, and Penn received almost identical numbers of early applications in both years. Early applications remained relatively constant at prominent liberal arts colleges as well: Amherst, Swarthmore, and Williams received an average of 392 Early Decision applications in 2002–03 and an average of 401 Early Decision applications in 2003–04.

Looking over a longer period, however, the growing importance of early applications is clear. Yale received more than twice as many early applications in 2003–04 as it had when it last offered Early Action in 1994–95. Swarthmore received 137 Early Decision applica-

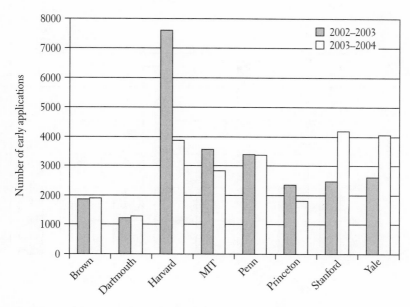

Figure 1 Early applications, 2002–2004. (College newspapers)

tions in 1994–95 and more than twice as many, 310 Early Decision applications, in 2003–04.[10] These examples represent a national trend. Across all Early Decision colleges that report their data to the College Board, early applications increased an average of 67 percent in just six years from 1995–1996 to 2001–2002.[11]

Early Admission Decisions in 2003–04

Despite some dramatic shifts in application numbers, the number of students admitted early to elite colleges remained stable in 2003–04. Figure 2 compares the number of students admitted early to eight highly selective colleges in 2002–03 and 2003–04. Only Harvard, Stanford, and Yale exhibit more than marginal differences in the number of early admits from one year to the next, with Harvard falling and Stanford and Yale rising—logical changes given application

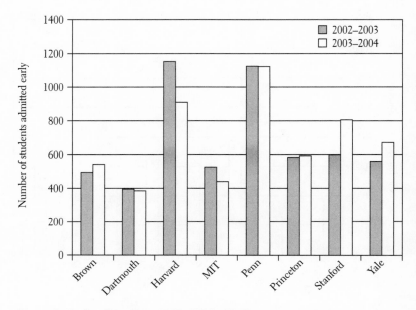

Figure 2 Early admissions, 2002–2004. (College newspapers)

numbers. Though Princeton had 23 percent fewer early applicants in 2003–04 than in 2002–03, it admitted approximately the same number of students as early applicants in each year. Thus, its admission rate for early applicants jumped from 25 percent to 33 percent in one year. (Harvard's admission rate also jumped, from 15 percent to 23 percent, but this was not sufficient to offset its large decline in applicants. It admitted 1,150 students early in 2002–03 and 906 in 2003–04.)

The results at Stanford and Yale in 2003–04 are harder to judge. Unlike 2002–03, their early admits were not committed to enroll. Assuming a 75 percent matriculation rate, Stanford will enroll a few more students and Yale about 50 fewer in 2004 through Early Action programs than they did through Early Decision the prior year.

Figure 3 compares the admission rates for early and regular applicants at eight highly selective universities and three highly selective

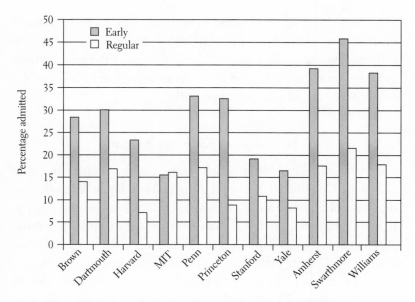

Figure 3 Early vs. regular admission rates, 2003–2004. (College newspapers)

liberal arts colleges for 2003–04.[12] Most of these colleges' admission rates for early applicants are about twice as high as their admission rates for regular applicants. The pattern is similar to that of Figure 2.7, which depicts admission rates for early and regular applicants in 1999–2000, suggesting that our statistical findings in Chapter 5 still hold today.

Applicants, however, should consider absolute admission rates, not merely the ratio of early to regular admissions. Applying early to an elite institution to raise one's chance from 4 percent to 8 percent does not accomplish much. Except for the strongest students, the trend is discouraging. In merely four years, from 1999–2000 to 2003–04, admissions became much more competitive. The early and regular admission rates fell by nearly a quarter at Dartmouth, MIT, and Penn. Karl Furstenberg, dean of admissions at Dartmouth, observed that the average SAT score of early admits to

Dartmouth went up by 13 points in one year. "Each year we have to squeeze from not only a larger but also a stronger pool, while the first-year class stays the same size."[13] The tougher the competition, the more important it is for students to make a careful choice in deciding whether and where to apply early.

The Future of Early Applications

We highlight several reforms that seem possible to enact in Table C.2 of the Conclusion. Some progress has been made. We welcome the move of Stanford and Yale from Early Decision to Early Action. It is also reassuring that *U.S. News* has revised its ranking criteria, and that Senator Kennedy has called attention to the need for verifying and publicizing information on early application programs.

In one respect, these developments, and the ongoing debate about the value of early application programs, represent tremendous progress. In another respect, they simply underscore how entrenched early admissions programs are. The change in the *U.S. News* methodology, for example, hardly affected actual rankings (only one new college moved into the top 20 "Best National Universities"—Vanderbilt, which simply moved from 21st to 20th in the rankings), and had no discernible influence on the advantage of applying early.

One systemic reform remains elusive: the possibility that many more colleges will adopt Early Action, or entirely eliminate their early programs. Yale's well-publicized decision to change from Early Decision to Single-Choice Early Action had significant reverberations, with Stanford and Harvard changing their programs in response, and others beginning to consider change. With much criticism levied against Early Decision programs because they appear to favor students from wealthy backgrounds, other colleges may feel pressure to abandon Early Decision as well. Charles Deacon summarized the public relations value of Georgetown's program: "I think we still have the high ground[,] being early action."[14] Similarly, Larry Summers, the president of Harvard, commented: "I have been an advocate of open and competitive markets in college admissions, as in many other spheres. In that regard, the recent shift by some leading colleges from Early Decision to Early Action is an important and welcome development."[15] Three factors are likely to limit the effect of Yale's decision and the responses to it by others. First, many Early Decision colleges have commented that they are very happy with their programs. For example, Swarthmore's admissions dean Jim Bock echoed the prevailing view of many of his colleagues with his comments: "We don't always change policy just because another school has done it. . . . We look at what we're doing . . . and [if] it works for Swarthmore."[16]

Second, Early Action is most attractive for highly ranked colleges, such as Stanford and Yale, which can be confident that if they offer Early Action, most admitted students will still enroll. Figures 2 and 3 suggest that Stanford and Yale may have gained a competitive advantage by adopting Early Action in 2003–04. But lesser-ranked colleges might fear that they would reduce their ability to attract and enroll students by switching from Early Decision to Early Action.

Third, even if a significant group of colleges would welcome a change to a less binding world, few would be willing to give up their binding programs if others did not. Yet there is no mechanism for coordinating rule changes across colleges, because colleges are prevented from making joint decisions by antitrust concerns. Without the ability to coordinate, Karl Furstenberg of Dartmouth describes the increasing reliance by colleges on their early application programs as a "classic arms race." In his view, the recent actions of individual colleges, with colleges "flip-flopping" between Early Action and Early Decision, has simply escalated competition when it would have been preferable for all to find some way to disarm.[17]

Two national organizations, the College Board and the National Association for College Admissions Counseling (NACAC), have sufficiently large memberships that they could conceivably develop guidelines and rules to govern early applications and coordinate change. But both organizations already have trouble enforcing their existing guidelines. Fewer than half of colleges reporting Early Decision programs to the College Board follow the College Board's Early Decision plan and the College Board provides no guidelines whatsoever for Early Action (see Chapter 2 for more details). As we describe in Chapter 2, NACAC made a subtle change in its rules in 2001, when its membership amended its "Definitions of Admission Decision Options" as part of its "Statement of Principles of Good Practice" to include the statement that Early Action applicants can apply to other colleges "without restriction," meaning that they are allowed to submit early applications to more than one college.

NACAC's revised guidelines were quickly challenged. Within two years, Yale, Stanford, and Harvard directly violated these stipulations by adopting Single-Choice Early Action programs. In addition, a number of Early Decision colleges violate NACAC's rules by prohibiting their early applicants from submitting Early Action applications to other colleges.[18] NACAC, like the United Nations, is somewhat helpless when some of its major members choose not to follow its proposed policies. NACAC responded by declaring a moratorium on enforcement of its new rule and appointed a "Steering Committee on Admission Standards" to review its broad set of admissions rules. "It has become apparent that the complexities of the issues and the rapidly shifting nature of the admissions landscape make it increasingly difficulty to find workable, 'one-size-fits-all' definitions . . . It is clear that there is not common agreement within our membership about whether or not such restrictions [required by Single-Choice Early Action] are appropriate."[19] The conundrum is obvious. NACAC is the most likely body to clarify the rules of early application programs and to guide change in the system. Yet colleges, particularly major colleges, have made it clear that they will choose their own path.

Whatever reforms NACAC adopts when its Steering Committee

completes its review in the next year, it is likely that the process of change will be driven by the actions of individual colleges. Some Early Decision colleges, most notably Brown and Princeton, have stated publicly that they are contemplating a change to Early Action.[20] What will the early admissions landscape look like a few years down the road? Two years after his original declaration against Early Decision, Richard Levin, president of Yale, assessed the possibilities as follows:

> With Harvard, MIT, Stanford, and Yale now in alignment, others are likely to follow, lest they be perceived as unfriendly or indifferent to the welfare of students. I doubt that Princeton or Penn will move soon, since their presidents have staked out strong positions in favor of binding early decision. Although I have not communicated with any of my counterparts on this subject, I would not be surprised to see highly competitive schools like Columbia, Brown, Amherst and Williams move toward non-binding early action.[21]

These changes would be significant, and Levin acknowledged the possibility that his projection could be "over-optimistic." Yet even if this projection comes true, the pressures to apply early will still remain. And applying to a Single-Choice Early Action school will send a powerful signal. As one independent counselor observed of Yale's adoption of Single-Choice Early Action: "This isn't reducing the frenzy . . . Students at competitive high schools are still saying, 'I need to apply early somewhere.'"[22]

Janet Rapelye, dean of admissions at Princeton, commented that the larger questions regarding early application practices are still far from resolved: "I think that the question that is being posed to us isn't whether Early Action or Early Decision is the better system, it's whether we should be having early programs at all. That's a philosophical question, not a policy question."[23]

Whatever the answer to that question, the evidence is clear: Barring a collective decision by a large number of colleges—which would quite possibly be illegal—early admissions will remain a prominent feature of the admissions landscape. Individually, colleges gain from offering early admissions, as we discuss in Chapter 6, and will not unilaterally abandon these programs. Different colleges facing different circumstances will offer different programs, some may switch programs to reverse poor choices from the past, particular early programs may wax and wane, and applications and acceptances may take time to settle down when rules change. But major programs will remain that allow some students to apply early to show commitment to a college, and that allow colleges to reward such commitment with an easier admissions standard.

Appendixes

Notes

Acknowledgments

Tables and Figures

Index

Appendix A

Median SAT-1 Scores and Early Application Programs at Various Colleges

College	Score	Program
Alfred University	1100	Early Decision
Allegheny College	1210	Early Decision
American University	1195	Early Decision
Amherst College	1400	Early Decision
Arizona State University	1090	Early Action
Assumption College	1095	Early Decision
Auburn University	1105	
Augustana College	1180**	
Babson College	1205	Both EA and ED
Bard College	1230	Early Action
Barnard College	1320	Early Decision
Bates College	1330	Early Decision
Baylor University	1180	
Beloit College	1245	Early Action
Bennington College	1215	Early Decision
Bentley College	1120	Both EA and ED
Birmingham-Southern College	1185	Early Action
Boston College	1305	Early Action
Boston University	1270	Early Decision

College	Score	Program
Bowdoin College	1360	Early Decision
Bradley University	1190	
Brandeis University	1320	Early Decision
Brigham Young University	1195**	
Brown University	1390	Early Decision
Bryn Mawr College	1300	Early Decision
Bucknell University	1275	Early Decision
Butler University	1150	Early Action
California Institute of Technology	1515	Early Action
California Polytechnic State University: San Luis Obispo	1170	Early Decision
California State Polytechnic University: Pomona	995	
California State University: Chico	1025	
California State University: Fullerton	970	
California State University: Long Beach	960	
Carleton College	1375	Early Decision
Carnegie Mellon University	1370	Early Decision
Case Western Reserve University	1345	Early Decision
Catholic University of America	1165	Early Decision
Claremont McKenna College	1390	Early Decision
Clark University	1180	Early Decision
Clemson University	1180	
Colby College	1320	Early Decision
Colgate University	1320	Early Decision
College of Charleston	1160	
College of the Holy Cross	1235	Early Decision
The College of New Jersey	1250	Early Decision
College of William and Mary	1320	Early Decision
College of Wooster	1170	Early Decision
Colorado College	1245	Early Action
Colorado State University	1110	
Columbia University: Columbia College	1410	Early Decision
Connecticut College	1140	Early Decision
Cooper Union	1375	Early Decision
Cornell University	1365	Early Decision
Creighton University	1160	
Dartmouth College	1425	Early Decision
Davidson College	1330	Early Decision
Denison University	1205	Both EA and ED

College	Score	Program
DePaul University	1115	Early Action
DePauw University	1170	Both EA and ED
Dickinson College	1220	Both EA and ED
Drake University	1135	
Drew University	1215	Early Decision
Drexel University	1140	
Duke University	1400	Early Decision
Duquesne University	1185	Both EA and ED
Earlham College	1195	Both EA and ED
Eckerd College	1155	
Elon College	1115	Early Decision
Emerson College	1185	Early Action
Emory University	1380	Early Decision
Eugene Lang College / New School for Social Research	1235	Early Decision
Evergreen State College	1120	
Fairfield University	1175	Early Decision
Florida International University	1100	
Florida State University	1160	
Fordham University	1150	Early Decision
Franklin and Marshall College	1260	Early Decision
Furman University	1255	Early Decision
George Mason University	1075	
George Washington University	1235	Early Decision
Georgetown University	1365	Early Action
Georgia Institute of Technology	1335	
Gettysburg College	1200	Early Decision
Gonzaga University	1160	Early Action
Goucher College	1180	Both EA and ED
Grinnell College	1330	Early Decision
Guilford College	1135	Both EA and ED
Hamilton College	1250	Early Decision
Hampshire College	1250	Both EA and ED
Hartwick College	1095	Early Decision
Harvard and Radcliffe Colleges	1485	Early Action
Harvey Mudd College	1480	Early Decision
Haverford College	1355	Early Decision
Hobart and William Smith College	1160	Early Decision
Hofstra University	1095	Early Decision
Howard University	1105	Early Action

College	Score	Program
Illinois Institute of Technology	1315	
Illinois State University	1045**	Early Action
Illinois Wesleyan University	1255	
Indiana University (Bloomington)	1095	
Iowa State University	1210	
Ithaca College	1150	Early Decision
James Madison University	1170	Early Action
Johns Hopkins University	1390	Early Decision
Johnson and Wales University	920	
Kalamazoo College	1290	Both EA and ED
Kansas State University	1065**	
Kenyon College	1290	Early Decision
Knox College	1225	Early Action
Lafayette College	1250	Early Decision
Lake Forest College	1140	Both EA and ED
Lawrence University	1255	Early Decision
Lehigh University	1270	Early Decision
Lewis & Clark College	1245	Early Action
Louisiana State University	1085**	
Loyola College in Maryland	1215	
Loyola Marymount University	1130	
Loyola University New Orleans	1175	
Loyola University of Chicago	1155	
Macalester College	1335	Early Decision
Marist College	1110	Early Action
Marquette University	1160	
Mary Washington College	1200	Early Decision
Massachusetts Institute of Technology	1485	Early Action
Merrimack College	1090	Early Action
Miami University (Ohio): Oxford Campus	1210	Early Decision
Michigan State University	1115	
Middlebury College	1410	Early Decision
Montana State University	1115	
Mount Holyoke College	1265	Early Decision
Muhlenberg College	1200	Early Decision
New Mexico Institute of Mining and Technology	1180**	
New York University	1335	Early Decision
North Carolina State University	1185	Early Action
Northeastern University (Mass.)	1125	
Northern Illinois University	1045**	

College	Score	Program
Northwestern University	1380	Early Decision
Oberlin College	1315	Early Decision
Occidental College	1210	Early Decision
Ohio State University: Columbus	1160	
Ohio University	1090	
Oregon State University	1080	Early Action
Penn State University Park	1185	
Pepperdine University	1250	Early Action
Pitzer College	1225	Early Action
Pomona College	1435	Early Decision
Princeton University	1490	Early Decision
Providence College	1180	Early Action
Purdue University	1130	
Quinnipiac College	1085	
Reed College	1325	Early Decision
Rensselaer Polytechnic Institute	1275	Early Decision
Rhodes College	1280	Early Decision
Rice University	1410	Both EA and ED
Roanoke College	1100	Both EA and ED
Rochester Institute of Technology	1195	Early Decision
Rose-Hulman Institute of Technology	1295*	
Rowan University	1105	
Rutgers University	1195*	
San Diego State University	1045	Early Action
San Jose State University	995	
Santa Clara University	1220	
Sarah Lawrence College	1245	Early Decision
Scripps College	1280	Early Decision
Seattle University	1115	
Simmons College	1070	Early Action
Skidmore College	1225	Early Decision
Smith College	1265	Early Decision
Southern Methodist University	1160	Early Action
Spelman College	1050	Early Action
St. Joseph's University	1215	
St. Lawrence University	1140	Early Decision
St. Louis University	1200*	
St. Olaf College	1265	Both EA and ED
Stanford University	1460	Early Decision
State University of New York at Albany	1130	Early Action

College	Score	Program
State University of New York at Binghamton	1210	Early Action
State University of New York at Buffalo	1115	Early Decision
State University of New York at Geneseo	1225	Early Decision
State University of New York at New Paltz	1090	Early Decision
State University of New York at Oswego	1100	Early Decision
State University of New York at Purchase	1090	
State University of New York at Stony Brook	1130	Early Action
Stevens Institute of Technology	1285	Early Decision
Stonehill College	1165	Early Decision
Swarthmore College	1435	Early Decision
Syracuse University	1205	Early Decision
Temple University	1030	
Texas A & M University	1180	
Texas Christian University	1150	Early Action
Texas Tech University	1075	
Trinity College (Conn.)	1270	Early Decision
Trinity University (Tex.)	1280	Both EA and ED
Truman State University	1225	Early Action
Tufts University	1325	Early Decision
Tulane University	1235	Both EA and ED
Union College	1215	Early Decision
United States Air Force Academy	1270	
United States Coast Guard Academy	1250	Early Action
United States Military Academy	1255	
United States Naval Academy	1295	
University of Alabama	1100	
University of Alabama: Birmingham	1025**	
University of Arizona	1095	
University of California: Berkeley	1320	
University of California: Davis	1175	
University of California: Irvine	1145	
University of California: Los Angeles	1285	
University of California: Riverside	1060	
University of California: San Diego	1180	
University of California: Santa Barbara	1185	
University of California: Santa Cruz	1145	
University of Central Florida	1140	
University of Chicago	1385	Early Action
University of Cincinnati	1060	
University of Colorado at Boulder	1155	

College	Score	Program
University of Connecticut	1140	Early Action
University of Dayton	1140	
University of Delaware	1150	Early Decision
University of Denver	1115	Early Action
University of Florida	1210	Early Decision
University of Georgia	1210	
University of Hartford	1050	Early Action
University of Hawaii at Manoa	1080	
University of Idaho	1105	
University of Illinois at Chicago	1085**	
University of Illinois at Urbana-Champaign	1245	
University of Iowa	1175	
University of Kansas	1140**	
University of Maryland: Baltimore County	1180	
University of Maryland: College Park	1250	Early Action
University of Massachusetts Amherst	1125	
University of Miami (Fla.)	1175	Both EA and ED
University of Michigan	1280	
University of Minnesota: Twin Cities	1203	
University of Missouri: Columbia	1195**	
University of Missouri: Rolla	1245	
University of Nebraska–Lincoln	1145	
University of Nevada: Reno	1050	
University of New Hampshire	1120	Early Action
University of New Mexico	1080	
University of North Carolina at Chapel Hill	1235	Both EA and ED***
University of North Carolina Charlotte	1035	Early Action
University of Notre Dame	1350	Early Action
University of Oklahoma	1125**	
University of Oregon	1115	
University of Pennsylvania	1425	Early Decision
University of Pittsburgh	1165	
University of Puget Sound	1245	Early Decision
University of Rhode Island	1085	Early Action
University of Richmond	1310	Early Decision
University of Rochester	1320	Early Decision
University of San Diego	1170	Early Action
University of San Francisco	1080	Early Action
University of Scranton	1125	Early Action
University of South Carolina	1110	

College	Score	Program
University of Southern California	1305	
University of Tennessee	1115	Early Action
University of Texas at Austin	1195	
University of the Pacific	1120	Early Action
University of the South	1225	Early Decision
University of Tulsa	1205	Early Decision
University of Utah	1085**	
University of Vermont	1135	Both EA and ED
University of Virginia	1305	Early Decision
University of Washington	1160	
University of Wisconsin–Madison	1245	
Utah State University	1060	
Valparaiso University	1195	Early Action
Vanderbilt University	1310	Early Decision
Vassar College	1350	Early Decision
Villanova University	1245	Early Action
Virginia Commonwealth University	1030	Early Decision
Virginia Tech	1175	Early Decision
Wake Forest University	1300	Early Decision
Washington and Lee University	1350	Early Decision
Washington State University	1060	
Washington University (St. Louis)	1370	Early Decision
Wayne State University	965**	
Wellesley College	1355	Early Decision
Wesleyan College (Ga.)	1145	Both EA and ED
Wesleyan University (Conn.)	1365	Early Decision
Westmont College	1190	Early Action
Wheaton College (Ill.)	1320	Early Action
Wheaton College (Mass.)	1200	Early Decision
Whitman College	1310	Early Decision
Willamette University	1205	Early Action
Williams College	1410	Early Decision
Wittenberg College	1180	Both EA and ED
Worcester Polytechnic Institute	1270	Early Decision
Xavier University (Ohio)	1135	
Yale University	1465	Early Decision

Note: This table includes four-year academic institutions in the United States with at least 5 applications from participants in the College Admissions Project.

The numbers in this table are computed from the College Board's database for 1999–2000. Each college reported the twenty-fifth and seventy-fifth percentile of SAT-1 verbal and SAT-1 math scores for its current students. We average each pair of scores separately to get an (approximate) average SAT-1 verbal and an average SAT-1 math score for each college, and then add these two scores together to get an (approximate) average overall SAT-1 score. Information about the early application programs for the colleges was compiled from the *U.S. News* website for 2001–02.

*This SAT information was taken from the 2003 *U.S. News* database (data were based on applications submitted in 2001–02), since the college's SAT information in missing from the 1999–2000 College Board database.

**This SAT information was converted from the composite ACT scores for the college in the 2003 *U.S. News* database (using a standard conversion chart for ACT-SAT scores), since the college's SAT information is missing from both the 1999–2000 College Board database and the 2003 *U.S. News* database.

***University of North Carolina at Chapel Hill announced that it will eliminate ED in 2002–03.

Source: College Board database (median SAT scores) and *U.S. News* website (early application programs).

Appendix B

Data Sources

We used five primary sources of information for this project: data on admissions results from colleges and from a student survey, and interviews with counselors, college students, and high school students.

1. Admissions Office Data from Colleges

The admissions office data we utilized consists of complete applicant records and decisions from each of fourteen well-known colleges over at least five years. Thirteen colleges provided us with a copy of their databases given two conditions: that we use the data only to analyze early applications, and that we maintain the anonymity of the participating colleges. The fourteenth college, also requiring anonymity, conducted its own data analysis using computer programs that we wrote, and then provided us with the results.

We had limited ability to compare applicants across colleges in the admissions office data because formatting and data definitions varied from college to college. The most critical variables, however—for example, SAT scores or whether the applicant was a legacy—were consistently defined across colleges.

2. Student Survey Data from the
College Admissions Project

The College Admissions Project, run jointly by Avery and Professor Caroline Hoxby of the Harvard Economics Department, surveyed more than 3,000 graduating high school seniors. The project asked guidance counselors at 500 prominent high schools around the country to survey 10 students each over the course of their senior year. Counselors at public schools selected students at random from the top 10 percent of the graduating class, whereas counselors at private schools selected students at random from the top 20 percent of the graduating class.

In total, 3,294 students from 396 high schools completed the surveys. Each of these students provided standard information from the Common Application (available at www. commonapp.org) and additional information about their accomplishments, applications, and application outcomes. We used this information to identify (1) alumni children; (2) athletic recruits; (3) applicants who are identified minorities; and finally the so-called unhooked applicants who did not fall into any of these categories. According to the categories included on the Common Application, minorities were those students who identified themselves as "African American, Black," "American Indian, Alaskan Native," "Hispanic, Latino," "Mexican American, Chicano," "Native Hawaiian, Pacific Islander," or "Puerto Rican."

For our analysis, we added two additional variables to the survey information: a high school rating and a student activity rating. We rated each participating high school on a scale of 1 to 5, where a higher score indicated that the school sent a high percentage of its graduates to the most selective colleges in the country. These ratings were estimates based primarily on Andrew Fairbanks's experience in the admissions field, particularly his tenure as the associate admissions director at Wesleyan. (The actual percentage of students from a given high school who attend a particular set of colleges is not generally available.)

Similarly, we compiled a student activity rating on a scale of 1 to 5 on the basis of each student's response to the question, "Please list your three most significant academic or extracurricular accomplishments." Since the survey only included very successful students from well-known high schools, the lowest rating, 1, still indicated considerable accomplishment. A rating of 2 indicated a leadership position in a high school club (for example, president of the debate club) or some success in an extracurricular activity. A rating of 3 indicated a leadership position at the high school level (for example, president of the class or editor of the newspaper) or outstanding success at the local level in an extracurricular activity (for example, Eagle Scout). A rating of 4 indicated success at the state level in an extracurricular activity (for example, member of an All State Orchestra or semifinalist in the Westinghouse Science Competition). A rating of 5 indicated success at the national level in some activity. Ratings of 4 and 5 were quite rare; only 6 percent of students in the survey received one of these two ratings. (These ratings were designed to follow the scale for applicants to Stanford described by Jean Fetter in her book *Questions and Admissions*, pp. 23–25.)

Both these variables were employed as additional measures of an applicant's attractiveness. This enabled us to refine our comparisons between early and regular applicants at each college. It also helped us to quantify the effect of applying early in terms of extracurricular activities—for example, how does the effect of applying early compare with the effect of extracurricular success that would improve one's activity rating from, say, 2 to 4?

3. Interviews with Counselors

In spring 1998, we interviewed fifteen high school guidance counselors at schools across the country and had further conversations with many of them over the next several years. A number of college admissions officers helped us to identify counselors who were experienced and thoughtful about early applications. These officers then recommended individual counselors to represent different parts of the country and both private and public schools. In spring 1999, we interviewed ten head counselors at public schools in Massachusetts (each of which was selected at random from a list of all Massachusetts public high schools) using the same interview format. Tables B.1 and B.2 list the counselors we interviewed and provide further information about their schools.

4. Interviews with College Students

We interviewed college students at five schools over the course of three academic years, from 1997–98 through 1999–2000; most of the interviews were completed in 1997–98 and 1998–99. We aimed to interview twenty-five students from the classes of 1998, 1999, 2000, and 2001 at Harvard, MIT, Princeton, and Yale. (At Wesleyan, we primarily interviewed freshmen in the classes of 2001 and 2002.) Students in the classes of 1998 and 1999 applied when all four of these colleges offered Early Action programs. Students in the classes of 2000 and 2001 applied when Harvard and MIT offered Early Action and Princeton and Yale offered Early Decision.

In general, we selected students at random from the undergraduate phone book and then asked them by phone or by e-mail to participate in a thirty-minute interview about their experiences applying to college. In some cases, undergraduate research assistants selected students at random from a particular dormitory (for example, research assistants at Harvard interviewed students who lived in the same undergraduate house). As a result, the students selected may not have been a fully random sample of all undergraduates at these institutions. The response rates varied by school, ranging from a low of about 30 percent to 50 percent or more.

Table B.1 List of interviews with counselors at nationally prominent high schools

Counselor	High school	Type of school	No. of seniors	% of students applying early (1997–98)
Carlene Riccelli	Amherst Regional (Mass.)	Public	240	12
Rory Bled	Berkeley (Calif.)	Public	550	3
Phyllis McKay	Oyster River (N.H.)	Public	140	18
Eileen Blattner	Shaker Heights (Ohio)	Public	400	13
Carol Katz	Stuyvesant (N.Y.)	Public	734	27
Alice Purington	Andover (Mass.)	Private	346	60
Terry Giffen	Choate (Conn.)	Private	250	50
Bruce Breimer	Collegiate School (N.Y.)	Private	50	15
Cathy Nabbefeld	Colorado Academy (Colo.)	Private	55	51
Kathy Giles	Groton (Mass.)	Private	90	94
Stephen Singer	Horace Mann (N.Y.)	Private	150	50
Scotte Gordon	Moses Brown (R.I.)	Private	55	40
Alan Crocker	New Hampton (N.H.)	Private	100	30
Larry Momo	Trinity (N.Y.)	Private	95	58
Nancy Beane	Westminster (Ga.)	Private	200	53

Table B.2 Interviews with Massachusetts public school counselors

Counselor	High school	No. of seniors	% students to four-year colleges	% of students applying early (1998–99)
Elaine Gelinas	Boston English	300	30	0
Louis Valenti	Brockton	700	80	<5
Steven Sarantopoulos	Bridgewater	356	69	10
Gerry Gerrard	Holyoke	200	40	5
Gail Roycroft	Marshfield	262	84	15
Thomas Pellucia	Mount Greylock	90	65	17
John DeFlumeri	North Andover	192	76	5
Don Cranson	Oakmont Regional	150	65	2
Bill Frazier	Pittsfield	255	40	4
Gary Watson	Springfield	400	40	3

The students we interviewed appeared to be broadly representative of the student body at each college in terms of the percentage of students who applied and were admitted early. For example, Harvard admitted approximately half its enrollees in the early process throughout this period, and just under 50 percent of the Harvard students we interviewed had been admitted early (see Table B.4). Similarly, the 1997 *U.S. News College Guide* estimated that MIT admitted 32 percent, Princeton admitted 49 percent, and Yale admitted 29 percent of the class of 2000 as early applicants. These numbers suggest that we interviewed students who were slightly more likely than average to have applied early, but any disparities are small.

All interviewers followed the protocols listed in Appendix C and took written notes during the course of the interviews. They then complied a typed summary of each interview. (Most written summaries for thirty-minute interviews were about two single-spaced pages.) Each interviewer made a record of noteworthy quotations and included them in the summaries. However, we do not have a word-for-word transcript of any of the interviews. Thus, we could not check the precise student quotations included in this book. In some cases, therefore, we had to make a best guess at the literal words of the original comment. Tables B.3 and B.4 provide details about these college students and their early application decisions. Two people coded each interview independently on the basis of rules for

Table B.3 Summary of interviews with college students

College	No. from class of 1998	No. from class of 1999	No. from class of 2000	No. from class of 2001	Total
Harvard	19	22	16	8	65
MIT	15	18	15	21	69
Princeton	26	32	26	16	100
Yale	16	21	28	33	98

Table B.4   Early applications for interview subjects

College	Applied early to any college	Applied early to this college (%)	Admitted early to this college (%)
Harvard	69.2	52.3	47.7
MIT	63.8	52.2	44.9
Princeton	79.0	64.0	59.0
Yale	53.1	34.7	27.6

forty separate aspects of the interviews. We then checked for discrepancies in the two coding results and resolved them by detailed analysis of the interview summaries.

5. Interviews with High School Students

In summer 1998 we selected students from Choate Rosemary Hall and students from Needham High School to be followed throughout their senior year. Guidance counselors at each school provided a list of students ranked by grade point average at the end of their junior year. Each school has a rising senior class of approximately 250 students. At Choate, we selected thirty students at random from the top hundred in the class, and twenty-eight participated in the project the following year. At Needham, we selected thirty students at random from the top fifty in the class and all thirty participated in the project the following year. Chapter 4 provides information about the applications and outcomes for each of the fifty-eight high school seniors who participated in the project.

Appendix C

Interview Formats

Guidance Counselors

A. *Open-Ended Questions*

1. Describe your high school to me. Is it common to go out of state to college? Is it common to go to Ivy League schools (or MIT, Chicago, Stanford, etc.)? What percentage of students go to four-year colleges?

2. How do you advise students who are considering an early application? Under what conditions do you believe that it is advisable for a student to apply Early Action (EA)? Under what conditions do you believe that it is advisable for a student to apply Early Decision (ED)?

3. Do you think that your students are in competition with each other for admission to highly selective colleges? If so, do you think that this affects their decisions to apply early? How does it affect the way that you advise them?

4. Do you believe that applying early makes a difference to a student's chances of admission? Do you think that applying early to an ED school has a different effect than applying early to an EA school?

5. How do you advise students who think that it will hurt their chances of admission if they do not apply early?

6. Do you think that EA and ED have an effect on financial aid?

7. Do you think that students receive accurate information regarding Early Decision from admission counselors? How well informed do you think that students are about Early Decision and Early Action? How well informed are you about Early Decision and Early Action?

8. What do you believe are the advantages and disadvantages of Early Action and Early Decision?

9. Have you witnessed a change over time in the difference between ED admission standards and RD [regular decision] admission standards? Have you witnessed a change in the way that students and colleges use ED and EA?

10. How would you change the current system of early admissions, if at all?

11. How much are parents involved in the choices of your students?

12. Do you have further comments?

B. Numerical Questions

How does applying Early Action affect a student's chance of admission?

   1. Disadvantage   2. Slight disadvantage   3. Neutral
   4. Slight advantage   5. Advantage

How does applying Early Decision affect a student's chance of admission relative to applying Early Action?

1. Disadvantage   2. Slight disadvantage   3. Neutral
4. Slight advantage   5. Advantage

Considering all factors, rate the overall value of Early Action for applicants.

1. Disadvantage   2. Slight disadvantage   3. Neutral
4. Slight advantage,   5. Advantage

Considering all factors, rate the overall value of Early Decision for applicants.

1. Disadvantage   2. Slight disadvantage   3. Neutral
4. Slight advantage,   5. Advantage

College Students

Note: This specific set of questions was used for Princeton students. An analogous set of questions was used for interviews at each of the other colleges.

A. *Open-Ended Questions*

1. Describe your high school to me. Is it common to go out of state to college? Is it common to go to Ivy League schools (or MIT, Chicago, Stanford, etc.)?

2. How did you end up attending Princeton?

3. Where did you apply to college?
Did you apply early?

4. How did you decide to apply early vs. regular?
Where did you get information about early admissions?
Did financial aid play a role in determining whether or not you applied early?

5. Did the distinction between Early Action and Early Decision affect your choice of where to apply?

Seniors: Would it have made a difference to your decision if Princeton had ED rather than EA when you applied?

Sophomores and Juniors: Would it have made a difference to your decision if Princeton had EA rather than ED when you applied?

6. Do you think that applying early helps your chances of being admitted? Do you think that applying early to an ED school has a different effect on your chances than applying early to an EA school?

Where did you get your information about this?

What did college admissions officers and guidance counselors tell you?

7. What are the advantages and disadvantages of EA? What are the advantages and disadvantages of ED?

8. Suppose that a student from your high school asked for your advice on the application process and early admissions. How would you advise him/her?

8a. Under what circumstances would you advise someone to apply early under EA?

Under what circumstances would you advise someone to apply early under ED?

9. How would you advise someone who says, "I'm not sure if I want to go to Princeton, but I'm worried that it will be a disadvantage if I don't apply ED"?

10. Do you have any further comments?

B. Numerical Questions

Rank on a scale from 1 to 5 (where 1 = not very influential, 5 = very influential) the following in terms of their helpfulness and importance in the college application process.

Parents
Teachers
Guidance counselor
Friends
College admissions officers

Rank on a scale from 1 to 5 whether Early Action provides an admission advantage or a disadvantage for an applicant.

1. Disadvantage   2. Slight disadvantage   3. Neutral
4. Slight advantage   5. Advantage

Rank on a scale from 1 to 5 whether Early Decision provides an admission advantage or a disadvantage for an applicant relative to Early Action.

1. Disadvantage   2. Slight disadvantage   3. Neutral
4. Slight advantage   5. Advantage

Rank on a scale from 1 to 5 whether Early Action is beneficial or harmful (overall) for an applicant.

1. Harmful   2. Slightly harmful   3. Neutral
4. Slightly beneficial   5. Beneficial

Rank on a scale from 1 to 5 whether Early Decision is beneficial or harmful (overall) for an applicant, relative to Early Action.

1. Harmful   2. Slightly harmful   3. Neutral
4. Slightly beneficial   5. Beneficial

C. Scenario Questions

1. Your friend says that his top choice is Stanford (which has Early Decision) and his second choice is Brown (which has Early Action), but he thinks that it is possible that he will change his mind. He is worried that applying ED to Stanford may be too committing, but he is also worried that not applying early may hurt his chances of admission. He is a strong candidate, but not one who is certain to be admitted to either school. Which of the following things would you recommend?

    a. apply ED (binding) to Stanford

    b. apply EA (non-binding) to Brown

    c. do not apply early

2. How would you advise your friend in the same situation if his preferences were reversed so that Brown is his first choice and Stanford is his second choice.

    a. apply ED (binding) to Stanford

    b. apply EA (non-binding) to Brown

    c. do not apply early

3. How would you advise your friend in the same situation if he is only considering Early Decision schools, with Stanford as his first choice and Amherst as his second choice?

    a. apply ED (binding) to Stanford

    b. apply ED (binding) to Amherst

    c. do not apply early

High School Students

A. Interview 1: Summer 1998

1. Are you planning to go to college?

2. Thus far, what has been your main source of information about college?

3. Thus far, what has been the most influential source of information?

4. Do you have family connections anywhere? Do you feel pressure in that direction?

5. Do you have any thoughts on what type of school you're looking for?

6. Are there any specific schools you have in mind at this point? Why those?

7. Is cost a factor?

8. How do you plan to proceed with applications?

9. Can you give me a list of your extracurricular activities?

B. *Interview 2: Mid-December 1998*

1. How is the college applications process going for you?

2. What sources of information have you been using to learn more about colleges? (Have you used the Internet to learn more about schools? Have you visited any colleges—which ones?)

3. Do you know what school you would most like to attend?

4. Have you applied anywhere? (Early?)

5. What are your plans for applications from this point on?

6. How is your senior year? Has your senior year been busy or easy so far?

C. *Interview 3: Mid-March 1999*

1. Where have you applied / what is the status of your applications?

2. What are your top choices at this point?

3. How has the application process affected your senior year?

D. *Interview 4: June 1999*

1. What did you hear from the schools you applied to and where are you going?

2. In retrospect, would you have done things differently?

3. Do you think applying early affects people's chances at admission? Do you think the effect is different for Early Ddecision vs. Early Action?

4. Under what circumstances would you advise someone to apply early?

Notes

Introduction

1. These calculations are based on the rankings in the 2003 *U.S. News College Guide* and on the College Board database of applications for 1999–2000. Of these 281 private colleges, 200 (71.1 percent) offer an early admissions program, with 114 offering Early Decision, 52 offering Early Action, and 34 offering both programs.

2. Larry McMurtry, *Roads* (New York: Simon and Schuster, 2001), pp. 166–167.

3. Radio interview, "The Battle over Early Decision," *The Connection*, National Public Radio, January 3, 2002 *(http://www.theconnection.org/archive/2002/01/0103b.shtml)*.

4. "Early Decision: The View from Different Perspectives," presentation at National Association for College Admissions Counselors Meeting, October 2000.

5. Robert Klitgaard, *Choosing Elites* (New York: Basic Books, 1985), catalogs a vast array of studies, concluding, "To recapitulate, the literature shows status across occupations is substantially correlated with both academic ability and education" (p. 217).

6. George W. Pierson, *The Education of American Leaders: Compara-*

tive Contributions of U.S. Colleges and Universities (New York: Praeger, 1969), p. 251, quoted in Klitgaard, *Choosing Elites,* p. 124.

7. In 1970 Steven Kelman wrote in his book about student protests at Harvard: "Harvard students are concerned about their futures, and they are happy because they have every reason to be optimistic. I'll never forget the freshman from Indiana who once said to me, 'You know I read an article recently that really impressed me. It said that if you go to a state college your chances of becoming a corporation president are one in fifteen thousand, at Columbia they're one in five hundred, and at Harvard they're one in fifty.' I don't know how figures like that could be computed, but the important thing is that they were cited, and cited with a velvety smile of contentment." Steven Kelman, *Push Comes to Shove: The Escalation of Student Protest* (New York: Houghton Mifflin, 1970), p. 187.

In 1990 *Fortune Magazine* surveyed 1,891 (then) current and former CEOs of major companies ("Where the CEO's Went to College," *Fortune Magazine,* June 18, 1990, pp. 120–122). It found that 19 percent of current CEOs and 14 percent of former CEOs had graduated from Ivy League colleges. Six of the eight Ivy League colleges ranked in the top ten in number of graduates who had risen to the rank of CEO (the exceptions were Brown and Penn).

8. These data were compiled by the Andrew W. Mellon Foundation (New York, N.Y.) and are known as the College and Beyond data. See also William G. Bowen and Derek Bok, *The Shape of the River: Long-Term Consequences of Considering Race in College and University Admissions* (Princeton, N.J.: Princeton University Press, 1998).

9. See, for example, Caroline Hoxby, "The Return to Entering a More Selective College: 1960 to the Present" (Cambridge, Mass.: Harvard University, 1998, mimeograph), and Dominic J. Brewer, Eric R. Eide, and Ronald G. Ehrenberg, "Does It Pay to Attend an Elite Private College? Cross Cohort Evidence of the Effect of College Type on Earnings," *Journal of Human Resources,* 34 (Winter 1999): 104–123. Hoxby writes that "people who invest in education at a more selective school generally earn back their investment several times over during their careers." Brewer, Eide, and Ehrenberg write, "We find a large premium to attending an elite private institution and a smaller premium to attending a middle-rated private institu-

tion relative to a bottom-rated public school." See Philip J. Cook and Robert H. Frank, *The Winner-Take-All Society: How More and More Americans Compete for Fewer and Bigger Prizes, Encouraging Economic Waste, Income Inequality, and an Impoverished Cultural Life* (New York: Free Press, 1995); David Karen, "Who Gets into Harvard?: Selection and Exclusion at an Elite College" (Cambridge, Mass.: Harvard University, Ph.D. diss., 1985); and Klitgaard, *Choosing Elites*, for references to earlier studies with similar findings. For the dissenting study see Stacy Berg Dale and Alen B. Krueger, "Estimating the Payoff to Attending a More Selective College: An Application of Selection on Observables and Unobservables," National Bureau of Economics Research Working Paper, August 1999 (available at *http://papers.nber.org/papers/W7322*).

10. See Robert Putnam, *Bowling Alone: The Collapse and Revival of American Community* (New York: Simon and Schuster, 2000).

11. This finding was first demonstrated in 1974 by the sociologist Mark Granovetter in *Getting a Job: A Study of Contacts and Careers* (Cambridge, Mass.: Harvard University Press, 1974). Granovetter discovered that more than half of professional and technical workers had found their current jobs through a personal contact, but that almost all of those contacts were through people whom the workers saw only occasionally. For a more popular discussion of this topic, see Malcolm Gladwell, "Six Degrees of Lois Weisberg," *New Yorker*, January 11, 1999.

12. See, for example, "The Harvard Lampoon's Media Mafia," *Brill's Content*, June 2001, and "The Industry: An Ivy League of Their Own," *Los Angeles Magazine*, July 1998.

13. Bowen and Bok, *The Shape of the River*, p. 131.

14. The estimate of $400 million is from Patricia McDonough, Anthony Lising Antonio, Mary Beth Walpole, and Leonor Perez, "College Rankings: Democratized College Knowledge for Whom?" *Research in Higher Education*, 39 (1998): 513–537. The $30,000 estimate comes from *Time* and was provided to those researchers by John Katzman, the CEO of Princeton Review.

15. These tabulations are based on calculations from the College Board's database. Since the strongest students in the pool may have applied and been admitted to more than just Ivy League colleges, the chances of a

student's getting into a particular Ivy League college are worse than the ratio of acceptances to applications.

16. "Inside the Meritocracy Machine," *New York Times Magazine,* April 28, 1996.

17. We identify subjects from our interviews with high school and college students by first name. Though we use pseudonyms to ensure that none of the subjects can be identified, we do report the correct college and graduating class for each college student. In addition, we maintain the gender of each subject, choosing female pseudonymous first names for women and male first names for men.

18. *http://www.infoplease.come/ipa/A0112636.html.*

19. We classify applications by academic year, so that 1991–92 refers to applications that were submitted in the fall of 1991 for entry into college in the fall of 1992.

20. The survey was conducted by Christopher Avery, one of this book's authors, together with Caroline Hoxby, a professor in the Harvard Economics Department. We are grateful to Professor Hoxby for allowing us to use the survey information for part of our data analysis.

21. We also interviewed sixty-eight students at Wesleyan, primarily freshmen in the class of 2002 (interviewed during the 1998–99 school year). Since these interviews were conducted using an interview format slightly different from those employed at the other four colleges, we use them primarily for background information and do not include them in most of the tabulations in the rest of the book.

22. Groucho never applied to college. He left school at age eleven and became a professional performer.

23. The College Board database lists 1,818 four-year colleges enrolling an average of 691 entering students who applied in 1999–2000—a total of more than 1.25 million students enrolling in four-year colleges in the fall of 2000.

24. Ronald G. Ehrenberg, *Tuition Rising: Why College Costs So Much* (Cambridge, Mass.: Harvard University Press, 2000), p. 90.

25. "Yale Proposes That Elite Colleges Abandon Early-Decision Admissions," *New York Times,* December 13, 2001, p. A1.

26. Beloit and North Carolina had previously offered both plans; they

eliminated Early Decision for applications in 2002–03, while maintaining Early Action. Stanford and Yale previously offered Early Decision; each will switch from ED to EA for applications in 2003–04. See Chapter 1 for further details.

1. The History of Early Admissions

1. One important exception was the policy at several Ivy League colleges to limit enrollment of Jewish students. These colleges, notably Columbia, Harvard, and Yale, excluded a certain number of qualified Jewish applicants on nonacademic grounds from about 1925 through at least the mid-1930s. For details, see Marcia Graham Synnott, *The Half-Opened Door: Discrimination and Admissions and Harvard, Yale, and Princeton, 1900–1970* (Westport, Conn.: Greenwood Press, 1979), and Dan A. Oren, *Joining the Club: A History of Jews and Yale* (New Haven, Conn.: Yale University Press, 1985).

2. *The Harvard Admission and Scholarship Committee Report*, 1952–1953.

3. Harold S. Wechsler, *The Qualified Student: A History of Selective College Admissions in America* (New York: Wiley, 1977). See Nicholas Lemann, *The Big Test: The Secret History of the American Meritocracy* (New York: Farrar, Straus and Giroux, 1999), for discussion of the development of the College Entrance Examination Board tests. See Edwin Cornelius Broome, *A Historical and Critical Discussion of College Admission Requirements* (New York: Macmillan, Berlin, Bayer, and Muller, 1903), for details of admission practices before 1900.

4. Jerome Karabel, "Status-Group Struggle: Organizational Interests and the Limits of Institutional Autonomy—The Transformation of Harvard, Yale, and Princeton, 1918–1940," *Theory and Society*, 13 (January 1984): 1–40. Karabel reports that in 1930, Harvard admitted 93.8 percent of the applicants from twelve leading prep schools, as opposed to 76.7 percent of all other applicants. In 1940, Harvard admitted 98.6 percent of the applicants from these same twelve schools, as opposed to 82.8 percent of other applicants.

5. Synnott, *The Half-Opened Door*, pp. 155–157.

6. See, for example, Lemann, *The Big Test*, p. 29. On a related note, James Tobin, a Nobel Prize–winning economist, recalled in a conversation in 1998 that he was recruited by Harvard early in the summer after he graduated from a public high school in Illinois. He applied after his high school graduation, won a Harvard National Scholarship, and enrolled in September.

7. George Wilson Pierson, *Yale College: An Educational History, 1871–1921* (New Haven, Conn.: Yale University Press, 1952), p. 388.

8. Ibid., pp. 402–411. See also Karabel, "Status-Group Struggle"; David Karen, "Who Gets into Harvard?: Selection and Exclusion at an Elite College" (Cambridge, Mass.: Harvard University, Ph.D. diss., 1985); and Morton Keller and Phyllis Keller, *Making Harvard Modern: The Rise of the American University* (New York: Oxford University Press, 2001), for more details of Harvard's admission practices during this period.

9. *The Harvard Admission and Scholarship Committee Report,* 1955–1956, records totals of 3,391 applications in 1952–53 (for entry in the fall of 1953), 3,320 in 1953–54, 3,816 in 1954–55, and 3,623 in 1955–56. By convention, throughout the remainder of this chapter applications are listed for the academic year they were received, meaning that they are for entry to college in the following fall.

10. Elizabeth Duffy and Idana Goldberg, *Crafting a Class: College Admissions and Financial Aid, 1955–1994* (Princeton, N.J.: Princeton University Press, 1998), pp. 35–36.

11. *The Harvard Admission and Scholarship Committee Report,* 1957–1958.

12. *The Harvard Admission and Scholarship Committee Report,* 1952–1953.

13. Duffy and Goldberg, *Crafting a Class*, p. 37.

14. Ibid., p. 36. Duffy and Goldberg document these ratios for ten of the most selective colleges in Massachusetts (Amherst, Williams, Mount Holyoke, Smith, and Wellesley) and Ohio (Denison, Kenyon, Oberlin, Ohio Wesleyan, and the College of Wooster).

15. Ibid., p. 38.

16. These yield figures were documented by Duffy and Goldberg, *Crafting a Class*, for the independent liberal arts colleges and by admission reports for Harvard.

17. In 1954–55, the fifth consecutive year in which Harvard's yield rate languished near 60 percent (its current yield is just under 80 percent), Harvard surveyed the 620 students who turned down its offer of admission to attend another college. About half of those students turned down Harvard to attend one of its five closest competitors—Yale, Princeton, Dartmouth, MIT, and Amherst, in that order (*The Harvard Admission and Scholarship Committee Report*, 1954–1955).

18. Duffy and Goldberg, *Crafting a Class*, p. 39.

19. See, for example, ibid., p. 40, quoting the 1953 Williams College Admissions Report.

20. Ibid., pp. 38–39.

21. Ibid., p. 40.

22. "Colleges Have Chosen, Now Await 'Voting by Prospective Students,'" *Boston Sunday Herald*, May 28, 1961.

23. Ibid.

24. Ibid.

25. Lemann, *The Big Test*, p. 145, suggests that much of the rating was determined by recommendations of headmasters at the feeder schools.

26. These definitions for the ratings are taken from *The Harvard Admission and Scholarship Committee Report*, 1954–1955.

27. *The Harvard Admission and Scholarship Committee Report*, 1955–1956. This yield rate of 69.2% includes all applicants, both those in the A-B-C program and those who were not.

28. *The Harvard Admission and Scholarship Committee Report*, 1954–1955.

29. Ibid.

30. Duffy and Goldberg, *Crafting a Class*, pp 40–41.

31. Catherine R. Rich and Thomas Garrett, eds., *Philosophy and Problems of College Admissions* (Washington, D.C.: Catholic University of America Press, 1963), p. 16.

32. *The Harvard Admission and Scholarship Committee Report*, 1954–1955.

33. Duffy and Goldberg, *Crafting a Class*, p. 41.

34. *The Harvard Admission and Scholarship Committee Report*, 1954–1955.

35. Duffy and Goldberg, *Crafting a Class*, p. 40.

36. Minutes of the Yale Committee on Admissions and Freshman Scholarships, October 26, 1964.

37. Letter dated April 22, 1965, and available in Yale Archives.

38. "Harvard's Admissions Committee Work Load Nearing 'Crisis,'" *Boston Sunday Globe*, April 4, 1965; Fred Glimp, personal interview, August 2000.

39. "Yale's President Raps Harvard on Admissions," *Harvard Crimson*, October 31, 1966.

40. "Harvard's Admissions Committee Work Load Nearing 'Crisis.'"

41. Quoted in "Yale Battles Harvard for Scholars," *Boston Globe*, October 31, 1966. Nicholas Lemann suggests that Yale eliminated the A-B-C program as part of an effort to change the demographics of its class; the percentage of alumni sons in the freshman class at Yale fell in one year from 20 percent to 12 percent (Lemann, *The Big Test*, p. 149).

42. Harvard's admissions deans made a similar argument in a 1998 editorial: William Fitzsimmons, Marlyn Lewis, and James Miller, "Preserving Access in Changing Times," *Harvard Crimson*, March 17, 1998.

43. This quote appears both in "Yale's President Raps Harvard on Admissions" and in "Yale Battles Harvard for Scholars."

44. "Yale's President Raps Harvard on Admissions."

45. Yale Archives, Draft Proposal for National Scholars Program, May 17, 1966.

46. "Yale's President Raps Harvard on Admissions." See also "Yale's Word to Harvard: Fie!" *Boston Sunday Herald*, October 30, 1966.

47. Yale Archives, Draft Proposal.

48. Duffy and Goldberg, *Crafting a Class*, p. 51.

49. Ibid.

50. "Early Decision: The View from Different Perspectives," presentation at National Association for College Admissions Counselors Meeting, October 2000.

51. Worth David, dean of admissions, Yale College, 1972–1992, personal interview, fall 1997.

52. Derek Bok, president of Harvard College, 1971–1991, personal interview, fall 1996.

53. "Harvard Admissions to Start Early Acceptance Next Year," *Harvard Crimson*, February 18, 1976.

54. "College Takes 150 Fewer Early Admits," *Harvard Crimson*, December 14, 1979.

55. "A Cure for Application Fever: Schools Hook More Students with Early-Acceptance Offers," *U.S. News and World Report*, April 23, 1990.

56. James W. Monks and Ronald G. Ehrenberg, "The Impact of *U.S. News and World Report* College Rankings on Admissions Outcomes and Pricing" (Cambridge, Mass.: National Bureau of Economic Research, Working Paper no. 7227, July 1999).

57. Ronald G. Ehrenberg, *Tuition Rising: Why College Costs So Much* (Cambridge, Mass.: Harvard University Press, 2000), p. 52.

58. An Early Decision commitment is enforced informally. Colleges share lists of students admitted under Early Decision with the understanding that once admitted to one college they should not be considered subsequently for admission to other colleges. Chapter 2 provides further details.

59. The Overlap Group included all eight Ivy League colleges, plus MIT and about twenty other selective private colleges.

60. Ehrenberg, *Tuition Rising*, pp. 76–79, provides a detailed account of the Overlap case and how its settlement influenced the nature of financial aid packaging throughout the 1990s.

61. Brown's historical practices are described in an internal administrative report. ("Alper Committee on Financial Aid: Final Report," May 5, 2000, section 3; see *http://www.brown.edu/Administration/President/ACFA/ACFA1.htm*). Brown changed to need-blind admissions in spring 2002 ("Brown Adopts Need-Blind Admissions Rule," *New York Times*, February 24, 2002).

62. Radio interview, "The Battle over Early Decision," *The Connection*, National Public Radio, January 3, 2002 *(http://www.theconnection.org/archive/2002/01/0103b.shtml)*.

63. Warren W. Willingham and Hunter M. Breland, with Richard I. Ferrin and Mary Freun, "The Status of Selective Admissions," in *Selective Admissions in Higher Education: A Report of the Carnegie Commission on Policy Studies in Higher Education* (San Francisco: Jossey Bass Publishers, 1977), p. 82 (emphasis added). COFHE consists of many highly selective, mostly Eastern, colleges. There are currently 31 members of COFHE (see, for example, *http://www.swarthmore.edu/Admin/institutional_research/cofhe.html*). As of 2002–03, 27 of the COFHE schools (including Stanford

and Yale, which will switch to Early Action in 2003–04) offer Early Decision, and the remaining four offer Early Action.

64. "How to Survive the Admissions Maze," *U.S. News and World Report,* October 26, 1987.

65. "Locking Up Students," *U.S. News and World Report,* December 23, 1996.

66. "Colleges Filling More Slots with Those Applying Early," *New York Times,* February 14, 1996, citing statistics from the College Board. The article states that 471 colleges had early admissions programs in 1995–96. Unfortunately, the College Board's current database for early admissions programs dates only to 1997–98, so those figures cannot be verified independently now.

67. *Early Decision/Early Action Summary Report,* National Association for College Admission Counseling, Merrifield, Va., 1997.

68. More than half of the less selective colleges—those with admit rates of 60 percent or less—using Early Action had introduced those programs since 1990, and nearly a quarter of them introduced them between 1994 and 1996. Similarly, just less than half of the moderately selective colleges using Early Decision had introduced those programs within the past five years.

69. "Colleges Filling More Slots with Those Applying Early."

70. Ibid.

71. "The Wisdom of Early Action," *Harvard Crimson,* December 6, 1995; "Record Number Apply Early," *Harvard Crimson,* [date to come].

72. "Acceptance Rate Rises to 19%," *Yale Daily News,* April 17, 1995; "Binding Admissions May Deter Yale Applicants," *Yale Daily News,* October 24, 1995.

73. "Early Apps Decline with New Policy," *Yale Daily News,* November 16, 1995.

74. "Yale Drops Early Action Admissions," *Yale Daily News,* March 1, 1995.

75. "Early Apps Decline with New Policy"; "Crowding Nightmare, How It All Happened," *Yale Daily News,* September 5, 1996.

76. For example, the College Board's database records 1,493 early applicants and 546 early admits for Yale in 1998–99.

77. "College Takes 150 Fewer Early Admits."

78. *Report to the President*, MIT, 1999–2000, http://web.mit.edu/communications/pres00/06.00.html.

79. "New Early Policy Yields Record Admit Numbers," *Brown Daily Herald*, January 26, 2000.

80. "Brown Adopts an Early Decision Policy for Early Applicants," press release, Brown News Office, February 24, 2001.

81. "Ties That Bind: Brown Considers a Change to Early Decision," *George Street Journal*, November 10, 2000.

82. "Yale Proposes That Elite Colleges Abandon Early-Decision Admissions," *New York Times*, December 13, 2001.

83. "The Waiting Game on Early Decision," *Yale Daily News*, April 22, 2002.

84. "Yale Proposes That Elite Colleges Abandon Early-Decision Admissions."

85. "The Battle over Early Decision" *(http://www.theconnection.org/archive/2002/01/0103b.shtml).*

86. University of North Carolina website: *http://www.ais.unc.edu/sis/admissions/uga/ed.html.*

87. "Harvard May Ignore Early Decision," *Harvard Crimson*, June 6, 2002; "Harvard Plans to Sidestep Early Admission Restriction," *Boston Globe*, June 7, 2002, p. A1.

88. "Yale, Stanford to End Binding Early Admissions," AP report, November 7, 2002.

89. "Stanford Joins Yale in Dropping Early Admissions Policy," *Boston Globe*, November 7, 2002.

2. The State of the Game

1. We cross-checked information about early application programs provided in individual college listings in the 2003 *U.S. News College Guide* with the College Board's database for 1999–2000 to compile a list of early application programs in fall 2002. (Where these two sources provide different information about the existence of a program for a given college, we checked that college's website to determine if the school offered an early

application program.) The College Board's database included 1,764 colleges that were listed for both 1998–99 and 1999–2000, but only about 1,400 of these were listed in the *U.S. News College Guide*. Among these 1,400 or so colleges, 460, or approximately one-third, offered early application programs for 2002–03: 196 offered Early Action, 208 offered Early Decision, and 56 offered both programs.

2. That survey of 421 four-year institutions, reported in the January 2002 *NACAC Bulletin*, found that 32.7 percent of private institutions offered Early Decision and 26.8 percent of private colleges offered Early Action. In contrast, the survey found that only 11.4 percent of public institutions offered Early Decision and 8.8 percent of public institutions offered Early Action.

3. For instance, Maryland, Miami (Ohio), and Truman State (Missouri) admit more than half of their entering classes early. According to the College Board's database, Miami (Ohio) admitted 9,069 students in 1999–2000, including 4,581 early admits. Similarly, Maryland admitted 10,340 students in 1999–2000, including 7,526 early admits. Truman State did not report its early application numbers for 1999–2000, but in 1998–99 it admitted 2,226 early applicants—more than half of the 4,000 or so students that it admits on average each year.

4. As we described at the end of Chapter 1, the University of North Carolina announced in April 2002 that it was eliminating its Early Decision program but retaining its Early Action program.

5. This information is based on a comparison of the College Board's databases for the application years 1997–98 and 1998–99. The four colleges that added a program were Dickinson, Lawrence, North Carolina, and Tulane. Dickinson, Lawrence, and North Carolina used Early Decision in 1997–98 and then offered both programs in 1998–99; Tulane used Early Action in 1997–98 and then offered both programs in 1998–99.

6. The NACAC guidelines are published in official NACAC materials and are also listed on the NACAC website *(http://www.nacac.com/downloads/policy_admission_options.pdf)*.

7. Additional text in these Early Action guidelines notes that "the application must be initiated by the student, and not by the institution"; and "Colleges that solicit commitments to offers of Early Action admission and/

or financial assistance prior to May 1 may do so provided those offers include a clear statement that written requests for extensions until May 1 will be granted, and that such requests will not jeopardize a student's status for admission or financial aid."

8. Additional text in these Early Decision guidelines notes that "the application must be initiated by the student, and not by the institution"; "Students should not be encouraged by counselors or institutions to pursue Early Decision solely as a strategy for admission, but instead should utilize this option only if they are very sure of the college they wish to attend"; "Admission offices of postsecondary institutions should communicate promptly and directly to secondary schools all decisions made on their Early Decision applicants"; "A student applying for financial aid must adhere to institutional Early Decision aid application deadlines"; and "An institution may not offer special incentives (such as scholarships, special financial aid, or special housing opportunities) to encourage students to apply under an Early Decision plan."

9. The College Board's Early Decision Plan Agreement is published in *The College Board College Handbook, 2001* (New York: The College Board, 2000), p. 1903.

10. According to the College Board's database, 122 of the 253 colleges with Early Decision programs in 1999–2000 subscribed to the EDPA.

11. According to the College Board's database, 69 of the 253 colleges with Early Decision programs in 1999–2000 reported notification dates that fall after December 15.

12. *The College Board College Handbook, 2001*, p. 15.

13. Gerald Pope and Penny Oberg, personal interviews, June 2001. Pope and Oberg served as co-chairs of a joint committee on behalf of NACAC and the College Board, respectively.

14. For example, several MIT students told us that they had applied early to both MIT and Cal. Tech. However, the Cal. Tech website does not reveal whether this is permissible; we had to call the Cal. Tech admissions office to verify that its Early Action program has always allowed multiple early applications.

15. See Chapter 1 for details.

16. See "Stanford Joins Yale in Dropping Early Admissions Policy,"

Boston Globe, November 7, 2002, for a discussion of the Brown and Princeton policies. In 2001–02, Georgetown stated the following policy on its website: "Students who apply under the Early Action program may apply to other non-binding Early Action programs, but they may not apply to binding Early Decision programs at the same time." In 2002–03, Georgetown softened this rule: . . . "it is our hope that students applying under our Early Action program will not apply at the same time to other binding Early Decision programs since they then would not be free to choose Georgetown if admitted" *(http://www.georgetown.edu/undergrad/admissions/general.html#early).*

17. An incident that came to light in July 2002 underscores the degree to which admissions offices guard the privacy of their decisions. In April 2002, Princeton surreptitiously logged into the Yale admissions database eighteen times and looked at the admissions decisions for eleven regular applicants. When Yale learned of the offense, it notified federal officials, and the FBI began an investigation. "Yale Accuses Princeton of Hacking," AP wire report, July 25, 2002; "F.B.I. to Investigate Princeton Admissions Hacking Incident," *Yale Daily News,* July 26, 2002; "Yale Accuses Princeton of Web Prying," *Boston Globe,* July 26, 2002.

18. Worth David, dean of admissions, Yale College, 1972–1992, personal interview, fall 1997.

19. We compiled the number of colleges offering both Early Decision 1 and Early Decision 2 programs by counting the number of colleges listed with two ED deadlines on the College Board website for 2001–02.

20. *Committee on Undergraduate Admission and Financial Aid, Annual Report 1997–1998,* Stanford University website, *http://www.stanford.edu/dept/facultysenate/archive/1998_1999/reports/106136/106137.html.*

21. Ibid.

22. "First Year Admission," Wesleyan University website: *http://www.admiss.wesleyan.edu/frosh.html.*

23. These priority groups include some highly rated athletes, students of color, sons and daughters of alumni, students from geographically underrepresented areas, and top students from schools with only one application.

24. *The College Board College Handbook,* 2001, p. 15.

25. *Early Decision/Early Action Summary Report,* National Association for College Admission Counseling, Merrifield, Va., 1997.

26. "Harvard May Ignore Early Decision," *Harvard Crimson*, June 6, 2002.

27. It is conceivable that courts would find the sharing of lists of accepted ED applicants to be collusive and illegal. There have been no court cases on this matter, and the legal scholars we consulted disagreed about the legality of the practice.

28. Michele Hernandez, *A Is for Admission: The Insider's Guide to Getting Into the Ivy League and Other Top Colleges* (New York: Warner Books, 1997), p. 218.

29. "Harvard Plans to Sidestep Early Admissions Restriction," *Boston Globe*, June 7, 2002.

30. "Early Decision Policy Clarified," *Harvard Crimson*, July 26, 2002.

31. Bill Paul, *Getting In* (New York: Addison-Wesley, 1995), p. 168. This story dates to a time when Princeton offered Early Action.

32. "Early Action and Early Decision Plans," College Board website, *http://www.collegeboard.com/article/0,1120,4-24-0-104,00.html?orig=sub.*

33. Jean H. Fetter, *Questions and Admissions: Reflections on 100,000 Admissions Decisions at Stanford* (Stanford, Calif.: Stanford University Press, 1995), p. 52.

34. Charles Guerrero, personal interview, spring 2000.

35. All of these numbers are skewed toward early applicants, because we only interviewed students who were attending one of these four highly selective colleges.

36. We identified the per capita income and college-graduation rate for each zip code on the basis of information from the 1990 U.S. Census.

37. In 1998–99 North Carolina State reported 8,468 Early Action applications and Miami University (Ohio) reported 5,843. An additional fifty-four institutions that ranked in the top four tiers in the *U.S. News* rankings for national universities or liberal arts colleges did not report to the College Board the number of applications for their early programs for 1999–2000.

38. Unfortunately the College Board's database dates only to 1997–98, so it is difficult to determine in any systematic fashion the trend in early applications before 1997–98.

39. Part of the increase in early applications in 1999–2000 is due to the large increases in early applications to Brown, Georgetown, Harvard, and MIT, as that was the first year that it was legal to apply Early Action to more

than one of these colleges. Even removing these schools from this calculation, however, Early Action applications still increased considerably from
1997–98 to 1999–2000.

40. The only exception is the University of North Carolina at Chapel
Hill, which did not report its number of Early Decision applications for
1998–99.

41. The two colleges receiving fewer than ten Early Action applications
were Husson College (Maine), Lyndon State College, St. Joseph College
(Connecticut), and the University of Puerto Rico: Aguadilla. The five colleges receiving fewer than ten Early Decision applications were Franklin
College: Switzerland, Massachusetts College of Pharmacy and Health Sciences, University of Judaism, Webb College, and Wesley College.

42. Among the colleges ranked in the top two tiers of national universities or liberal arts colleges by the *U.S. News Guide* in 2001, the thirty-three
institutions that offered Early Action and reported their application numbers to the College Board for 1999–2000 admitted an average of 694 applicants in Early Action and admitted a total of 2,696 applicants overall, for
a percentage of 25.7 admitted early. This calculation excludes two additional schools, Miami (Ohio) and the University of Maryland, which admitted a disproportionate number of early applicants (each admitted more than
4,000 Early Action applicants).

43. Bruce Breimer, personal interviews, spring 1998 and spring 1999.

44. When we compared the numbers reported to us by admissions offices for 1998–99 with the numbers in the College Board's database, we
found a close match for the number of early applications at each college. Upon further inspection, it appeared that none of these institutions
counted its deferred admits in the number of early admits reported to the
College Board.

3. Martian Blackjack

1. After watching all day, the old man discovers the rules: unless the
high score wins by 2, it loses, at least for now.

2. We classified the understanding of subjects on the basis of their responses during a thirty-minute interview. Students with a "good" knowledge

of the process knew the rules of early applications and had considered the possibility that an early application might influence an admissions decision. Students with a "fair" or "poor" knowledge of the process were misinformed about an important element of early applications at the colleges they were considering—hence their high schools were like those invited to participate in the survey.

3. Some students were poorly informed in more than one of these ways, so the overall percentage of students who did not have a full understanding of early applications is less than the sum of these three percentages.

4. While the College Admissions Project ultimately included responses from students from 396 of 500 participating high schools, we classified an additional 300 or so similarly prominent schools as "in the CAP survey" for the purposes of this tabulation.

5. See Ronald G. Ehrenberg, *Tuition Rising: Why College Costs So Much* (Cambridge, Mass.: Harvard University Press, 2000), chapter 4, for further details.

6. The 2002 *U.S. News Guide* switched positions again, citing our research as evidence that it is advantageous to apply early.

7. These were the books available at the Wordsworth Book Store in Harvard Square, Cambridge, Mass., on October 23, 1999.

8. *www.collegeboard.com/article/0,1120,4-24-0-104,00.html?orig=sub.*

9. This guide described Early Action in four bullet points: 1. colleges using EA are very discriminating; 2. Early Action applicants can be rejected as well as deferred; 3. no financial aid awards are given in December (early admits must wait until April for a financial aid package); and 4. applying Early Action does not show interest. Even if applying EA did show interest, *Peterson's* concluded—offering a remarkable observation that we have never heard elsewhere—that "Early Action schools are so competitive, that your desire to attend is not important to them."

10. http://admissions.cornell.edu/apply/firstyear_edp.cfm. This statement has been on Cornell's website since at least 1998–99.

11. Brown announced during the 2001–02 academic year that it was returning to need-blind admissions starting in 2002–03.

12. We also looked at these same websites each year from 1998–99 to the

present. Throughout this period, these colleges maintained similar statements about the effect of applying early.

13. *http://www.upenn.edu/admissions/undergrad/applying/early.html.*

14. These figures exclude applicants to Columbia's School of Engineering and Applied Sciences.

15. See, for example, Ballon's editorial "For Some Students, Early Decision Is Best," Opinion, *New York Times*, December 18, 2001.

16. *http://www.dartmouth.edu/admin/admissions/admissions/early.html.*

17. *http://www.yale.edu/admit/freshmen/application/early_decision.html.*

18. As this quote was highlighted in a variety of public forums in 2001–02, both by us and by others, we thought Princeton might change the statement. But this remained the text as of April 2002.

19. *http://www.princeton.edu/pr/admissions/u/QandA.html.*

20. William Wharton, the headmaster of the Commonwealth School in Boston, suggests an alternate interpretation that might clarify this statement. He believes that the second sentence ("A candidate to whom we otherwise would not offer admission . . .") is directed toward noncompetitive applicants, so that it need not imply that all early admits would also be admitted in the regular process. Further, he interprets the last sentence ("And in part, it's undoubtedly . . .") as a subtly accurate statement that Princeton favors early applicants among the group of students who are broadly qualified for admission.

21. Scotte Gordon, personal interview, spring 2000.

22. See, for example, Thomas J. Kane, "Racial and Ethnic Preferences in College Admissions," in *The Black-White Test Score Gap*, Christopher Jencks and Meredith Phillips, eds. (Washington: Brookings Institute, 1998).

23. Kathy Giles, the college counselor at the Groton School in Massachusetts, offers an alternate explanation. She thinks that colleges withhold information about the difference between early and regular standards for admission in order to preserve the signal of enthusiasm contained in early applications.

24. The students could not always remember which admissions officer made a particular comment, thus some of them might have been remembering comments made by admissions officers at schools other than Harvard.

25. "Early Admission Changes the Rules for College Applicants," *Boston Sunday Globe*, June 15, 1997. In a subsequent phone interview with the authors, Matthews commented that some of the numbers of applications and acceptances in the quoted passage were incorrect, but that his comparison between the results of early and regular applicants still indicated that colleges favored early applicants from St. Paul's over the school's regular applicants.

26. There is substantial overlap between these numbers; more than half of those college students who remembered a high school counselor's saying that applying early would help the chances of admission also said that the high school counselor explicitly encouraged early applications.

27. Phyllis MacKay, personal interview, spring 2000.

28. The Technical Appendix includes the precise language of these questions.

29. Michele Hernandez, *A Is for Admission: The Insider's Guide to Getting Into the Ivy League and Other Top Colleges* (New York: Warner Books, 1997), explains, "Most colleges will talk to applicants, so I definitely recommend that the student call the admissions office himself, ask to speak to the regional officer in charge of his high school, and try to get a sense of what his weaknesses are and if there is any advice the officer would suggest" (pp. 33–34).

30. The percentages in this paragraph are based on the coding of the verbal responses, particularly to question 6 in the interview protocol (see Appendix C).

31. The percentages in this paragraph are based on the answers to the numerical questions in the interview protocol (see Appendix C). We did not include clashes between the verbal and numerical responses of a subject as contradictions when we computed the statistic that 25 percent of subjects made contradictory statements or described themselves during the interview as poorly informed.

32. "Preserving Access in Changing Times," *Harvard Crimson*, March 17, 1998.

33. Radio interview, "The Merrow Report," *National Public Radio*, November 15, 2000 (transcript available at *http://www.pbs.org/merrow/tmr_radio/pgm12/*).

34. Ibid.

35. For example, throughout the 1990s it was acceptable to submit more than one Early Action application if you applied to some pairs of Early Action colleges, but not to others.

4. The Innocents Abroad

This chapter is coauthored with Emily Oster.

1. This ranking is based on the summed scores on three different components of the statewide assessment test, known as the MCAS, given to tenth-graders in 1998. As a school district, Needham placed 10th of 208 districts in aggregate scores for fourth-, eighth-, and tenth-graders. These rankings can be found at the following website: *http://www.boston.com/mcas/index98.shtml*.

2. One difference between the Choate and Needham interviews should be noted, though we do not believe it significantly affects the analysis. The Choate interviews were conducted by a single person, Emily Oster, who graduated from Choate in 1998, one year ahead of the interviewed students. The Needham students, by contrast, were interviewed by several different people during the year, and the interviewers were unknown to them in a social setting.

3. The U.S. Naval Academy is sometimes classified as an Early Action school because it accepts applications as early as August and notifies some students of admission on a rolling basis. Andrew was never officially classified as an early applicant, but he applied in September and was given "Early Notification" of his admission before Thanksgiving, conditional on passing a physical examination.

4. We interviewed these high school students in 1998–99, the last year that Brown, Georgetown, and Harvard stipulated that Early Action applicants could not apply early to any other college. Thus, applicants from both Choate and Needham had to choose a single college if they wanted to apply Early Action to one of these three institutions.

5. According to Terry Giffen, Choate's director of college counseling (personal interview, spring 1998), Choate students who are admitted in Early Action are restricted to no more than three additional applications,

though one of the six such students in the study actually applied to four additional colleges.

6. This ranking is based on admission rates calculated from the College Board's database for 1999–2000.

7. The Morehead Scholarship provides full tuition and expenses for four years of study at North Carolina, amounting to more than $100,000 in funding for out-of-state recipients.

8. Each of these three students was admitted to the less selective colleges early, but deferred and later rejected by the more selective college. All three seemed to prefer the more selective college at the early application deadline.

9. "The American Freshman: National Norms for 2001," summarized in *NACAC Bulletin*, March 2002. Earlier studies such as Charles F. Manski and David A. Wise, with Winship C. Fuller and Steven F. Venti, *College Choice in America* (Cambridge, Mass.: Harvard University Press, 1972), produced similar historical findings.

10. Leon Festinger, *Theory of Cognitive Dissonance* (Evanston, Ill.: Row, Peterson, 1957), introduced the concept of cognitive dissonance to describe mechanisms that people use to rationalize earlier decisions in the aftermath of disappointment. Herbert Simon, *Models of Man: Social and Rational; Mathematical Essays on Rational Human Behavior in a Social Setting* (New York: Wiley, 1957), introduced the concept of "satisficing" to describe behavior in which people seek to get a result that is "good enough" though not necessarily the best.

11. See, for example, "Tipping the Athletic Scale," *Chronicle of Higher Education*, March 8, 2002, vol. 48, issue 26, p. A37.

12. Elinor Adler and Thomas Dorney, Needham High School college counselors, personal interview, May 1998.

13. Daniel Kahneman, Amos Tversky, and Paul Slovic, eds., *Judgment under Uncertainty: Heuristics and Biases* (New York: Cambridge University Press, 1982).

14. Elinor Adler and Thomas Dorney, personal interview, May 1998.

15. Terry Giffen, personal interview, spring 1998.

16. Earlier in the chapter we mentioned that 90 percent of college freshmen in 2000–01 reported that they were attending a first-choice or second-

choice college. Although these numbers are even greater than those for the high school students in our study, they do not suggest that the results should have been even better for those at Choate and Needham. First, the Choate and Needham students in our study were applying to highly selective colleges. Despite their outstanding qualifications, they were more likely to be rejected by their first-choice college than was the average high school student, whose first choice was presumably less selective. Second, once on campus, freshmen are likely to increase their original preference for the college that they are attending.

5. The Truth about Early Applications

1. We list applications according to the academic year they were received, meaning that the data for 1990–91 refers to applications for college entrance in the fall of 1991. We had data for 1990–91 to 1995–96 for ten of the fourteen colleges. For the remaining four colleges, we had data for at least 1991–92 to 1995–96 or 1992–93 to 1996–97.

2. Counselors at public schools selected students at random from the top 10 percent of the senior class, and counselors at private schools selected students at random from the top 20 percent of the senior class.

3. We define minorities according to the categories listed on the Common Application, excluding applicants who identify themselves as "African American, Black," "American Indian, Alaskan Native," "Hispanic, Latino," "Mexican American, Chicano," and "Puerto Rican." It was not always possible to identify each subcategory in the admissions data, and in some cases, a college grouped some of these categories together. We have performed the analysis both excluding and including "Asian" and "Asian American" applicants with little effect on the results; the results reported throughout the book include both categories of Asian applicants. Excluding these applicants would have little effect on our findings. In addition, we excluded foreign citizens who do not have a permanent U.S. visa, since it is difficult to compare the qualifications of these applicants with the qualifications of U.S. applicants (some colleges apply openly different standards to international and domestic applicants). Finally, we excluded applicants who withdrew from consideration before learning any admission decision, applicants

whose materials were incomplete, and a small number of applicants whose records appear to contain errors in coding.

Thomas J. Kane, "Racial and Ethnic Preferences in College Admissions," in Christopher Jencks and Meredith Phillips, eds., *The Black-White Test Score Gap* (Washington, D.C.: Brookings Institute, 1998), finds that the most selective colleges give an advantage to black and Hispanic applicants in admissions decisions that is equivalent to an increase of nearly 400 points on the SAT-1. Similarly, James L. Shulman and William G. Bowen, with Lauren A. Meserve and Roger C. Schonfeld, *The Game of Life: College Sports and Educational Values* (Princeton, N.J.: Princeton University Press, 2001), find that selective colleges favor recruited athletes significantly.

4. This averaging method has a statistical danger; if the colleges are sufficiently different in terms of the strength of their applicants and their standards for admission, then the "average" results may produce false patterns that do not apply to any of them individually. But this danger does not seem to affect the results presented in this chapter. For example, our separate analysis for the fourteen colleges in the admissions office data indicates that each of them significantly favors early applicants in admissions decisions.

5. There is no need to eliminate "hooked applicants" from the sample for regression analysis, since these traits (for example, recruited athlete) can be used as control variables in the regression framework. We performed these regression analyses in two ways: (1) for the full sample, using characteristics such as "alumni child" and "recruited athlete" as additional control variables; (2) for the restricted sample. The results are substantially the same for each of these methods. The text reports the results from method (1), using the full sample.

6. "Colleges Filling More Slots with Those Applying Early," *New York Times*, February 14, 1996.

7. *http://www.brown.edu/Administration/Admission/guidance.html*.

8. *http://adm-is.fas.harvard.edu/Eareg.htm*.

9. The average scores are somewhat higher for survey participants than for the students in the admissions office data in Figures 5.1 and 5.2. This difference reflects the fact that the survey only selected very good students from very good high schools to participate.

10. This group of fourteen colleges overlapped to some degree with the set of fourteen colleges in the admissions office data, but the two sets of schools are far from identical. A fifteenth college, Rice University, also received more than thirty early applications from survey participants, but it was excluded from more detailed analysis because it offered both Early Action and Early Decision, and we could not distinguish between applicants of these two programs at Rice.

11. These calculations, once again, refer to the restricted sample of applicants, as described in note 3 above.

12. "Early Admissions Change the Rules for College Applicants," *Boston Globe*, June 15, 1997.

13. Michele A. Hernandez, *A Is for Admission: The Insider's Guide to Getting Into the Ivy League and Other Top Colleges* (New York: Warner Books, 1997), p. 31.

14. We count early applicants who were deferred and admitted as "[early] admits" in all calculations throughout the chapter.

15. See Appendix 2 at the end of the book for details about how we measured high school quality and extracurricular accomplishments.

16. Slightly more than half of the applicants fell into these seven rating categories.

17. These twenty-eight colleges consisted of eight Early Action colleges (Boston College, Brown, Cal. Tech, Georgetown, Harvard, MIT, Notre Dame, and the University of Chicago) and twenty Early Decision colleges (Amherst, Columbia, Cornell, Dartmouth, Duke, Middlebury, NYU, Northwestern, Penn, Princeton, Stanford, Swarthmore, Tufts, Vassar, Virginia, Washington University, Wellesley, Wesleyan, Williams, and Yale). We omit from this analysis six additional colleges that received at least ten early applications from survey participants. We omit North Carolina and Rice because they offered both Early Action and Early Decision, and we cannot be certain which early program each participant applied to at these colleges. We also omit four additional colleges: University of Florida, Georgia Tech, University of Illinois at Urbana-Champaign, and University of Maryland because each admitted more than 90 percent of survey applicants. All sixty-two applicants to the University of Florida from the College Admissions Project were admitted.

18. See *http://www.brown.edu/Administration/Admission/faq.html*.

19. See *http://adm-is.fas.harvard.edu/Eareg.html.*

20. Michael Robinson and James Monks, "Making SAT Scores Optional in Selective College Admissions," mimeo, 2002. Robinson and Monks studied the entire freshman class that entered Mount Holyoke College in fall 2001. Among the students in that class, Robinson and Monks found that early applicants were predicted to have a grade-point average 0.03 higher than regular applicants with similar academic credentials and demographic backgrounds. This difference in predicted GPA for early and regular applicants was not statistically significant. In comparison, a gain of one rating point in the admissions office's academic rating, which runs from 1 to 9, has a statistically significant effect of approximately 0.20 in predicted GPA—nearly seven times the effect of applying Early Decision. Similarly, students who chose not to submit their SAT scores to Mount Holyoke, the central focus of the study, had GPAs as much as 0.15 below the level that would be predicted on the basis of their characteristics other than SAT score. That is, not submitting an SAT score had a negative predicted effect as much as four times the effect of applying Early Decision.

21. It is also possible that the admissions office ratings are biased in favor of early applicants relative to regular applicants—as the theory of cognitive dissonance might suggest they would be, given that early applicants are admitted at higher rates than regular applicants. More generally, the determination of the rating may be a projection of the admissions outcome rather than an absolute standard for comparing candidates on an equal basis. If so, the admissions office ratings would actually exaggerate the attractiveness of early applicants, meaning that the advantage of applying early is even larger than our analysis of the admissions office ratings suggests.

22. "Preserving Access in Changing Times," *Harvard Crimson*, March 17, 1998.

23. In general, the 5 percent significance level has become the norm—this is used as a standard significance level in most instances. Occasionally, 1 percent might be used as a significance level in a case where very convincing evidence is desired (so that we would require results that would ordinarily occur less than 1 time in 100 rather than 1 time in 20 to proclaim statistical significance). A significance level of 0.1 percent is the most extreme level that we have ever seen employed in social science research.

24. A comparison between the results at Dartmouth and Harvard illus-

trates the workings of statistical significance. The observed effect for early applicants is greater at Dartmouth than at Harvard, but there are somewhat fewer applicants to Dartmouth (224 applicants) than to Harvard (402 applicants) in this analysis. This difference in number of applications explains why the results for Dartmouth are not as statistically significant as the results for Harvard.

25. We emphasize that we chose the coefficients in the regression equation strictly for illustrative purposes. They do not reflect any of the actual regression equations that we estimated in the course of our data analysis.

6. The Game Revealed

1. "Early Decision: The View from Different Perspectives," presentation at National Association for College Admissions Counselors Meetings, October 2000.

2. Robert Klitgaard, *Choosing Elites* (New York: Basic Books, 1985), p. 26.

3. Robin Mamlet, personal interview, spring 1997. Mamlet made clear that this was not her practice at Swarthmore; nor did she think that the most selective colleges needed to use Early Decision in this manner.

4. Elizabeth Duffy and Idana Goldberg, *Crafting a Class: College Admissions and Financial Aid, 1955–1994* (Princeton, N.J.: Princeton University Press, 1999).

5. "Crowding Nightmare: How It All Happened," *Yale Daily News*, September 5, 1996.

6. "At Cornell Medical: Stay Away One Year and Get One Free," *New York Times*, August 13, 1996.

7. Some colleges have changed their attitudes toward their waiting lists in recent years. Waiting lists provide colleges and universities with a device comparable to early admission for managing yield and selectivity. Many institutions, such as Wesleyan, only count a student offered a position from the waiting list as admitted if the student accepts the offer of admission. That sly accounting practice guarantees a yield of 100 percent for students who enroll from the waiting list, boosting the college's apparent statistical performance. Partly in response, in the 1990s Wesleyan planned to admit

thirty to fifty students, or 4 to 7 percent of its entering class, from the waiting list each year. This practice provided additional insurance against over-enrollment; in a year when an unusually high proportion of admitted students selected Wesleyan, the school could still achieve its targeted class size by reducing the number admitted from the waiting list.

8. When 2,000 students make independent enrollment decisions and each has a 50 percent chance of selecting the college, then the average enrollment is 1,000. With this many students admitted, the actual enrollment is approximately given by a Normal distribution with standard deviation of about 22 students. In this case, enrollment of 1,050 or more (which represents a result of at least 2.24 standard deviations above the mean in a Normal distribution) occurs about 1.3 percent of the time.

9. Half the time there is actually an expected yield of 52 percent rather than 50 percent. In this case, the average enrollment is 1,040 students ($2,000 \times 0.52 = 1,040$), so that enrollment of 1,050 represents only 10 students, or 0.44 standard deviations above the norm. (The standard deviation in enrollment remains about 22 students.) A result of at least 0.44 standard deviations more than the average result occurs about 33 percent of the time in a Normal distribution. The combination of events (true yield of 52 percent *and* more than 0.54 standard deviations above the mean in actual enrollment) occurs a bit more than 16 percent of the time (50% × 33%).

10. *The College Board College Handbook,* 2002 edition, p. 16.

11. We presume that these percentages refer to the percentage of students in each pool who apply for financial aid.

12. Ronald G. Ehrenberg, *Tuition Rising: Why College Costs So Much* (Cambridge, Mass.: Harvard University Press, 2000), chapter 5, provides a more detailed account of the decision by some colleges, such as Brown, to abandon purely need-blind policies.

13. Brown changed its policy to need-blind admissions in the spring of 2002; "Brown Adopts Need-Blind Admissions Rule," *New York Times,* February 24, 2002.

14. Advisory Committee on University Planning Meeting (October 18, 1999). A report in this meeting estimated that the number of students receiving institutional support at Brown could rise from 38 percent to 50 percent with a need-blind policy, an increase of about 30 percent over the cur-

rent rate. The minutes of the meeting are available at the following website: *http://www.brown.edu/Administration/Provost/acup101899.html.*

15. *Alper Committee on Financial Aid, Final Report* (May 5, 2000), section 5. The report is available at the following website: *http://www.brown.edu/Administration/President/ACFA/ACFA1.htm.* The report explains, "For the Classes of 1998–2001, the Office of Admission estimated the cost of moving to a need-blind policy by running a parallel process that simulated 'admitting' a class 'need-blind.' In those years, the cost estimates, to admit four classes on a similar basis, ranged from $3.2 million to $6 million." The report cited an upper-end estimate of $8 million to include the additional cost of a recession in implied financial need for admitting students.

16. Personal interview with William Fitzsimmons and Marlyn Lewis, October 1996. Many academic authors have studied the importance of the antitrust case. Caroline Hoxby, "Benevolent Colluders? The Effect of Antitrust Action on College Financial Aid and Tuition" (Cambridge, Mass.: National Bureau of Economic Research, Working Paper no. 7754, 1999), provides a systematic analysis of changes in financial aid practices resulting from the end of the Overlap agreement; see also Gordon C. Winston, "Subsidies, Hierarchy and Peers: The Awkward Economics of Higher Education," *Journal of Economic Perspectives,* 13:1 (Winter 1999), pp. 13–36, and Ehrenberg, *Tuition Rising,* chapter 5. Michael S. McPherson and Morton Owen Schapiro, *The Student Aid Game: Meeting Need and Rewarding Talent in American Higher Education* (Princeton, N.J.: Princeton University Press, 1998), provide a more general overview; see also Michael S. McPherson and Morton Owen Schapiro, "Reinforcing Stratification in American Higher Education: Some Disturbing Trends" (Williamstown, Mass.: Williams College mimeograph, June 2000). Charles T. Clotfelter, *Buying the Best: Cost Escalation in Elite Higher Education* (Princeton, N.J.: Princeton University Press, 1996), highlights the growing gap in tuition between public and private institutions, emphasizing (see especially chapter 3) that colleges account carefully for the effect of changes in their tuition and financial aid policies on the flow of future applications.

17. "Many Top Students Bargain and Often Get More Financial Aid," *Boston Globe,* June 12, 2002, p. A1. Ehrenberg reports a similar finding for 1997–98. That year, 800 students who had been admitted to Carnegie

Mellon faxed other (higher) financial aid offers to Carnegie Mellon, and it responded by increasing its offer to 460 of them (Ehrenberg, *Tuition Rising*, p. 78).

18. These practices were documented by Ehrenberg, *Tuition Rising*, p. 86. See also "Expensive Lesson: Colleges Manipulate Financial Aid Offers, Shortchanging Many," *Wall Street Journal*, April 1, 1996, and "The New Economics of Higher Education," *New York Times*, April 27, 1997.

19. David Hawkins and Kerry Cunningham, "Admissions Trend Update," *NACAC Bulletin*, January 2002.

20. It is not clear how colleges that use early admissions to limit financial aid would respond if such programs were curtailed. They might expand aid; alternatively, they might maintain aid levels by denying more requests or by admitting fewer financial aid applicants.

21. Carlene Riccelli, personal interview, spring 1998.

22. Nancy Beane, personal interview, spring 1998.

23. This program was described in both the 1997 and the 1999 *U.S. News Guide*. In 2002–03, Franklin and Marshall's website offered a different financial incentive to Early Decision applicants: "Assurance of Aid to Meet Need: You are assured that your demonstrated financial need will be met in full with financial aid" (*http://www.fandm.edu/departments/admission/apply/early_decision.html*). Franklin and Marshall also offers an "Early Read of Financial Aid" to early applicants, as well as access to school facilities to early admits before they enroll.

24. The NACAC guidelines are available on the NACAC website: *http://www.nacac.com/downloads/policy_admission_options.pdf*.

25. James W. Monks and Ronald G. Ehrenberg, "The Impact of *U.S. News and World Report*" (1999). "College Rankings on Admissions Outcomes and Pricing Decisions at Selective Private Institutions," *National Bureau of Economic Research Working Paper*, no. 7227 (July 1999).

26. Patricia McDonough, Anthony Lising Antonio, Mary Beth Walpole, and Leonor Perez, "College Rankings: Democratized College Knowledge for Whom?" *Research in Higher Education*, 39 (1998): 513–537. These authors defined "highest selectivity colleges" as those with a median freshman SAT score of 1300 or above and "high selectivity colleges" as those where the median freshman SAT score falls between 1000 and 1300.

27. See Ehrenberg, *Tuition Rising*, chapter 4, for further details about

the ranking process used by *U.S. News*, and the degree to which colleges respond to manipulate their own rankings.

28. "Early Decision: The View from Different Perspectives," presentation at National Association for College Admissions Counselors Meetings, October 2000.

29. Peter W. Cookson, Jr., and Caroline Hodges Persell, *Preparing for Power: America's Elite Boarding Schools* (New York: Basic Books, 1985), p. 175.

30. Worth David, dean of admissions, Yale College, 1972–92, personal interview, fall 1997.

31. "Glass Floor: How Colleges Reject the Top Applicants and Boost Their Status," *Wall Street Journal*, May 29, 2001.

32. Ibid.

33. Carol Katz, personal interview, spring 1998.

34. "Pushy Parents and Other Tales of the Admissions Games," *Chronicle of Higher Education*, October 6, 2000.

35. Steven Singer, personal interview, spring 1998.

36. Larry Momo, personal interview, spring 1998.

37. Leslie Miles, personal interview, June 2001.

38. Michelle Hernandez, *A Is for Admission: The Insider's Guide to Getting Into the Ivy League and Other Top Colleges* (New York: Warner Books, 1997), p. 33.

39. Historical figures are from Worth David, personal interview, October 1997. Information about "automatic deferrals" is from "Colleges Shut a Door to Early Applicants," *Boston Globe*, February 11, 2001.

40. "Colleges Shut a Door to Early Applicants."

41. Worth David, personal interview, fall 1997. For example, Harvard rejected 224, or 15 percent, of its 1,458 early applicants in 1979–1980 ("College Takes 150 Fewer Early Admits," *Harvard Crimson*, December 14, 1979).

42. Worth David, personal interview, fall 1997.

43. "Some Saying 'No' Sooner to Their Early Applicants," *New York Times*, December 25, 1996.

44. "Colleges Shut a Door to Early Applicants."

45. All of our figures on deferred applicants for 1999–2000, both in Fig-

ure 6.1 and in the text, were reported to us in phone conversations with admissions offices in the summer of 2000.

46. "Colleges Shut a Door to Early Applicants."

47. "Moments of Truth Come by Mail for Seniors at Great Neck South," *New York Times*, April 19, 1984.

48. David Karen, "Who Gets Into Harvard?: Selection and Exclusion at an Elite College" (Ph.D. diss., Harvard University, 1985).

49. Cookson and Persell, *Preparing for Power*, pp. 167–168.

50. Ibid., pp. 174–177.

51. Ibid. Cookson and Persell, citing earlier research by Coleman and others, estimate that the average caseload for public school counselors is 323.

52. Ibid., p. 183.

53. Ibid., p. 182. Cookson and Persell claim that private schools began to suppress information about class rank when they realized that most of their students were in the top 25 percent of their previous public school classes. They felt that the class ranking was thus unfair to students below the average in their classes because these students would likely have had significantly higher class rankings had they stayed at their previous schools.

54. Eileen Blattner, personal interview, spring 1998.

55. Rory Bled, personal interview, spring 1998.

56. Steven Singer, personal interview, spring 1998.

57. "Glass Floor: How Colleges Reject the Top Applicants and Boost Their Status."

58. Eileen Blattner, college counselor, Shaker Heights High School (Ohio), personal interview, spring 1998.

59. One of our research assistants believes that she was admitted to a particular college because her counselor was retiring, and without a next year to worry about, the counselor was willing to express excess enthusiasm about her students, in effect "cashing in" her long-time reputation.

60. Phyllis MacKay, college counselor, Oyster River High School, personal interview, spring 1998.

61. Eileen Blattner, personal interview, spring 1998.

62. Bruce Breimer added that he is not certain if the rule would stand up to legal scrutiny; no one has ever challenged it.

63. This exception was explained to us by a student who applied Early Action to Princeton and then to Stanford at the regular deadline. This practice created some confusion; another Exeter student told us that she was not allowed to apply to Stanford after applying Early Action to Yale. Whatever the historical practice of Exeter, this question is moot now that Stanford has adopted Early Decision.

64. The negative inference, not always caught, is that if Singer is silent, then the Early Action admit has not applied to other schools and will be accepting the offer of admission.

65. Cookson and Persell, *Preparing for Power*, p. 169.

66. As mentioned in the Introduction, Patricia McDonough, Anthony Lising Antonio, Mary Beth Walpole, and Leonor Perez, "College Rankings: Democratized College Knowledge for Whom?" *Research in Higher Education*, 39 (1998): 513–537, report an estimate that students and their families spend $400 million on college-preparatory products each year.

67. Harry Payne, "In My View: The Problematic Rush to Early Decision," *Alumni Review*, Williams College, Winter 1999.

68. These percentages do not add up to 100 because of rounding.

69. Larry Momo, personal interview, spring 1998.

70. Terry Giffen, college counselor, Choate Rosemary Hall, personal interview, spring 1998.

71. Kathy Giles, college counselor, Groton School, personal interview, spring 1998.

72. "Inside the Meritocracy Machine," *New York Times Magazine*, April 28, 1996.

73. This comparison was relevant when we conducted our interviews, but as of 2001–02, Brown has switched from Early Action to Early Decision.

74. Darva Conger achieved her fifteen minutes of fame as the bride on the infamous "Who Wants to Marry a Millionaire" television show. The quote is from "Early Admissions Madness," *Time Magazine College Guide* 2001.

75. Hernandez, *A Is for Admission*, p. 33.

76. A recent *Boston Globe* article ("Many Top Students Bargain and Often Get More Financial Aid," *Boston Globe*, June 12, 2002, p. A1) cited one private counselor who said that he advises all his students to appeal their

financial aid awards once they have been admitted to two or more colleges as regular applicants. About half of them receive increases in their financial aid packages, with the increase ranging from $500 to $5,000 for the freshman year.

77. Bruce Breimer, personal interview, spring 1998. More recently, in September 2002, Breimer noted that he is no longer so categorical in counseling strong minority candidates to avoid Early Decision; the continuing trend toward early applications has caused him to soften his view.

78. "Early Admissions Change the Rules for College Applicants," *Boston Globe*, June 15, 1997.

79. *http://www.princeton.edu/pr/aid/estim.shtml.*

80. One of the worries expressed by counselors such as Nancy Beane is that even if colleges give Early Decision admits a financial aid package based on a standard formula, those ED admits will still get less financial aid than regular admits—that is, regular admits may gain more financial aid through negotiations or merit scholarships because the college is eager to entice them to enroll.

81. Larry Momo, personal interview, spring 1998.

82. Payne, "The Problematic Rush to Early Decision."

7. Advice to Applicants

1. Charles Clotfelter and Jacob Vigdor, "Retaking the SAT," *Journal of Human Resources* (forthcoming). Critics of the *U.S. News* rating system, such as Ronald Ehrenberg, often assert that colleges use the most generous method of computing SAT scores because that will improve the median SAT score of the entering class, which is one factor in the *U.S. News* ranking.

2. A great advantage of well-connected high schools, as we emphasized in Chapter 4, is that they keep close records of the applications and outcomes of past graduates. This allows current applicants to gauge the range of colleges where they are most likely to be admitted and also the set of colleges where they are unlikely to be admitted.

3. We omit colleges from Table 7.2 if they did not report an interquartile range for SAT-1 scores to the College Board for 1999–2000.

4. The median SAT-1 scores in Table 7.2 are computed by taking the

average of the interquartile range (the twenty-fifth percentile and the seventy-fifth percentile of SAT-1 scores for the current students at a college) reported by colleges to the College Board in 1999–2000. Note that the median SAT figures reported in these tables refer to all freshmen at these colleges (these numbers do not refer to students in the survey data—those who participated in the College Admissions Project).

5. Thomas J. Kane, "Racial and Ethnic Preferences in College Admissions," in Christopher Jencks and Meredith Phillips, eds., *The Black-White Test Score Gap* (Washington, D.C.: Brookings Institute, 1998).

6. See, for example, James L. Shulman and William G. Bowen, with Lauren A. Meserve and Roger C. Schonfeld, *The Game of Life: College Sports and Educational Values* (Princeton, N.J.: Princeton University Press, 2001), for information about the advantages given to recruited athletes in the admissions process.

7. The odds are not much worse, because less than half of the applicants fall into these priority categories at most colleges.

8. The interquartile range reported in the *U.S. News Guide* and other college guides slightly underestimates the twenty-fifth percentile for total SAT-1 scores and slightly overestimates the seventy-fifth percentile for total SAT-1 scores. The reason is that these interquartile numbers are calculated by summing the twenty-fifth percentile score for the SAT-1 verbal section and the twenty-fifth percentile score for the SAT-1 mathematical section to get the twenty-fifth percentile for the total SAT-1 score. If all students were equally strong or weak on these two sections, then this calculation would be exactly correct, for the student at the twenty-fifth percentile on the verbal section would also score at the twenty-fifth percentile on the math section and fall at the twenty-fifth percentile for total score. But the student who scored at the twenty-fifth percentile on the verbal section is likely to have scored somewhat above the twenty-fifth percentile on the math section, meaning that the twenty-fifth percentile of total scores should be somewhat greater than the sum of the two twenty-fifth percentile scores. By similar reasoning, the seventy-fifth percentile of total scores should be somewhat less than the sum of the two seventy-fifth percentile scores. For example, applicants to Harvard in the College Admissions Project had an interquartile range of (690, 770) for the SAT-1 verbal section and an interquartile range

of (700, 790) for the SAT-1 math section. The sum of these individual numbers would give an interquartile range of (1390, 1560) for total SAT-1 score for these applicants, but the actual interquartile range for these applicants was (1410, 1530).

9. Michele A. Hernandez, A *Is for Admission: The Insider's Guide to Getting Into the Ivy League and Other Top Colleges* (New York: Warner Books, 1997), p. 32.

10. In addition, these numbers are probably slight overestimates of your chances with an SAT score of 1200 since they are based on results for students with SAT scores in the range of 1200 to 1290.

11. Remember, most Early Action colleges now permit you to apply EA to other colleges as well.

12. If you attend a high school that limits regular applications once students have been admitted in Early Action, you might want to approach the process as though every early program is Early Decision.

13. *http://www.nyu.edu/ugadmissions/uga/apply/apply.html?1.*

14. Some readers will observe that you could send such a letter to more than one college. We do not recommend taking such a chance. You may "get away with it" and improve your chances of admission at more than one college. But if you are caught, you risk angering the colleges where you have applied, and you may lose your chance of admission entirely.

15. Hernandez, A *Is for Admission*, p. 34.

16. This assumption of independence simplifies the calculation dramatically but is probably somewhat unrealistic. For example, Albert might be admitted to Stanford because his essay is outstanding, but that would also likely improve his chances of admission to Penn.

17. Another simplification in this calculation is that it does not allow for the possibility that an Early Decision applicant could be deferred and admitted from the regular pool.

18. See John S. Hammond, Ralph L. Keeney, and Howard Raiffa, *Smart Choices: A Practical Guide to Making Better Decisions* (Boston, Mass.: Harvard Business School Press, 1999), for further information on this topic.

19. Here, a score of 8 means that he puts the same value on (1) a certainty of being admitted to Stanford only; and (2) an 80 percent chance of

being admitted to both colleges and a 20 percent chance of being admitted to neither of them.

Conclusion

1. The current set of deadlines often does not work so well for students as it does for colleges, since the notification date for early admissions programs and the submission deadlines for regular decision are so close. Most students must begin their applications to other schools well before they learn whether they have been admitted to the early admission school.

2. "How to Get Your Kid into Princeton," *New Jersey Monthly Magazine,* December 1996.

3. "The Early Decision Racket," *Atlantic Monthly,* September 2001.

4. See "Binding Admissions May Deter Yale Applicants," *Yale Daily News,* October 24, 1995. Brown moved to Early Decision in 2001, allegedly to spread the admissions workload. Harvard is highly unlikely to do so in the foreseeable future. Its admissions directors are passionate in their views that Early Action is preferable to Early Decision. (See, for example, "Preserving Access in Changing Times," *Harvard Crimson,* March 17, 1998.) Harvard may also derive benefits in competition with its Ivy League rivals because it is the only one of them that continues to offer Early Action.

5. "Yale Changes Its Approach to Admissions," *New York Times,* November 7, 2002.

6. "The Early Decision Racket."

7. Ibid.

8. Our Prisoners' Dilemma formulation assumed equally matched colleges. A different result would occur if college 1 is substantially more attractive than college 2. Then college 1 would prefer that both schools have Early Action, since it will then end up with most of the best students. College 2, however, would prefer that both have Early Decision, which would likely lead some of the best students to apply Early Decision to college 2, fearing that they would not be admitted to college 1. The game-theory equilibrium would likely have college 1 offering Early Action (since most applicants prefer college 1, college 1 does not need to require them to make a

binding commitment through Early Decision) and college 2 offering Early Decision, its best means for combating college 1's advantage in appeal.

9. This argument is slightly oversimplified, for the Nonpartisans may gain somewhat at the expense of the Partisans by applying early—if enough Nonpartisans apply early, that waters down the signal of the Partisans and may also take some prime admissions slots from them.

10. Personal interview, spring 1998.

11. Indeed, two of the Choate students who did not apply early explained that they had attended the Choate Abroad program, one in the spring of junior year and the other in the fall of senior year.

12. This quotation is taken from Harvard's "Early Action Statement," available at the following website: *http://adm-is.fas.harvard.edu/Eareg.htm.*

13. See, for example, Alvin E. Roth, "The Evolution of the Labor Market for Medical Interns and Residents: A Case Study in Game Theory," *Journal of Political Economy*, 92 (1984), pp. 991–1016; Susan Mongell and Alvin E. Roth, "Sorority Rush as a Two-Sided Matching Mechanism," *American Economic Review*, vol. 81 (June 1991), pp. 441–464; and Alvin E. Roth and Xiaolin Xing, "Jumping the Gun: Imperfections and Institutions Related to the Timing of Market Transactions," *American Economic Review*, 84 (September 1994), pp. 992–1044.

14. "Yale Moves to Early Action for 2008," *Yale Daily News*, November 7, 2002. The headline refers to students admitted in 2003–04 for Yale's class of 2008.

15. "The Early Decision Racket."

16. Ibid.

17. "Yale Moves to Early Action for 2008." Administrators at Stanford, including its president, John Hennessey, provided similar explanations for Stanford's decision. See "Yale, Stanford to End Binding Early Admissions," AP report, November 7, 2002.

18. See "Yale, Stanford to End Early Decision Policy," *Harvard Crimson*, November 7, 2002; "The Early Decision Racket."

19. "Yale Moves to Early Action for 2008."

20. Roth, "The Evolution of the Labor Market."

21. Students complete a set of standardized forms, choose six programs

for application, and provide all of this information to the UCAS, which then submits their applications. The UCAS keeps track of the offers of admission for each student and makes certain that no applicant holds more than two offers at any time, but it does not take the extra step of matching students and colleges by comparing their preferences. The UCAS website, *www.ucas.ac.uk*, provides further information about its rules and practices.

22. The colleges, even if they wished, could not have a uniform financial aid formula since that was barred by the settlement of the Overlap case. The United States medical match does not have to contend with these problems because salaries are set by position in advance of the match.

23. England is able to avoid this problem because most of its financial aid is allocated through national programs.

24. "Early Decision: The View from Different Perspectives."

25. Letter from an admissions dean to Bruce Breimer, personal interview, spring 1998.

26. Nancy Beane, college counselor, Westminster Schools (Ga.), personal communication, spring 1998.

27. Joanna Schultz, director of college counseling, the Ellis School (Pa.), "The Early Decision Racket."

28. "The Early Decision Racket."

29. "Ivies Differ on Limiting Early Admittance," *Yale Daily News*, February 11, 1999.

30. These figures are based on the College Board's database for 1997–98. The yield rates are based on all admitted applicants, including early applicants.

31. Forty-seven of the fifty-one colleges ranked as the "Best Liberal Arts Colleges" in the *U.S. News* ranking, including all of the top twenty-five in the list, offer Early Decision. Four of these colleges (Centre College, DePauw, Dickinson, and Wabash) offer both Early Action and Early Decision. Among the four colleges in this list that do not offer Early Decision, three (Bard College, Colorado College, and Willamette) offer Early Action and one (Illinois Wesleyan) has no early program.

32. Karl Furstenberg, the dean of admissions at Dartmouth, explained: "We are each obligated to make those decisions individually. Any concerted action with regard to admissions would seem inappropriate. The only ac-

tion we are allowed to take in a concerted effort has to do with athletics" ("The Waiting Game on Early Decision," *Yale Daily News*, April 22, 2002). See also "Yale Seeks Approval for Early Admissions Pact," *Yale Daily News*, May 6, 2002; and "Stanford Joins Yale in Dropping Early Admissions Policy," *Boston Globe*, November 7, 2002.

33. "Yale Moves to Early Action for 2008."

34. Christopher Avery, Christine Jolls, Richard A. Posner, and Alvin E. Roth, "The Market for Federal Judicial Law Clerks," *University of Chicago Law Review*, 68: 3 (Summer 2001), pp. 793–902.

35. This incident actually happened after the NCAA dropped Pick-Em Day, but before it instituted a formal qualifying system.

36. Roth and Xing, "Jumping the Gun."

37. Alvin E. Roth. "A Natural Experiment in the Organization of Entry Level Labor Markets: Regional Markets for New Physicians and Surgeons in the U.K.", *American Economic Review*, vol. 81 (June 1991), pp. 415–440.

38. "Yale Will No Longer Require Early Applicants to Commit to Attend," news release, Yale Office of Undergraduate Admissions, November 6, 2002 *(http://www.yale.edu/admit/freshmen/news/earlyaction.html)*.

39. The college would have somewhat less power in this situation than with a formal Early Decision program, because it would not be allowed to contact other colleges to ensure that the student withdraws all her other applications.

40. Roth and Xing, "Jumping the Gun."

41. In 1997–98, only about 15 percent of Collegiate graduates applied early to college. In the last five years, that number has grown to about one-third, though this is still a relatively small number compared with some of the other private high schools in New York (Bruce Breimer, personal interviews, spring 1998 and September 2002).

42. "Glass Floor: How Colleges Reject the Top Applicants and Boost Their Status," *Wall Street Journal*, May 29, 2001.

43. Leslie Miles, personal interview, May 2001.

44. This argument has been made in a number of popular articles and books. See, for example, Ronald G. Ehrenberg, *Tuition Rising: Why College Costs So Much* (Cambridge, Mass.: Harvard University Press, 2000); Nicholas Thompson, "Playing with Numbers," *Washington Monthly*, Sep-

tember 2000; "The Early Decision Racket"; and Amy Graham and Nicholas Thompson, "Broken Ranks," *Washington Monthly*, September 2002.

45. The main components of the student selectivity rating are the standardized test scores and the high school class rank of incoming students.

46. For example, Amy Graham, the former director of data research at *U.S. News*, and the journalist Nicholas Thompson have advocated for a ranking system that emphasizes studies of student satisfaction at different colleges. See "Broken Ranks" at *http://www.washingtonmonthly.com/features/2001/0109.graham.thompson.html*.

47. Of course, a de-emphasis on admissions statistics in the selectivity rating would mean that greater weight would then be placed on test scores and class-rank statistics. It is possible that this change would lead colleges to overemphasize those figures in admissions decisions, but we believe that the net effect of the change would be positive. As it is, colleges have an extra incentive to admit both students with high test scores and students who are most likely to enroll—eliminating admissions statistics from the rating would eliminate one set of pernicious incentives entirely.

48. "Early Decision: The View from Different Perspectives," presentation at National Association for College Admissions Counselors Meeting, October 2000.

49. Radio interview, "The Battle over Early Decision," National Public Radio, *The Connection*, January 3, 2002 *(http://www.theconnection.org/archive/2002/01/0103b.shtml)*.

50. These calculations are based on the figures in the 2001 *U.S. News Guide*.

51. "The Battle over Early Decision."

52. This letter was responding to the article "Playing with Numbers." The letter is available on the *Washington Monthly* website: *http://www.washingtonmonthly.com/features/2000/norc.cary.html*; the article can be found at *http://www.washingtonmonthly.com/features/2000/0009.thompson.html*.

53. Charles Clotfelter and Jacob Vigdor, "Retaking the SAT" (Durham, N.C.: Sanford Institute of Public Policy Working Paper, Duke University, July 2001).

54. In the fall of 2001, the highly regarded U.S. accounting profession suffered a severe blow when the Enron–Arthur Andersen scandal came to

light. In the year that followed, accounting scandals emerged at a number of other major firms, and Arthur Andersen collapsed completely. Despite these disturbances, the U.S. financial system still runs on certified accounting information that is overwhelmingly regarded as accurate.

55. The gain to the college in improving yield and selectivity would be the same as for round 1; the enthusiasm advantage would be somewhat less than for round 1.

56. "Early Decision: The View from Different Perspectives."

57. Louis D. Brandeis, *Other People's Money and How the Bankers Use It* (New York: Stokes, 1914), p. 92.

Early Admissions 2004

1. "Pressure is on Early Admissions," *USA Today*, December 8, 2003.

2. At the time, they all just referred to the program as "Early Action."

3. The rankings still consider acceptance rate, the percentage of applicants admitted by a college. Increasing the number of early admits helps a college's score for both yield and acceptance rate because it increases the percentage of admitted students who will enroll and reduces the number of students who need to be admitted to fill the entering class. The rankings thus still provide an incentive for colleges to favor early applicants.

4. http://www.usnews.com/usnews/edu/college/rankings/about/cofaq _brief.php#this

5. See, for example, http://www.gwu.edu/~action/2004/edwards/ edw112102sp.html, which contains the text of Edwards's November 21, 2002 speech on education policy.

6. http://www.nacac.com/downloads/earlydecision.pdf; http://www .aacrao.org/federal_relations/position/kennedy.htm; http://www.acenet.edu/washington/letters/2003/09sept/Kennedy_HEA.cfm

7. The application numbers cited in the text for 2003–04 are drawn from college newspapers. See also "Change on Early Admission Produces Application Shifts," *New York Times*, November 13, 2003.

8. "Early Applications Down by 25 Percent," *The Hoya* (Georgetown University), November 14, 2003.

9. "Number of Early Applications Drops," *Daily Princetonian*, November 14, 2003.

10. "Early Decision Results," *The Phoenix* (Swarthmore College), February 7, 1997; http://phoenix.swarthmore.edu/2004-04-01/news/13902.

11. Tabulation provided by Renee Gernand, Senior Director, College Planning Services. An average of 226 early applications in 1995–1996 were reported by 184 Early Decision colleges, and 209 Early Decision colleges reported an average of 377 early applications in 2001–2002.

12. We compiled these numbers from college press releases and newspaper articles. We were unable to identify the number of students who were deferred admits at each college, so these students were counted as regular admits in each case. As a result, the graph slightly overestimates the percentage of regular admits and slightly underestimates the percentage of early admits.

13. "For Class of 2008, Early Admit Rates Dip," *Dartmouth Online*, January 7, 2004.

14. "Early Applications Down By 25%," *The Hoya* (Georgetown University), November 14, 2003.

15. Personal communication, April 23, 2004.

16. "37 Percent of Class Admitted Early," *The Phoenix* (Swarthmore College), February 6, 2003.

17. Personal communication, April 22, 2004.

18. For example, as of April 2004, the Brown University admissions website included the following statement from October 19, 2002: "We are longstanding members of NACAC and are currently seeking clarification from the organization vis-à-vis our Early Decision plan within the context of more recent policy shifts by NACAC. Until we have clear, unequivocal direction from NACAC, we request that applicants respect the guidelines of our Early Decision plan."

19. "Announcing a NACAC Moratorium on Enforcement: Early Action 'Without Restriction,'" *NACAC Bulletin*, August-September 2003.

20. "U. Debate Early Admit Programs," *Daily Princetonian*, February 18, 2004. "Early Decision Applications Hold Steady," *Brown Daily Herald*, January 28, 2004.

21. E-mail communication, April 11, 2004.

22. "Change in Early Admission Procedures Produces Application Shifts," *New York Times*, November 13, 2003.

23. Personal communication, April 7, 2004.

Acknowledgments

This book is the product of several years of research and the advice and help of dozens of individuals. Many college admissions officers and guidance counselors gave freely of their time to share their knowledge and understanding of the admissions process. Literally hundreds of high school and college students served as interview subjects for the project. Many skilled research assistants and advisors lent a hand over the course of the project. Without them, this book would never have appeared.

The Mellon Foundation generously provided financial support for our research. Bill Bowen and Harriet Zuckerman, its officers, provided intellectual guidance. In the early stages of our work, Michael Behnke, Bill Fitzsimmons, Marlyn Lewis, Larry Momo, and Barbara-Jan Wilson—all leading professionals in the admissions field—served as an advisory board to help us design the various aspects of our study. Dick Light, college interviewer extraordinaire, advised us throughout on the tricky business of interviewing students effectively. Chris Avery's interest in this topic was sparked by a series of conversations with his high school classmate Laura Attardi.

Among the many experts who helped us, a few were most generous with their time and advice. They are Michael Goldberger from Brown; Derek Bok, Fred Glimp, and Gus Reed from Harvard; Bette Johnsen from MIT; Robin Mamlet from Swarthmore (now at Stanford); Russ Adair, Margit Dahl, Worth David, and Chris Murphey from Yale; and Renee Gernand from the College Board.

Minnie Avery, Bonnie Gordon, and Jesse Shapiro read early drafts of the book and made extensive suggestions that greatly improved the text, while Bill Brainard, Jim Cooney, and Miriam Jorgensen paved the way for us to interview a number of admissions deans. Miriam Avins and Christine Thorsteinsson edited various drafts of the book and improved our exposition tremendously. When we had completed much of our work, James Fallows and Nicholas Lemann provided expert advice on the publication process, and Michael Aronson supervised the publication process at Harvard Press.

Chapter 1 relies heavily on information compiled by three undergraduate research assistants, Kirsten Trainer, Emily Oster, and Jane Risen. In addition, while we conducted our research, Anne Joseph, Antonio Rangel, and Al Roth alerted us to many important sources of information and news articles as the early application system continued to evolve; Kristin Wiley tracked down last-minute news sources in November 2002. Chapter 2 is primarily based on our analysis of data compiled by the College Board. Renee Gernand, Rick Ziehler, and Cathy Serico from the College Board made it easy for us to understand and analyze this data. Chapter 3 is the result of more than four hundred interviews with college students, each lasting thirty minutes or longer. Chris Avery conducted sixty-one of these interviews, and the remainder were completed by research assistants at five different colleges: Harvard (Gabriel Kaplan, Emily Oster, Kirsten Trainer, and Joanna Veltri); MIT (David Hellmuth, William LeBlanc, and Neha Sharma); Princeton (Christina Barkauskas, Kasey Evans, Julia Lee, Jaynie Randall, Genevieve Schaab, and Mony Singh); Wesleyan (Meredith Orren and Matt

Goldstein); and Yale (John Katsarakis, Julia (Yun) Kim, Isabelle Kinsolving, and Joshua Marks). We received invaluable logistical support and help with recruiting research assistants from Susan Athey, Sara Ellison, and Jim Snyder as MIT, from Helen Levy at Princeton, and from John Geanakoplos, David Pearce, and Dee Smitkowski at Yale. Clara Chan and Eric Meyer, Jonathan Feng and Szu Wang provided hospitality at Princeton. We owe special thanks to Aaron Siskind for supervising the interview process at Princeton, to Dan Benjamin and Gabriel Kaplan for testing and commenting on our interview format, and to Julia Kim, William LeBlanc, Genevieve Schaab, and Kirsten Trainer for helping us to develop our system for coding the interviews. Lisa Halpern, Emily Oster, and Jane Risen also coded interviews and double-checked our results. (Appendix C lists the questions used in each interview format, and Appendix B provides further details of our interview procedures.)

Chapter 4 is based on more than two hundred interviews with fifty-eight high school seniors. Emily Oster conducted all the interviews with students from Choate Rosemary Hall. William LeBlanc, Joann Park, and Joanna Veltri completed the interviews with students from Needham High School. Emily coded and analyzed the results of these interviews. She is a coauthor of Chapter 4.

Chapter 5 builds on the analysis of applicant information from the fourteen colleges that allowed us access to their databases on all college applications over multiple years. We thank the many individuals at these colleges who helped compile and translate the data; alas, we cannot identify them because we promised to preserve the anonymity of the colleges that agreed to participate. Sylvanie Wallington and Jonathan Wilwerding helped us with our initial data analysis. Chapter 5 also uses data from the College Admissions Project, described in Appendix B. We are grateful to the hundreds of high school counselors who participated in this project, and to the many research assistants who helped with subsequent data collection and coding, especially Jim Barker, Michael McNabb, and Scott Resnick. We thank Caroline Hoxby (a co-principal investigator with Chris Avery on this project) for allowing us to use these data.

Chapter 6 reports on interviews with college admissions deans, high school counselors (listed individually in Appendix B), and college students. Chris Avery and Andy Fairbanks interviewed fifteen counselors at nationally prominent schools; Anim Steel interviewed counselors at ten public schools in Massachusetts. We are grateful to these counselors for their time and interest, and also to the many other counselors who provided comments and suggestions over time, notably Michael Denning, Brad MacGowan, Leslie Miles, Dan Murphy, and Penny Oberg.

The concluding chapters of the book synthesize all that we have learned during the course of the project to provide advice to applicants, as well as to policy makers interested in improving the early admissions system. Our colleagues Susan Athey, Truman Bewley, Bill Brainard, Charlie Clotfelter, Suzanne Cooper, Matt DeGreeff, Ronald Ehrenberg, David Ellwood, Jerry Green, Caroline Hoxby, Rob Jensen, Tom Kane, David Laibson, Nolan Miller, Katherine Newman, Bill Nordhaus, Anne Piehl, Michael Rothschild, James Tobin, Sarah Turner, Gordon Winston, and David Zimmerman were patient listeners and thoughtful advisers. College Presidents Richard Levin (Yale) and Lawrence Summers (Harvard) generously shared their insights into the operation of early admissions and the potential for reform. Finally, we acknowledge Howard Raiffa and Al Roth, whose research endeavors inspired us and provided an intellectual foundation for much of this book.

Tables and Figures

Tables

Figures

Index